HEAVEN'S HA

HEAVEN'S HARLOTS

◐ ◐ ◐

My Fifteen Years
as a Sacred Prostitute
in the Children of God Cult

◐ ◐ ◐

Miriam Williams

EAGLE BROOK
William Morrow and Company, Inc.
New York

Published by Eagle Brook
An Imprint of William Morrow and Company, Inc.
1350 Avenue of the Americas
New York, N.Y. 10019

It is the policy of William Morrow and Company, Inc., and its imprints and affiliates,
recognizing the importance of preserving what has been written, to print the books we
publish on acid-free paper, and we exert our best efforts to that end.

The Library of Congress has cataloged a previous edition of this title.

Library of Congress Cataloging-in-Publication Data

Williams, Miriam.
   Heaven's harlots : my fifteen years as a sacred prostitute in the
Children of God cult / Miriam Williams.—1st ed.
      p.   cm.
   ISBN 0-688-17012-9 (alk. paper)
   1. Williams, Miriam.   2. Children of God (Movement)—Biography.
3. Ex-prostitutes—Biography.   4. Children of God (Movement)—
Controversial literature.   5. Prostitution—Religious aspects—
Controversial literature.   I. Title.
BP605.C38W55   1998
299'.93—dc21
[B]   97-48644
                                                                      CIP

Paperback ISBN 0-688-17012-9

Printed in the United States of America

First Paperback Edition 1999

3   4   5   6   7   8   9   10

BOOK DESIGN BY BERNARD KLEIN

www.williammorrow.com

To the women of the cult
and to the men who loved them
and lost them.
May we all find inner peace.

With the exception of Jeremy Spencer, Moses David, and myself, all the legal names and Bible names of Children of God members in this book have been changed in the interest of confidentiality.

Acknowledgments

I would like to thank:

My five children, who helped me through the sometimes painful process of writing this book, simply by being themselves; especially my oldest son, with whom I share my fears and joys, and my oldest daughter, who was often a fill-in mommy, helping the others with homework and meals.

My mother, who has always been the prayer warrior of the family and a caring grandmother.

My best friends, who are all former members of this cult and contributed valuable insight: Sharon, Pope, Tracy, and Billy. May we continue to walk our separate journeys together.

My sisters, who helped me out.

My ex-husbands, who have been supportive during the writing of this book.

My friends who helped me with suggestions, strength, and understanding: Jef, Dollie, Ann, Jean, Anne, Malati, Sterling, Simon, Cindy, and the abhyasis.

My many contacts among former members who remain faithful in the support network.

The scholarship donors who helped me make it through school: the local chapters of the National Honor Society, Golden Key, American University Women, and Beck/Kiwanis.

And my editor, Joann Davis, who asked me all the questions I would never think to write about, since I am just beginning to see in the light, and her lovely colleague Michelle Shinseki.

Contents

Introduction

Why would a mother of five healthy, well-adjusted children write a book about her former life as a sacred prostitute? The question torments me. At age forty-four, I am now on the verge of receiving a master's degree in sociology that will allow me to work and pull my family out of relative poverty. I have no reason to expose myself to the publicity this unusual autobiography could generate. Worse still, I could be undermining the stability that my children now enjoy.

My own life, as you will see, has never been stable. This book relates the story of a girl from Lancaster, Pennsylvania, who fell through the cracks into what became one of the most bizarre sex cults of our time, the Children of God, which at its peak had eighteen thousand members. Numerous documentaries have been made about this controversial cult by the major networks in America, and it has been the subject of various sociological and psychological studies. Celebrities such as Fleetwood Mac's original slide guitarist, Jeremy Spencer, made headlines when he left the popular musical group to join the cult. And River Phoenix, the disillusioned young movie star who died from drug abuse, spent years of his childhood in the Children of God.

The leader of the Children of God, Moses David, has been described by cult expert Dr. Steve Dent as a "lustful prophet," who used the group to unleash his repressed sexuality. Kent writes that the most abused and sexually manipulated people in all the cults he studied were the women of the Children of God, who were instructed to demonstrate God's love by giving sex first to the men in the group and then to the "lost" of the world. According to Moses David, "God was a pimp," and we were the "loving whores of God."

I married twice in the cult and bore five children. Eventually, the ugly weed of child abuse was creeping through the camp. Fearful it might touch my own children, I snapped out of my delusional state and we left the cult for good. But acknowledging previous pain, and accepting responsibility for my actions, proved to be a long and difficult journey back to sanity. I reentered American culture as a forty-year-old single mother who spoke three languages and had been in over twenty countries, but who had never had a checking account, credit line, car, or home of my own. I started work as a waitress at a truck stop to help support my family as I went back to college.

After graduating in June of 1996, I kept a promise I made to myself four years earlier that when I finished college I would write my story. Working without an agent, I photocopied two pages out of a huge directory of publishers and sent off five query letters to editors I chose at random from this haphazardly selected list.

A few weeks later, as I was shopping for groceries, I picked a paperback book off the shelf. Although I had never heard of the book or the author before, I was interested because the cover said it was a true story. The next morning, while sitting on my porch finishing the book, I received a call from one of the editors I had contacted.

"Your letter struck me," said the woman on the phone, "and I usually don't read unsolicited material. Exactly what kind of book do you want to write?"

I wasn't exactly sure, but I found an answer immediately. "Well, I was thinking of writing an honest and personal book, something like the one I'm reading right now."

"Oh, what book is that?" the woman asked.

"*The Eagle and the Rose*, by Rosemary Altea," I replied, checking the cover to make sure of the name again.

"*I* edited that book" came the quick response.

My heart jumped into my throat. Coincidences like this one, the equivalent of a one-in-a-million chance, don't just *happen*. I checked the acknowledgments page. There was her name in the book I had randomly picked up the day before.

Had it not been for that incident of serendipity, I would have not had the courage to continue this far.

But now all my angst and confusion have been transferred from my heart and mind to a computer disk. The unexplainable driving force is gone. I fluctuate between hoping for the best and preparing for the worst. But I decide to keep believing in a higher purpose than I know today.

At present, I am engrossed in literature about the problems of society. As I read stories of bewildered, despairing young adults, I remember my own adolescence and share in their collective pain. Confusion about sexuality and identity prompts many young people to look for solutions through alcohol, drugs, promiscuity, subservience, anorexia, and even suicide. Deeply troubled teens come from all types of families and socioeconomic classes, and upper-middle-class, two-parent homes are affected as much as single-parent homes and households living below the poverty line. We are reminded that our society has to change. I believe that the first step to change is awareness. Each individual must take responsibility for personal actions, but the responsibility often begins with awareness.

This book was written to shed light on one of the escape routes taken by sensitive youth growing up in a troubled society—the path to cult involvement. It is probably one of the most drastic, claims the lives of the most naive idealists, and usually requires the most help along the road to recovery. Unfortunately, there is little knowledgeable help available. While the actions of these people are worthy of contempt, cult members realize that they were motivated by blind idealism.

This is also a story of self-discovery written for those who have lost their self. My journey out of hell came through incremental steps, which were guided by what I can only call fate. Now that I have made it back to reality and can finally lead a normal, fulfilling life, I feel a responsibility, especially to the children born and raised in the cult, to add to awareness of cult involvement. Perhaps one day I can provide practical assistance to ease the transition back to society for others, but for now, I offer hope.

HEAVEN'S HARLOTS

1

○ ○ ○

"God Is a Pimp"

I smiled at the uniformed man operating the hotel elevator. I usually smiled at everybody. It had become a habit. But this time, when he smiled back, I thought to myself, "He must know what I just did."

The elevator opened into one of the most elegant establishments in Monte Carlo, the distinguished Hôtel de Paris. Walking through the plush lobby, I felt a little self-conscious in my worn jeans. I also wondered if the money that Salim had just stuffed in my back pocket could be seen. I crossed the marble floors and went through the revolving door. This was the first time I had received hard cash for giving God's love, and I felt sensations of shame, confusion, and anger.

Passing the limousines and Rolls-Royces unloading in front of the hotel, I did not pause in curiosity to identify any famous faces, but instead I walked with my face turned in the other direction. I intentionally avoided eye contact with anyone for fear they might recognize the turmoil in my soul. Walking quickly around the tree-lined island in the middle of the majestically landscaped cul-du-sac, I headed for the Café de Paris, a popular, upscale café-restaurant. There I could sit down with a cappuccino and try to make sense of what had happened. The café was crowded, and while I hesitated at the entrance, my thoughts reviewed the previous day's events.

I had met Salim the night before at Le Pirate, a well-known restaurant on the Côte d'Azur. One of the women I was living with, Sharon, had a date with an older German gentleman, and since she had met him only recently she asked me to come along. Normally, we never went alone on dates until at least one other member of our group had met the person we were going out with.

Sharon and I were surprised to be taken to Le Pirate, which had a reputation for being patronized by millionaire swingers. We had both put on our nicest clothes, hand-sewn dresses made of a soft muslin material that we had bought at a discount store in Nice. The gentleman was older than I expected, surely past sixty, and I wondered if this bothered Sharon. Our policy was to show God's love to everyone—rich or poor, handsome or ugly, young or old—but I knew from experience that it was hard to physically practice such an abstract ideal.

Sharon was a talented and dynamic singer, but she was somewhat shy on dates. She had been raised in a very traditional Catholic family and had studied to become an opera singer before she joined our group. She was tall, blond, and constantly on a diet in order to control a voluptuous figure. Her large, expressive eyes often portrayed alarm or amazement, like a little girl who had seen the roaring ocean for the first time. Sharon had a husband and young child at home, and I felt she would rather be back with them. Our tentative plan was to have an early dinner, give him "the message," and be home on time for me to go out again. But as soon as we arrived at the celebrated restaurant, I sensed that it would be a long evening.

Le Pirate was located on the striking coast of Roquebrune-Cap-Martin, with a view made famous by a Monet painting. The waiters were attractive young men dressed in romantic pirate costumes. They had been trained to perform little dramas such as breaking up chairs and throwing the pieces into the fire. It was all part of the Le Pirate experience. Violin players, and the owner himself, came by our table occasionally, entertaining us with Gypsy-style music.

Our German friend was enjoying himself in our company, and the evening dragged on. Only a few other guests were present when we arrived, and soon I noticed that we were alone except for another group at the other end of the room. They were having some sort of party, and as the night wore on, the noise from their table grew louder. Just as our gentleman friend said that he might send a message over to their table, asking them to quiet down, a bottle of champagne arrived with a note for me. It was from the man at the other table.

Out of courtesy, I walked over to thank him. He was a dark-haired man with deep, piercing eyes that smiled ambiguously, although his expression was quite serious, almost severe.

"Who is the grandfather?" he asked me.

"Oh, just a friend of ours," I replied, caught a little off-guard by his abruptness.

"Well, come and sit with us. He is too boring to have beautiful girls at his table alone."

I thought to myself, "You're right." I was practically falling asleep, and Sharon had already given me anxious looks as if to say, "Let's wrap this one up."

Before I could answer, the man moved over to make room for me next to him. Glancing at the lady who had been sitting beside him previously, an attractive brunette with red-painted lips and wearing a dress that revealed an ample cleavage, I tried to assess the situation. With an inviting smile, she indicated that I should sit down, and I did so while signaling to Sharon.

"This really might not be polite to the gentleman over there," I said. "We hardly know him."

"Yes, I understand that you do not know him," the dark-haired man replied in what I now recognized as a Lebanese accent. "And do not worry about his feelings. He will be honored to be at this table. But your friend looks worried. Tell her to come here. No, wait, I will send for both of them."

He called for a waiter and gave him a message. Within minutes we were all seated together. The ambience at the table was charged with fresh energy, and immediately we were integrated into their party. Sharon was radiant as she sang some of her original songs for our new acquaintances, while I played my usual role as interpreter of the spiritual message behind the words. We were so different in our approach, so zealous, so genuinely naive and open, that everyone immediately responded as if we were longtime friends.

The Lebanese man who had called me over was obviously the host. His name was Salim, and at one point the beautiful brunette told me that I should remain beside him because he liked me. She said this as if she were my confidante offering her best advice.

We stayed on till nearly dawn, singing, laughing and dancing, and although our German friend was having a great time, his strength eventually wore out. He was much older than we were, and he gave no indication of desiring further intimacy. Sharon looked relieved to be able to go home. As we were leaving, Salim took my number and told me he would call. Sure enough, when I woke up the next day, already after noon, he had called and left a message with Sharon that he was sending a chauffeur and car to bring me to the Hôtel de Paris.

It had happened so quickly that I did not have time to discuss the plans with anyone. Sharon, already awake with her baby, advised me to go. She assured me that she "got a good witness on him," and that everything would be all right. Within an hour a chauffeur driving a Mercedes-Benz arrived, and I was driven to the hotel. Although I had been there a few times, this was my first encounter upstairs. As I walked through the ornate lobby, I realized that I was socially unprepared; I would be playing with the pros without ever having been an amateur.

Taking the elevator to the floor Salim had indicated, I walked down the wide hallway thinking that, in just the steps between two doors, this corridor covered more square feet than my entire bedroom. I admired the fine inlaid woodwork on the walls and thought I might try to do something like that to the room I was fixing up at that time. My mind definitely was not on the imminent sexual activity I would probably soon experience. Perhaps I had taught myself the stress-relieving technique of not thinking about it right before you do it. I had been well prepped for these types of encounters. I would show physical evidence of love, touching his hands, stroking his back, then perhaps kiss him gently. He would respond by opening up and becoming more intimate. I would then bring in the message about God's Love, how I was merely a form of God's immense love for each and every human being, and that if he had never been shown the extent of God's Love for him, he had it before him now. That was our group's basic philosophy, and interjecting any reality into the ethereal picture would taint it in my mind. I kept reality and my mission in separate rooms that had no connecting door, and as I entered Salim's suite that early afternoon, I was still a twenty-three-

year-old American girl who was more shamelessly curious than
selflessly loving.

Salim had left the door to his suite slightly ajar, and he called for
me to come in when I knocked lightly. I did not see him in the
spacious blue sitting salon that opened out to a balcony with a view
of the casino entrance. Then I heard him call from a darkened room
to my right.

"I am in here. Come," he said in a tone that only partially dis-
guised the commandlike quality of his words. In my mind, I imagined
him to be saying, "I am a searching soul, and I need your love." I
entered what appeared to be the master bedroom. The curtains were
tightly drawn, and the only light came from an adjacent bathroom.
Salim was in bed. He lay on his stomach with his face toward the
pillow.

"Can you give a good massage?" he asked.

It soon became evident that Salim wanted all I could offer, and he
wanted it now. I have no recollections of what I thought during the
most intimate moments. It is not as if I blacked out or put these
experiences into a subconscious holding area; simply, I do not believe
that I thought much at all during the act. I followed Salim's dictates.
He asked me to do nothing unusual, and it must have lasted less than
ten minutes because I didn't have time to tell him the message.

As usual, I was concerned that he would hear our message of salvation. The previous night had offered no opportunity, and things
heated up so quickly once I arrived at his hotel suite that I feared
the moment had passed. That was becoming all too typical for me as
the time between meeting a man and giving him love was becoming
continually shorter. I don't know how other girls in our group felt,
but I felt awkward telling him about God and Jesus in the midst of
intimate sexual exchanges. For years I never thought about getting
any pleasure for myself since I was so truly concerned to "give" God's
message of love.

"I want you to know that God loves you," I said, walking into
the pretty sunlit room, "and that is why I am here." Salim, standing
by the balcony, was already cleaned and dressed in a suit, and I
noticed through an open door to the left that there was another bedroom suite attached to this one.

"Yes, I am a Christian Lebanese, you know," he answered, which seemed to settle the matter, at least for him. "Do you have a way to get home?" he asked, adding, "I need the chauffeur right now."

"I could take a taxi, but I did not bring money with me."

"Of course." He walked over to a highly polished desk by the balcony window, and pulled out some French bills.

"Oh, really, I don't need that much," I protested.

"Okay, darling. I am going to Zurich tonight. But I will be back in a few days and give you a call. I gave your name and number to my secretary, Kahlil, so he might be calling to set another date. Now, please, go down before me," he commanded in a businesslike manner.

As I walked to the elevator, I wanted to pull out the bills and see what he had given me, since I thought it was too much for a short taxi ride. But I decided to wait until I was out of the hotel.

At the entrance to the Café de Paris, I finally pulled the colorful French bills out of my pocket. There were four 500-franc bills. A hundred francs would have been enough for a taxi. Salim had given me this money for sex! What did he think I was—a prostitute? I gave him my body to show God's Love, not for money. Maybe he did not understand. Maybe I should go back to his fancy suite and tell him I did not want his money. I decided to call home first.

"Would you like a table?" the waiter at the Café de Paris asked, breaking my thoughts.

I suddenly realized that I must have been standing at the entrance-way for quite some time.

"Oh, no, I'm looking for someone," I replied. I did not want to break a 500-franc note to call home, since I fully intended to give it back to Salim. However, I did not bring even small change with me. I would have to borrow a few francs from someone. I searched the café for someone I knew and spotted Jean outside on the patio.

Jean had been one of the first men in Monte Carlo to whom I had given sex. He was about twenty years older than I and divorced. At that time I had been careful to explain that what I was doing was showing God's Love, but he did not understand. In fact, not many people did. Jean was no longer one of my "fish," but he had remained a friend.

I walked over to his table and said a few words of greeting in French. He responded pleasantly and asked me to sit down. We talked casually for a while, but I was anxious to call home before Salim left the hotel. Finally, I just came out and asked Jean to lend me a few francs.

"I have only five-hundred-franc bills," I explained, "and I don't want to break them for a phone call."

Immediately, I felt foolish for mentioning the 500-franc bills. I never carried that much money with me, and Jean knew it. He gave me a wink, which I assumed meant he knew what was going on, and he emptied a pocketful of change into my hand. I thanked him and went down to the ladies' room where the phones were located.

Timothy, the only man who lived at our home, answered the phone. Timothy was married to Sharon, and since there were three women in our home, he became our "fisherman"—the one who would give advice on which "fish" to give sex to and which ones were not ready. He was only twenty years old. The women were all about my age, ranging from twenty-three to twenty-five, yet this younger man was considered our authoritative figurehead. I was sure that Sharon had already told him about Salim.

"Timothy, it's me," I started excitedly. "Yeah, everything was okay. I'll tell you about it when I get home. But Timothy, Salim gave me money. Lots of it. He gave me two thousand francs!"

"Why did he do that?"

"He stuck a few bills in my pocket for taxi money. I didn't know how much it was until I got outside. Listen, Tim, I want to give it back. I feel dirty. I feel like he thinks I do this for money. I mean, I told him it was for God's Love, and I thought he understood. Timothy, I'm angry. It's not like when someone buys us groceries or a gift. This is hard cash—you know, filthy lucre."

By now I was barely holding back tears. It all seemed so ugly. I wanted Timothy to help me out of this.

"No, Jeshanah, don't give it back. We need it, and I think God touched his heart to give you that money. He must have. Salim doesn't even know us yet, but the Lord must have shown him we needed some financial help at this time."

"Are you sure, Timothy? I feel really bad about this."

"Listen, I just got some letters from headquarters, and they say that it's okay to take money. You haven't even read the letters yet, but they talk about getting paid for giving God's Love. Don't worry about it. You are doing all right."

"I don't know," I replied. "Are you sure you are not misinterpreting something?"

"No, really! Wait until you read the letter. It's heavy! Don't worry about it. Go get a drink and take a taxi home."

"But Timothy," I protested in exasperation, "I feel like a prostitute!"

"Yeah, that's what you are," he replied emphatically, "a prostitute for Jesus! And God is our pimp!"

◐

Seven long years before, in 1971, I had joined a religious group called the Children of God in upstate New York. At that time they were radical Christians who lived in a commune and spent most of the day witnessing about Jesus. Starting with the ideal of "From each according to his ability, unto each according to his need," we included the message of God's salvation through Jesus, and we believed that we were living true Christian communism. We supported ourselves with donations as we sought to help the drug addicts in New York City by bringing them to our commune and "turning them on to Christ." Sometimes it worked.

When I first joined, the group was very puritanical with strict rules about separating boys and girls. Now we shared sexually, not only within our group, but also with the lost souls outside. We witnessed by practicing self-sacrificial love including laying down our lives and our bodies. Only the dedicated stayed through this transition from Jesus People to radical "fishers of men." I was one of those who stayed, convinced that whatever was done for love could not be wrong. But now, I was doing it for money.

The more I thought, the more confused I became. There is a painful tension in situations caused by behaving in conflict with what one believes. Something has to change, either how one acts, or how one believes. The obvious solution is to stop behaving that way; however, such action is not always possible. I first joined this group to relieve the stress of living a material-centered, competitive life that appeared meaningless to me. For seven years, instead of working for money, I worked for love. I considered some several thousand fellow idealists my spiritual family. Now, I was poised to change again, but instead of changing my behavior, I changed what I believed. In a few months

I would accept the concept of "sacred prostitution" and become a person without universally established morals. We were supposed to be revolutionizing the world, and the old morality would have to be replaced. My entire worldview had been slowly changing, and this was the great leap. The words of our leader came to my mind: "If you think, think, think, you'll sink, sink, sink." I simply could not understand by thinking. This was a leap of faith. I took it!

By now the sun was setting and the sky had become a harmonious mélange of blues and pinks and purples. I stopped rationalizing about right or wrong and let the beauty of the evening envelop me.

2

○ ○ ○

A Curiouser and Curiouser World

My father sang to me as I played on the California beach. I remember him singing one of his favorite songs. "I'll have a little talk with Jesus/and I'll tell him all about my troubles." I guess he had a lot of problems, and so he drank and so he sang. And that's what I remember most about my father.

His family was from Ireland. They were struck by tragedy when his mother was hit by a car and killed when he was a little boy. The story was told to me by my father when he was drunk, and by my mother when she tried to explain why Daddy always drank. He had let go of his mother's hand when crossing a busy Philadelphia street. Whether she was hit because she ran after him, or he saved his life by letting go of her hand, I never understood. I only know that my father, and everyone in his family, were alcoholics by the time I came around, on June 27, 1953.

My father, John, was a tall, trim, handsome fellow who had served in World War II. Since he was a very good Linotype machine operator, he could always get a job wherever he went. But he could never hold on to it because of his drinking. Maybe that's why we moved across the United States and back, and I never went to one school for a whole year until I was in ninth grade. Sometimes we lived in nice suburban houses, and then we would move to a tiny apartment in the inner city. Often my mother sent my older brother, Steve, and I to the bars to look for my dad. If he did not come home from work, we went to remind him that he had a family. Since we didn't have a TV (it was too heavy to move around), this was always an exciting adventure for us. My memories of that early part of my life include Planters peanuts, bright orange soda, and dart boards, set around the many lounges my dad frequented. In the really bad days, they were on skid row.

My mother, on the other hand, was a fundamentalist Christian who had been raised in a loving family. Mother had come to America as a sixteen-year-old escaping Nazi Germany. Her father worked hard and made a good living for his family, and although he had been a prosperous carpenter in Germany, he became a gardener for wealthy German industrialists when he moved to America. Shrewd and frugal, he managed to buy five homes in America and became a landlord. My grandmother instilled strict Christian ideals in her daughter. She was a sweet, caring lady, but I never had a conversation with her since she never learned to speak English. She was blind when I was old enough to know her.

My mother and her family settled in Reading, Pennsylvania, in 1939. She eventually attended Temple University, but she left to work at a newspaper office, where she met my father. Although she had six children with him, she was not the typical 1950s housewife. When I was younger, I was always embarrassed by my mother because she spoke with a German accent, didn't perm her hair or wear makeup like other moms, and her name was Elfriede. Most of all, she did not know how to take care of the house.

"Why don't you know how to cook, or keep house?" I often asked her when I was a sassy twelve-year-old. Since I was the oldest girl among six children, many of these chores fell on me. "You were raised in Germany, and all the German women we know cook very well and keep spotless houses."

"You see, I went to the 'better schools' in Germany," she explained unashamedly. "And girls who went to those schools did not have to learn household chores since they would have maids to do them."

Obviously, being a housewife was beneath her since she had been given the dream of marrying above her middle-class status in Germany. But this was America, Mom. Wake up, the middle class here is huge.

Our family was a study of contrasts. We were often poor, but we usually lived in nice neighborhoods. My father drank, smoked, and cursed, whereas my mother was very religious and would not allow us to say so much as "Oh my God," which was taking the Lord's name in vain. My older brother and I, who bore most of the traveling hardships, excelled at school. Unfortunately, my brother used his extraordinary intelligence to obtain money through illegal methods, such as burglary and the unauthorized withdrawal of other people's bank money. Consequently, Steve spent most of his adult life in prison, while I spent most of my life trying to serve the Lord. Perhaps they are two sides of the same coin.

I entered McCaskey High School, Lancaster County, Pennsylvania, in 1968. By this time I had convinced my mother that for the sake of my four younger sisters, she should separate from Dad. I was fourteen years old. Steve was already in a reformatory, and I was beginning to get angry with my mom for allowing us to live such a dysfunctional life. My mom explained sweetly that she didn't believe in divorce but she might consider separation. I think she talked it over with her pastor, and since her six children were all in school now, she got a job and eventually bought a house in the town of Lancaster. She separated legally from Dad, but it only meant we didn't move so much. He still came around drunk.

Lancaster County, known as Amish country, was removed from the massive social upheaval sweeping the nation at the time. People in Lancaster were content. Many of them were Mennonites, and the ones who were not lived rather well with the traditional lifestyle encouraged by Amish and Mennonite philosophy, with little exposure to modern life. However, even Lancaster would not escape the unrest that infected American youth like a plague.

I was among the first to catch it, or perhaps my unrest was just waiting to express itself. I had thought it was my family's unusual gypsy lifestyle that was preventing me from feeling like one of the crowd among my peers. However, now that I had lived in one place for more than a year, and still felt like an outsider, I began to wonder. I always made good grades, but I could not find a niche. In addition,

I was beginning to be known as a rebel. Popular girls were wearing miniskirts at that time, and I thought it was more practical to wear pants. I remember being sent to the principal's office.

"Miriam, you are a smart girl. You will probably get some good scholarships to college, if you don't cause any trouble. Now you know the rules—girls cannot wear pants."

"Why?" I asked.

"Well, that's the rule."

"I know, but why was that rule made? I mean, don't you know that the boys spend half their time trying to look up the girls' dresses? And I believe some of the teachers do, too. With hemlines six inches above the knee, do you think it is a good rule to require girls to wear dresses?"

The principal was a sincere man. "No," he answered, "perhaps it is not a sensible rule anymore, but until it changes, you must obey it."

"I believe I must protest it. If the rule is ever to change, sir, someone has to challenge it."

I protested by wearing my unfashionable farmer jeans to school, and the principal suspended me for three days. That was the rule. But I continued to wear pants, and he never suspended me again.

I have always suspected that the real reason I wore pants was because I could not afford to dress fashionably. Wearing dresses or skirts meant having a different outfit every day. With jeans, I only had to change my shirts. However, the very next year the rule was changed. Girls could wear pants. By then I had discovered that thrift stores held a wonderful variety of lovely old dresses for literally nickels and dimes. For five dollars I could buy a wardrobe that lasted for months and was one-of-a-kind. I was especially fond of the 1940s-style silk dresses and anything with lace or bead work. I became a hippie before I knew what it was to be one.

Since the hippies had not yet come onto the scene in Lancaster, I had only one good friend until my junior year. She was a Jewish girl who was extremely intelligent, and though we came from completely different backgrounds, we had similar interests. I would ride my bike over to her upper-class neighborhood in my thrift store clothes and spend the evenings discussing existential thought. We remained in contact throughout high school.

By the time I was in eleventh grade, a group of hippies started to form at my school. They dressed like me, or I dressed like them—I'm not sure which—and other people lumped me in with them. Teachers knew that if I did not agree with a viewpoint, I would discuss it publicly. I had also taken to hitchhiking around town, since my brief tenure as a driver had resulted in the wreck of my long-awaited car. Most of all, I began smoking dope, on my own. I smoked it religiously, alone in my room, with candles and incense burning and music playing. It was a personal ritual, almost sacred, and I was reluctant to include others at that time. I also had been dabbling in philosophy and Eastern practices like yoga. I was at the door of discovering myself, when the hippies called at my window. They looked colorful, exciting, and adventurous, like I wanted to be. I guess I wanted company after all.

I soon met Jan, a classmate who had recently given up her role as cheerleader and boy-with-car-chaser to experiment in the sixties happening. A tall, thin, pretty, and stylishly dressed girl, she approached me one day out of the blue to ask where she could buy marijuana. I was surprised she thought I would know this information, but we became friends and we spent the next two years together sampling the culture of sex, drugs, and rock and roll that was born during the famous decade of the 1960s, and had come to Lancaster a few years later. Our hippie group was small, and for a short time I was under the illusion that we were sensitive, open, and caring. However, I soon discovered that these wonderful free freaks were just a new teenage clique. As in all cliques, it could be very alienating for anyone who did not fit in, and after a short time, I knew I did not belong here either. I believe that realization came from going to the Spruce Street house.

Someone, I never found out who, had rented a house on Spruce Street, near Franklin and Marshall College, which we used as a winter hangout. A fantastic stereo system was set up where the main bedroom should have been. I usually went to the music area, where there were bright pillows thrown around the wooden floor and candles pouring their multicolored wax over empty wine bottles. In the first months of its short existence, the Spruce Street scene was innocently experimental, but soon drug use and underage drinking began and decadence set in. It was a time of deep observation on my part. I noticed that free-loving hippies were never free from one high or another, and were certainly not very loving at all. When the music became too hard rock, I would slip down to the kitchen to sit with the hard drug users. In my naive state, I never knew what drug they were taking, and they never offered me any either.

I first went to the kitchen because it was the only room where I could practice guitar. I was not very good, so I did not want anyone to hear me, and being with the dopers was like being alone. However, after a while, I started observing them. Candy was a few years older than me, but she looked like a Holocaust survivor, all skin and bones, with stringy hair and dark bags under her eyes. I knew she had been in and out of the "nuthouse," a place they sent junkies before reha-bilitation homes became popular. These were the kind of people my older brother knew, and their lifelessness was horrifying to a budding flower child. For a student who had studied Timothy Leary's theory about drugs bringing one to a higher level of consciousness, I found these people consciousness-less.

The only person I became relatively close to at Spruce Street was another recluse called Mick. I was sixteen then, and Mick had already graduated from high school, but I found out that he did not use drugs often because they made him freak out. He had trouble handling real life, let alone the strange world of psychedelics. Slightly short and muscular, Mick hid behind a beard and long hair, rarely looking any-one in the eye. His primary love was music, and he was famous for his record collection. Ask him anything about music, bands, songs, musicians, or songwriters of the 1960s and '70s and he came alive. Otherwise, he hung around like a wet sock slung over a shower cur-tain rod. His vulnerability made him the object of childish pranks. I was unwittingly involved in one of these.

Spruce Street had lately become a place for lovers to try out their wings. I was still, surprisingly, a virgin, so I never made use of the room reserved for youthful experimentation. Neither did Mick. It was not long before some of the prank-playing boys thought Mick and I should be together. I can't remember how we got into the room, but Mick and I found ourselves facing one another over the disreputable bed. Mick was much more flustered than I, and what had seemed like an innocent joke suddenly had tragic implications. I saw that Mick's precarious position within this group could be at stake. In addition, his own bottled-up self-esteem was about to crack wide open before my eyes.

"Mick," I said, being careful not to look directly into his eyes. "What do you want to do?"

He blubbered something unintelligible, and I felt uncomfortable witnessing a blatant display of raw vulnerability. I walked over to the door and locked it from the inside.

"There, no one can come in. Why don't we pretend that we are doing it? Can you pretend?"

His face lit up in disbelief, but I detected a sense of relief.

"What do you mean, Miriam?"

"You know, we'll turn off the light and make a lot of noises as if we were in bed, doing what they put us in here to do. They'll believe it, and I won't tell them anything. Okay?"

He was game. He drank all the wine that was left in the bottle on the floor, and after loosening up, we play-acted without ever touching one another. Now our tormentors were knocking at the door, trying to get in. After a while they just left, seemingly content to believe that they had instigated a love affair. We waited until all was quiet outside the door, and then we swore ourselves to secrecy and exited the love chamber. We have remained friends ever since that uneventful night.

Soon, I tired of Spruce Street. The sex, drugs, and rock-and-roll scene was a dead-end street as far as I could discern. I drifted toward the music coming from Franklin and Marshall College. The campus was alive with high-bred, well-fed antiwar protestors. After attending evening classes at the underground "FREE" University to learn the truth about the Vietnam War, I became a full-fledged social activist. As a good revolutionary, I started wearing a black armband to school and inviting my friends to either quit smoking or steal their cigarettes, since everyone knew that most of the tax money went to the military-industrial complex. My idealism had caught fire.

By the end of the spring of 1970, the protest movement at Franklin and Marshall had degenerated into free concerts on the campus green. Music became the medium, but I doubt that many of the listeners understood the message. When it was time to go to a march, I was usually alone. Always looking for something new, I drifted toward the blues music that a small group of intellectuals started on campus in a place called the "AT." It was there that I would cross that last barrier that kept me from being one with others. I did the drugs, the protests, the music scene, but I had always avoided the "free love."

Pot, I believed, was opening my mind to new truths, and I began to feel that love would connect me with the community of truth seekers. Since I was fairly smart, I practiced birth control, and then waited for the opportunity to experience "free love."

The first time was disastrous. It hurt—in every sense. Jay had been in my philosophy class and captured my attention with his brilliant theories on thought, but I never saw him again after the class ended. Then I met him in the "AT." With sounds from a blues group called the Black Cat encircling the dark, smoky room, marijuana joints were shared and Boone's Farm wine flowed freely. I danced solo to the music, oblivious to anything but the movements of my body, and, finally exhausted, I sat down on the wooden floor with a group of boys passing around a pipe, surprised to find Jay among them. We talked until closing time about the ideas we had learned in our class, and, turned on more by his mind than his body, I walked home with him to listen to music in the privacy of his bedroom. I was seventeen years old, but since sex had never been a top priority for me, I really didn't know much about how to do it. I was surprised by the pain.

"Shit, I didn't know you were a virgin," Jay said almost contemptuously.

"This isn't free love," I thought, "it's free sex." I remember standing by the window in his attic room, and looking out on the darkened road. I suddenly recognized it as the same street where my sister had been born years ago—Ruby Street. Wiping the tears from my eyes, I left him silent on the bed and walked home alone through the empty, rain-drenched streets. As usual, my mom and sisters were in bed. It didn't matter. I couldn't talk to them anyway. Sex was a taboo subject in my house. I could picture my mom screaming and calling the pastor if I told her. I had no curfew and my mother thought I was mature enough to do what I wanted, so I walked the streets all night with a mixture of happiness to have had the experience and sadness to be alone again.

Feeling alienated from the drug and music scene, I looked around for something to feel close to and thought I would return to the familiar pews of the churches. I remember riding my bike one day to a church that advertised a special youth meeting with an internationally known missionary speaker. I was hopeful that perhaps my old love for religion would be reignited. After all, I wanted to be a missionary when I was a child, and I had asked Jesus into my heart when I was a twelve-year-old at a Bible camp. As I held hands with a dozen other campers around a campfire, a feeling of euphoria came over me. I felt I had been chosen by God for "His Ministry," but I was not sure what that meant. Having gone to Sunday school and church camps until I was a teen, I'm sure it was a Christian concept I had internalized. I never thought it would be easy to a Christian; in fact, I felt that perhaps I had left the church because it was too hard to obey all their rules. Maybe now I would be like the prodigal son/daughter. I imagined the missionary welcoming me with open arms. Ah, how wonderful it would be if someone pure hugged me. "What a friend we have in Jesus."

In my state of hopeful anticipation, it never occurred to me to dress up for church. I wore my jeans, the ones I had carefully embroidered to fill up the holes, and a lacy, old-fashioned blouse covered with a tapestry vest. My long blond hair was hanging free, barely brushed, and I wore no makeup or jewelry. My unkempt appearance became brutally obvious the minute I walked into the church, which was only a few blocks from where I lived.

Once inside, I walked hesitantly up to one of the front rows and took a vacant seat beside a group of girls about my age. They were all dressed nicely, with nylons on their legs and shiny shoes. I looked not only ragged next to these polished specimens of American youth; I looked dirty. My beautiful embroidery, which I had always admired for its colorful appearance, now looked dull and shabby.

A young boy with buzz cut turned around to whisper something to the girl next to me. She giggled and inched away from me. Was she making more room for me, or was my presence repulsive? I realized that most of these young people went to my high school, but I did not recognize anyone. Did anyone know me?

I focused my attention on the missionary. He was regaling us with his stories about his work in Africa. He launched into a diatribe about the sins of the youth in America, and how we were so lucky to have good parents who raised us differently. I kept my eyes on him the entire time, hoping he would look my way and notice the deep desire I had to serve the Lord. He glanced at me once briefly and never looked my way again. In fact, I felt that he avoided turning his eyes to the section I was sitting in altogether.

The missionary finished his talk. An extra collection was made, but I had no money to drop in the basket. The young people got up to sing some songs led by a young man playing guitar. The service would soon be over. I felt my heart beating excitedly. After all the wonderful songs about helping others and loving the world, surely someone would come over and talk to me. I had so much to ask, so much to convey, and so much I wanted to learn.

People started leaving. The girls next to me got up and went out the other way so they would not have to pass by me. The boys in the front row walked by without looking my way. Still, I remained in the pew. I would not leave until the church shut down. I wanted someone to talk to me. I wanted to feel like I belonged.

Finally, an older man came over to me. He handed me a paper that seemed to be the program for the evening.

"Young lady, you can go downstairs if you want to, but I am going to close up here, so you will have to leave the pew."

Tears had come to my eyes without my noticing it and I could hardly read the program. Did it say that there were refreshments being served downstairs? Is that where everyone went?

"No, thank you," I said, now visibly crying. "I want only food for the soul. Do you happen to know where to get that?"

He looked at me curiously, and I suddenly felt sorry for him. He did not have a clue what I meant.

I continued my quixotic quest after that church experience, but with less hope. Definitely, there was something different about me. I did not seem to fit in anywhere. I was an outcast like my poor brother, only I had not chosen the crime track. Fortunately, all my younger sisters were "normal." They were content with the typical little-town life that Lancaster offered. Maybe being in one place had helped them, or being raised without an alcoholic father always around. I didn't ask why then, only what—what do I do now?

Meanwhile, back at the hippie scene, Jan had a steady boyfriend, and we took different paths. She wanted to live a love-and-peace lifestyle with her "old man," and I was headed for college. Since I would have to get some scholarship money, I started staying home in the evenings to study.

"Miriam, we got a new history teacher at school today," my younger sister, Karen, told me one afternoon. "You would really like him. He talks like you, and he has long hair."

"What do you mean he talks like me?" I asked Karen, who was in junior high.

"Oh, he talks about ideas, and tells us to think about things and discuss the subject with each other. You know, like you tell us to do about the Vietnam War and all that stuff. I think he is against the war too."

"Surely he did not say anything against the war in school?"

"No, but he brought in some newspaper articles that said things about America that were not too good. In fact, some of the kids said they were going to tell their parents."

"No way!"

"Well, he lives right down the street from us—about three houses down. I thought you might like him."

When I finished my homework, I walked outside our town house and looked down the street. All the houses were exactly the same in the group of ten. The only difference was what the residents put on their porch. Three houses down, the porch was empty, but what gave him away was the VW bug parked in front. I knew that it would appear odd for me to introduce myself uninvited, but if this man was anything like me, as my sister said, he would not mind. I walked up to the door and knocked.

"Yeah?" said a young man of about twenty who answered the door.

"Hi, I live a couple houses down."

"Yeah?" he said again.

"Well, my sister said that her teacher lived here and . . ."

"Come on in," he said to me as he called up the stairs. "Sonny, some hippie chick's here to see you."

I walked into a living room similar to ours. There were two other older boys sitting on the couch watching television. One motioned for me to sit next to him. He was a big fellow with curly black hair, and he smiled as he put his hand on my shoulder.

"My, you are a young one, aren't you?" he said, sardonically sizing up what appeared to be jailbait.

"I'm a senior," I said, not sure what he meant. I was beginning to feel very uncomfortable around these boys, who obviously were more sophisticated than I was, and I hadn't been prepared for a roomful of older males.

A man with shoulder-length, brown wavy hair was coming down the steps. He had a slight build and wore a full mustache. I remember thinking he had a nice smile.

"I'm Sonny," he said to me as he extended his hand to welcome me, "but I guess you heard of me as Mr. Economopoulus."

I was glad to stand up and move away from the bear grinning at my side. I introduced myself and then sat on another chair, feeling tension inside me caused by indecision on whether to stay or run away. However, Sonny looked safe.

"So . . . you're Karen's sister. You don't look like her." It was evident he was trying to make small talk, but he seemed interested.

"I look like me," I retorted, knowing immediately it was a stupid thing to say.

The other boys howled with laughter at my less than brilliant comment, which made me feel a slight desire to crawl into a hole. I was beginning to think it was not such a good idea to be here, but Sonny smiled in a way that made me feel comfortable.

"Well, let's go up in my room and we can talk there," he said casually.

That drew a round of catcalls.

"Remember, she's a minor."

"Don't do anything I wouldn't do. Or maybe I should say, don't do anything I would *want* to do."

I followed Sonny upstairs to the front bedroom. He had music playing and a few albums lying out on the floor. I looked at his collection.

"Who do you like?" he asked.

"Dylan; Crosby, Stills and Nash . . ."

"Do you like Carole King?"

"I never heard her."

"Well, you'll have to listen."

I sat down on the floor while he put on an album called *Tapestry*. He sat behind me on the bed with his knees touching my back while he told me about his musical tastes, his graduation from elite Franklin and Marshall, his work as a teacher, and his desire to go back to graduate school. He was twenty-four years old and from Massachusetts, and I remember feeling special to have a handsome college graduate interested in talking with me. It was my first intimate experience with someone so educated to whom I could relate. Up to this point, I had always felt a chasm between myself and the radical intellectual. But then, I was still relatively new in this counterculture predicted by contemporary visionaries, such as Paul Goodman, Allen Ginsberg, and Charles Reich.

My own vision included a major societal shift from war to peace, from hate to love, from bondage to liberation. I don't know if Sonny felt the same way, but I saw him as a fellow freedom fighter. When he offered me a pipe of marijuana, I took a hit. I still wanted to believe that smoking pot was a ritual between the enlightened, and maybe love would secure the connection. I let him take me to bed without any resistance. Since I was no longer a virgin, it didn't hurt anymore. With relatively little experience under my belt, I knew that it should feel good, but I had no idea what an orgasm should be like. Therefore, I never knew if I had one or not.

"I guess it is getting late for you," he said, as he rose to change the album.

"No, I don't have a curfew, " I replied. "And my homework is finished."

"So, you are conscientious about your homework. Tomorrow you can bring it over here if you like."

I spent many evenings at Sonny's house after that. I told my mother I was at a friend's house, which was not a lie; he had become my best friend. Associating with Sonny, I was introduced to many of the Franklin and Marshall graduates, mostly rich kids from New York and New England states, and I met the members of the same blues band that I used to listen to in the "AT." Although it was nice to be accepted by this group, who were not only "cool" but wealthy also, I knew it wasn't due to my merit as an individual but only because of my close friendship with Sonny. That troubled me, whereas I should have been basking in my newfound fellowship with the privileged.

I admired Sonny's intelligence, but more than anything I appreciated his gentleness. He never pushed me to do anything, and never belittled any of my viewpoints. Instead, he told me his own views without getting patronizing or offensive. He challenged me to think about what I was saying, but he did not criticize my youthful nonsense. And at seventeen, one can be very stupid.

Even though I came to Sonny's every time I was free, I did not consider him my boyfriend. I did not tell anyone at school that I was seeing him, and he never gave me a ring or necklace, or anything that signified we were "going out." I was too inhibited to ask why this was, but I eventually assumed that he realized I was too young to make our relationship public, or perhaps he thought that since I was seven years younger than he, I still had a lot to experience. I thought I did too.

"I want to go to the Moratorium against the war in Washington," I told him one spring day.

"You know I can't come," he said.

"I know, but I thought I would ask."

"Even if I did not teach, I would not go to the Moratorium. I have different ways to express my discontent with government policy."

"And so do I. But I want to go for the experience. I want to be part of the movement to stop the war."

"You are part of it right here. Go if you want to, of course. But how will you get there? Who is going with you?"

"I'm taking my sister, and we'll hitchhike."

"I can't tell you what to do," he said with a sigh.

I knew he did not approve of me hitchhiking, but he would never say it.

The Moratorium, held in April 1971, was a huge peace march against the war in Vietnam. I went to Washington to participate, slept on the Quaker church floor with hundreds of other dreamers, and was detained in a park by the National Guard. While there, I met an intense boy who read Chairman Mao religiously. I never saw him smile. Of the thousands of young people who came to Washington for those days, I met no one else. I was too busy observing this profoundly concentrated boy. He left for California when the Moratorium was over, and I don't even remember his name. But I remember the determined look on his face. I admired his dedication to a cause, and I thought to myself that I wanted to be as serious about an ideal as he was. Now, with a standard to measure up to, I just had to find the right ideal for me.

Sonny was there for me when I returned, but he didn't press for conversation. He just held me in his arms like an ever-present father. Sex was nothing for me to give in exchange for his masculine kindness.

After graduation from high school in June 1971, I went to Wildwood, a New Jersey beach town frequented mainly by young people, to look for a job in order to earn money for college. I found work in a restaurant as a waitress; all of the waitresses had to wear hot pants and I hated the idea. While in Wildwood, I met a boy from Pittsburgh who told me he had been born again. He witnessed to me about being a good Christian, saying that I should not give love freely, drink or smoke, or even listen to rock music. I should read my Bible every day and that would give me strength to resist evil. My roots were still in Christianity; however, Christians were always so close-minded and usually boring. But this boy was exciting, and he hung around with me, an obvious hippie. Why? Maybe there was still hope in this Jesus stuff he talked about. Since he did not say anything about going to church, I decided to follow his counsel. It wasn't hard for me to give up drugs, sex, and music, and soon I felt I was on the path to dedication—a higher ideal. Why I was such an idealist, I will never know.

Returning to Lancaster before summer was over, and before Sonny came back, I called Mick, my only friend left over from the Spruce Street gang. Mick had started hanging out with the Jesus People, a traveling group of ex-hippies who preached about Christ. Following their lead, Mick had destroyed all his "worldly" albums and listened only to Christian music.

When Sonny returned to Lancaster, I related the story of the Christian boy and the Jesus People. He was not impressed, but he respected my decision to start living a more "godly" lifestyle of no drugs or sex. We didn't sleep together after that.

A few weeks later, Sonny dropped me off at the Penn State campus in Schuylkill Haven where I would spend my freshman year. In a few days, he would be leaving for Europe, where he planned to stay for an extended period of time, while I was feeling safe at a small campus, with a renewed faith and two part-time jobs. We made no promises about the future, and it was an uneventful parting.

Dorm life was terrible. The girls who lived there were frivolous and uninteresting, and I did not make friends until I met Daisy. Living off campus, she supported herself by singing folk songs at a local coffeehouse and took classes at the college. She was a short, quiet girl who hid her bright blue eyes and rounded face behind long blond hair. Her whispery voice never held a hint of aggression. And her independent spirit was in complete contrast to her seemingly submissive attitude.

Daisy and I became good friends. I told her about my renewed belief in Jesus, and she confided that as a Catholic, she had always believed in God. Since she had such fantastic memories of a visit to the Greenwich Village hippie scene, we decided to go to New York during our winter break.

A little while before the semester ended, I saw a sign on a church saying that a film about a Christian commune would be playing that night. I rode over on my bike to watch it.

The documentary film, called *The Ultimate Trip*, was an episode from the weekly television news program *First Tuesday*. It documented the lifestyle of a group of Christians in Texas called the Children of God. I watched in awe as ex-hippies gave their testimonies about being lost and finding peace with God and one another in this commune. They sang songs and danced. They read their ever-present Bibles and quoted scriptures by memory. They ate together, watched each other's children, cooked, cleaned, worked, and farmed collectively. They said that no one had need of anything because everyone shared all they had—and it was enough. Here was pure communism, but these people were happy, not severe, like that boy at the Moratorium in Washington. These people were Christians, yet they looked like hippies in long skirts and flowing hair. And they had a vision—to change the world! Leaving the church as soon as the film was over, I tried to hide the tears in my eyes. I felt I had just seen the living purity of Jesus' words. I wanted to be like these people—to love everyone; to give my life for others; to be part of a true community. Maybe, during the summer break, Daisy and I could go out to Texas. The thought of meeting the Children of God gave me a new vision. Life had always seemed so strange to me and somehow I had become addicted to the unusual, the extraordinary, the mysterious. I felt like I was searching for meaning constantly, and for the first time, I thought the search would soon be over.

3

○ ○ ○

Through the Looking Glass

Daisy and I took the bus to my house in Lancaster on the way up to New York. We hitchhiked the rest of the way with about twenty dollars between us in our pockets. I had a change of clothes in my backpack, and Daisy carried a guitar and an old army bag with a few things in it. After spending the first day looking for fellow bohemians in Greenwich Village, all we had found were drug users, drug pushers, prostitutes, busy people going back and forth without glancing at anyone, and college students on their way back home. No one offered the peace and brotherhood that Daisy remembered from a few years ago. I spent the little money we had that first day buying food.

Soon it was getting dark, and we still had no place to go. As we walked aimlessly along a street, a burly man with coarse features asked us if we were lost. He was the only friendly person we had met all day.

"No, but we really don't have a place to go to," I said.

"Well, I have a place, if you want to come with me," he said with a sly smile. Something in his manner made me feel uneasy.

"Both of us?" I asked, thinking that I was being prudent.

"Sure, it's right around the corner."

We followed him to a doorway that opened onto a dilapidated and trash-littered hallway. He led us up three flights of stairs, each landing become darker and more dismal. On the third floor he stopped to talk to a girl who reminded me of the grotesque groupies I had seen at big rock concerts in Philadelphia. A feeling of despair swept over me, since those heavily made-up groupies exposing their bodies had shattered my idealism of rock stars. She passed him something, and he turned and opened a door to the right.

"Here we are," he said, showing us the way into a room full of smoke and old dumpy chairs. There was a roll-away bed pushed up against one wall where another girl was slouched like a rag doll someone had discarded long ago. As she looked at us with mascara-laden, glazed eyes, I realized that we were not among hippies.

"Where did you pick these fresh apples?" she murmured, coming out of her drug-induced nod.

"Get off the bed, Mona. What are you doing all f——d up in here?" he barked at her like a dog.

"I brought your bag. It's over there under the chair," she said, too spaced out to break the gaze she had fixed upon us. She seemed quite transfixed with our presence, but after a few minutes of indiscreet staring, she got up and slithered out the door like a snake who had decided we were not worth her time or energy.

Our host sat on the bed and took a bag of white powder out from under the chair.

"Sit down," he said, patting the bed beside him.

Daisy and I took the chairs that were nearest the door. He noticed our move to safety.

"You aren't afraid of me, are you?" he asked as he walked past us and locked the door. "I just want to be sure no one comes barging in here."

He looked more like a bear than anyone I'd ever seen, but a dirty one. Plumping himself down again on the bed, he put the bag under the mattress. Looking us over with a mischievous grin, he pulled out a joint and lit it up, passing it to us after taking a long drag. I pretended to take some and passed it to Daisy, who I knew never took any drugs. She did the same and passed it back.

"Hey, you girls aren't taking any. Come on, you can't be like that. You want Uncle Charlie to get angry?"

For the first time, I began to be really afraid. I didn't know what Uncle Charlie did when he got angry, but I did not want to find out.

"Well, we're just very hungry, and this gives you the munchies, you know."

"Oh, you want some food? I'll find out what we have. Food is not our line of merchandise, you know, but I'll see what I can scrounge up."

Charlie swaggered to the hallway and summoned Mona.

"Hey, get these girls something to eat. What do we have here anyway?"

"What are you talking about? There ain't no food here," she replied.

"Well, go the hell out on the street and find something."

Charlie came back in and was puffing away until Mona returned with some hot dogs. By now, Charlie was so stoned he forgot to lock the door after she left. We ate our hot dogs and kept an eye on Charlie, who was talking about the great stuff he could get for us—anything we wanted. Now he was drinking from a bottle, and he lit up another joint as he lay back on the bed, totally wasted. I nudged Daisy, and we grabbed our stuff and bolted out the door, down the steps, and out onto the street without looking back. We couldn't hear Charlie or anyone else behind us, but we still ran through the street in the direction of any light. Finally, we found ourselves in front of a well-lit college dormitory.

By this time we were so desperate, we did not care what anyone thought. We started banging on all the doors until someone answered.

"Please, let us in," I asked. "Some man is chasing us, and we don't know where we are."

The boy who answered the door didn't seem to believe us, but he reluctantly agreed to let us stay. We bedded down for the night on the floor.

The next day we were back on the street. I suggested that Daisy sing in the cafés so we could make some money to get a train out of there. After searching in vain all morning for places to sing, we decided to give up on that idea and just bum money instead by panhandling on the street.

By nightfall, we had only collected about ten dollars. We decided to go to the train station, spend the night there, and start panhandling again in the morning. On our way we passed an art gallery, and I stopped to look at the paintings.

"Hi, do you believe in Jesus?" someone asked.

It was a boy about my age carrying a guitar. He had a short, smiling girl with him.

"Yes. In fact, I carry a Bible with me all the time," I responded gaily, happy to hear a kind voice.

"You do! Wow! What version is it?"

"New Revised."

"Oh," he said, looking disappointed, but his face quickly lit up again. "I have a King James Version with me. Do you want to compare verses?"

I looked to Daisy, who was engrossed in conversation with the girl. "What do you mean?" I asked.

"Here, I'll show you a verse in my Bible, and you look for it in your Bible, and we can see how they're different."

I thought he had some point that he really wanted to make, so I joined in. We sat on the edge of the curb and he took out a three-by five-inch King James Bible. I took out my paperbound New Testament.

For the next half hour, we looked up scriptures, which he was much better at than I. He explained the beauty and purity of the King James version, which is written in Shakespearean English, and I felt my puny New Revised Version was totally inadequate.

Daisy and the girl she was talking to came over to participate in the impromptu Bible study. The girl's name was Praise.

"Should we go get some coffee?" said the boy. "It is cold out here."

Daisy and I agreed, and we walked together to a diner, where we spent the next hour listening to their explanations of Bible verses over cups of hot coffee.

"Why don't you girls come home with us?" Praise said. "We have a big campground upstate, and there is plenty of room."

"Who are 'we'?" asked Daisy with a commandlike quality to her voice.

"Oh, we're a group of people trying to serve the Lord. Maybe you heard about us. The papers call us the Children of God."

"You are with the Children of God?" I asked. "The ones I saw in a documentary?"

"Yes, that was our camp in Texas. We have a camp here in New York now. Do you want to come up with us tonight?"

"How far is it from here?" asked Daisy.

"Oh, not far," said Praise. "We have a bus taking us up in about an hour."

Daisy seemed okay about it, so we followed them to an old yellow school bus surrounded by a large group of noisy young people. One boy from the crowd came over to us.

"Praise the Lord," he said, giving Praise and the boy a quick hug. "You found some sheep!"

"Yes. This is Miriam, and this is Daisy," piped up Praise, pushing her long brown hair out of her eyes with tiny cold fingers. "They want to come home with us."

"Hallelujah! Are they saved yet?'

"Yes," I said, thinking that this seemed to be the criterion for visiting them. I was thrilled to be going to a real Children of God commune.

"Great," said the boy. "Well, take them on the bus and get them filled with the Spirit. Oh, and give them some food if they are hungry." He seemed genuinely happy and concerned for us. This was a pleasant change from the treatment we had received since coming to New York.

I entered the bus with excited apprehension. All the seats had been taken out, and there were blankets and pillows all over the floor. Someone was handing out sandwiches from a cardboard box at the front. I took a sandwich and followed Praise to the back. Daisy had been taken by a girl to another part of the bus.

Once we sat on the floor of the bus, Praise quickly took control of the conversation. She was a totally spaced-out girl who punctuated every sentence with "Praise the Lord," or "Hallelujah." She talked to me nonstop about the Bible, the Holy Spirit, Jesus' message of telling the world about salvation, loving others like yourself, and every other spiritual lesson I had ever heard about in connection with the Bible. Only she said it with such sincerity and belief that it came alive.

The bus began to fill up, and after a while we were packed. The young man who had greeted us stood up at the front.

"Okay. Hallelujah! Praise the Lord. Is everyone here?"

Most of the crowd became quiet and looked at him with respect. He was obviously some kind of group leader.

"All right. Well, we are going to pull out of New York City now. So everyone who wants to stay in hell better get off, because we are going to heaven."

Half of the people on the bus started screaming, "Hallelujah—praise the Lord—we love you, Jesus," in a confused type of unison.

A few people left. Daisy and I stayed on.

"Praise the Lord," said the man again. "I see we have some new people coming up with us. I hope you are all saved and filled with the Spirit. If you have any questions, please ask the people sitting next to you. I want you to be sure you know where you are going."

I wasn't sure if he meant where we are going when we die, or right now. But since I knew both of these answers, I didn't ask anyone.

After a few minutes, some more people got off the bus.

"Okay. Let's say a prayer for this old bus and get going. I don't know if we have gas or not. The gauge doesn't work. But God is not bound by a gas gauge, is He?"

The bus gave an uproar of "Hallelujahs" again.

The man led us in a spirited prayer, which was interspersed with more "Praise the Lords" and emphatic "Amens" from the crowd.

I wrapped myself in a blanket I found next to me since it was getting cold and the prayer was long. Finally, the bus started up. Another round of praises!

Praise brought the other boy back to our corner. I found out that his name was Ezra. Evidently, he had been in the Children of God (COG) less time than Praise, indicated by the way he kept looking to her for approval of what he said.

"I think Miriam might want to ask the Holy Spirit in," said Praise, "and I thought you might like to be here, since she is your sheep."

Ezra and Praise quoted all the verses they knew on the Holy Spirit, what it meant to be filled with the Spirit, and what would happen to me afterward. They protested when I told them I had already been baptized, saying that was not really enough. I looked out the window at the dirty city going by, so happy to be leaving it. Why should I not ask the Spirit in again? It seemed to mean so much to them, and it certainly would not hurt.

"Okay," I said, "I'll ask the Spirit to fill me."

Praise gave a squeaky sound of delight, and she called over a few more people to pray with me. Suddenly there were about a dozen pair of hands on my head, shoulders, and back. While Ezra led a prayer asking the Holy Spirit to fill me, the people holding me captive began a praise session of "Hallelujah—praise the Lord—we love you, Jesus" that lasted at least twenty minutes. I had my eyes closed the entire time, and when I opened them, I looked out the window. It was snowing.

The event seemed so symbolic. I had closed my eyes when we were in the filth of the city, and now, after asking to be filled with the Spirit, we were driving by a clean, snow-white field. Maybe I really did get filled with God's Spirit after all. It reminded me of the Bible verse I had memorized recently, "Though your sins be as scarlet, they shall become white as snow."

The bus stopped frequently on the way up. Each time this happened, everyone would start praising the Lord while the leader and some boys got out to tinker with the motor. The story I heard was that the bus was really out of gas, but the Lord just made it start anyway, contingent on the amount of praising we would give Him.

Eventually, I fell asleep, but not before I had concluded that this was my fate. Had I not been searching for something to dedicate my life to, having found nothing for me in all the usual places? Had I not seen a film on this very group just weeks before, and even then decided I would like to live in such a place? Had I not gone through one of the most hellish and depressing experiences of my life and been rescued by these people—perhaps my spiritual family?

It was the middle of the night when we arrived at the campsite in Ellenville, New York. Awakened from a deep sleep, I followed Praise in a daze to a bunkhouse and crashed. I woke the next morning to a group of girls crying, "Hallelujah—praise the Lord—we love you, Jesus." This was a frequent event throughout the day, and soon I would participate in the praise sessions myself.

The camp was a beautiful nature retreat that would have been comfortable in the summer. Unfortunately, it was not built for winter use, and every room was freezing except in the main building. There were two bunkhouses: a large one that held the girls and a smaller one for the boys. There were also a few cabins down by the wooded area and a bungalow set off by itself. On that cold December morning, I was grateful to leave the freezing bunkhouse and go into the warmth of the main building.

The main building contained a large meeting hall, a huge industrial kitchen, some rooms reserved for special classes, one bathroom, and a second floor. I would not even see the second floor for months. I stayed in the meeting room or kitchen those first few days.

In the morning we had a collective breakfast in the meeting hall converted into a dining room. There were close to a hundred bedraggled young people forming a line. Ezra came in and took me through the food line, quoting verses to me that I later learned he was memorizing.

"Wow, we got some doughnuts this morning, praise the Lord," he exclaimed, referring to a big cardboard drum filled with squished pastries. "Don't you want any?"

I declined. Instead, I took a bowl of watery oatmeal and some very weak coffee. I was soon to learn that choice of food was limited, but in those early days, food was the last thing I was concerned about.

Ezra ate with an enthusiasm that struck me as rather exaggerated. He always came with me when we went through the food line, and when I realized he was hungry, I took everything allotted me and offered him what I could not eat. He seemed to really appreciate this, although he never said anything but "Thank you, Jesus!"

Someone talked with me every minute of the day. Either Praise or Ezra or one of the two hundred or more other people who lived there. By design, I was never alone, and I hardly ever saw Daisy alone either. However, when Praise came with me to the bathroom, I protested.

"Okay, praise the Lord! I'll be right out here," she said sweetly.

It was quite interesting. I had no idea what commune life would be like, but this seemed to be a prime example. We ate together, worked together, sang together, and (separated into boys, girls, and married couple dorms) slept together. The main purpose seemed to be training new disciples, like me, to become full-time witnessers for the Lord. I learned that the Children of God had set up witnessing homes in many big cities across the nation, and would soon be setting one up in Manhattan. In addition, they made weekly trips to New York City and came back with dozens of new recruits. Most of them were drugged-out hippies. Many stayed on for days, weeks, or months, and during this time no one touched any dope. Thorough searches for drugs were conducted frequently, and no smoking or alcohol was allowed.

A few days after I had arrived—I lost count of the exact number of days that had gone by—a "sister" suggested that I go to the "Forsake All" and get new clothes. She explained that like the early disciples in the Bible, we shared everything here, including our worldly possessions.

When I told her that I had brought enough clothes with me, she informed me that I would have to forsake those, or give them up. "Old things are passed away, all things become new," she said, quoting II Corinthians 5:17.

The Forsake All held the discarded clothes of all the people who had joined at this particular commune, or "colony," as they called it. The Forsake All room was large and orderly. Boys' clothes were neatly folded in one area and girls' in another. The sister who took me suggested I get a few skirts.

"We believe that girls should dress feminine and modestly," she said with authority, as if she were my fashion coordinator.

She chose two long, shapeless skirts that were similar to the ones that most of the other girls were wearing. She allowed me to pick two blouses and a sweater. Those five items, along with a few pairs of underwear, would be my clothes for the next couple of months. I was also allotted a long warm coat. My army jacket, along with my beloved embroidered jeans, were taken away. I later saw the army jacket on a boy, but I never saw my jeans again.

It seemed that the members who had been with the Children for a while "had the faith" and that I was a disciple. Being a college student and having some definite goals in life, I was quite different from the regular recruit they picked up in New York. They informed me that I was a "chosen one" of God, like the rest of them there. I felt a surge of pride and recognition. I knew I was different—no wonder they had found me! Then I brushed it aside out of ingrained humility, probably learned in Sunday school as a little girl. Instead, I should be thankful that He had chosen little, insignificant me. I would have to prove I was worthy. The Bible did say, "Ye have not chosen me, but I have chosen you" (John 15:16).

I eventually could have taken these thoughts further and come to the logical conclusion that God doesn't go around "choosing people" in this way, but I was never left alone to think for myself. As a new disciple, I constantly had a big brother or sister at my side, usually quoting scriptures that reinforced the Children of God lifestyle and beliefs. "All that believed were together and had all things in common; and sold their possessions and goods and parted them to all men" (Acts 2:44). "And be not conformed to this world: but be ye transformed by the renewing of your mind" (Romans 12:2). I learned that new disciples should never be left alone with their thoughts, and that I should not think like a "flatlander," who could only see in a flat dimension. I tried to discipline my mind to not think of anything but biblical, spiritual, higher thoughts.

Although I don't remember making any verbal decision to join or signing anything, I handed over to the group all my belongings, including my driver's license, which was never returned. In my purse, I'd had only the few dollars we had panhandled in New York, which was also handed over, and I never held money again for years. It would also be years before I went to a store to buy anything, read a book, listened to radio, or watched TV. How I spent every minute of my life was decided for me; or rather, I let them decide it for me.

Many nights as I lay in bed—the only time I was alone—I would review my past life, which now seemed so very distant. At first I was saddened that I would never finish college, but soon these thoughts receded further and further away, and finally they never appeared again. I missed my family, but I believed I had met God's True Family. After all, that was what I had been praying for, and didn't God answer prayers? I read a passage from a booklet that was given me, which said:

> We belong to the greatest Family in the world, the Family of God's Love. Surely God must think you worthy to give you such a priceless privilege to be a member of His Family! We're the mighty army of Christian soldiers, fighting a relentless war for the truth and love of God, against the confusion of Babylon, the anti-God, Antichrist systems of the world. . . . We are the hard-core, the spearhead, the avant garde of this last spiritual revolution. We are the Cadre, the leadership of it, that requires one hundred per cent dedication. . . .

We called ourselves "revolutionaries" in a spiritual and material sense combined. I knew it would be hard. It was like joining an army, giving up my personal desires for a greater cause. But I felt like I was meant to do this—it was my purpose in life. And as I was told, I was still young enough to change: In another few years I would have become so ingrained with "system" thoughts, I could never be a "revolutionary."

My life in those days as a new disciple meant waking up early to pray alone for one hour and then together with a group of girls led by our "tribe leader." After a breakfast of powdered milk, doughnuts, and oatmeal, I helped to clean the camp, which, considering that it sometimes housed up to three hundred people, was kept fairly clean. Then began a long day of Bible classes, broken only by a small lunch of a sandwich or sometimes a fruit salad. At the end of the day, we were given time to memorize verses, always with an older brother or sister to guide us, and then to read the Bible silently, but not alone. A late dinner was followed by "inspiration," which included a few hours of singing and then a message from our leader. It was after a few weeks of those messages that I understood that our top leader and founder was a man who called himself Moses David.

Moses, called Mo for short, based his philosophy of a Christian communal life—which he preached, taught, and enforced through writings called Mo letters—on the biblical scriptures. Just as the Russian Communists were inspired by *The Communist Manifesto*, and the Nazi movement by *Mein Kampf*, the Mo letters told us what to believe in, and how to live this belief. Like those other revolutionary works, the Mo letters gave us the hope that we would change the world. However, the big difference was—our leader heard straight from God, and God was still speaking!

Mo wrote that "ninety per cent of our ministry here is condemning the church and the church people and the damn system" ("A Sample, Not a Sermon" J:55). When he began preaching that to the hippies gathering in a coffeehouse in Huntington Beach, California, they listened to this strange man in his late forties wearing a beard and sunglasses. He looked like one of them, only older and wiser, and he had a plan taken from one of the greatest plans ever written for humanity—the New Testament.

But Mo wasn't always a bohemian prophet. He started his adult life in the shadow of his famous evangelist mother, Virginia Brandt Berg, whom he claimed had been paralyzed by a car accident and miraculously healed. She became a relatively successful Christian evangelist and eventually had her own radio program called *Meditation Moments*. Her third child (second son), David Brandt Berg, was born after the accident and healing on February 18, 1919, in Oakland, California. His father, Hjalmer Emmanuel Berg, was a handsome Swedish singer who met Virginia before he was converted to Christianity by her father, a wealthy preacher. Virginia and Hjalmer both dedicated their lives to Christian work. He became a pastor, but according to Mo's testimony, he played second fiddle to his more successful wife.

David Berg eventually became a pastor himself, ordained by the British-American Ministerial Federation in 1941. Berg details his personal history in a publication he wrote dated January 1976, titled "Our Shepherd, Moses David." In it he claims that he graduated from Monterey Union High School in California with the highest scholastic record in the school's eighty-year history, and was offered numerous scholarships for college. He was drafted into the Army a few days after the bombing of Pearl Harbor, but since he did not believe in killing, he claims, he served as a conscientious objector with the U.S Army Corps of Engineers at Fort Belvoir, Virginia, until he received a complete-disability discharge due to heart trouble. According to his story, the Army thought he was dying of double pneumonia, but when he promised God he would serve Him faithfully, he was instantly healed. After a few years of evangelistic work, he returned to college on the GI Bill, studying philosophy, psychology, and political science, and became seriously involved in the study of socialism and communism. He later wrote, "I soon saw that the purportedly unselfish goals of these political systems could never be achieved without the love of God in the hearts of men, as in the pure Christian communism of the Early Church" ("Our Shepherd, Moses David" 351: 18). After attending various colleges, with no record of ever obtaining a degree, he took a private teaching job for a few years and then several positions with television and radio evangelists. Finally, at forty-nine years of age, without a ministry or job, he brought his wife and four children to live with his retired mother in Huntington Beach, California, in 1968. There he began to preach in the small coffeehouse run by a church group called Teen Challenge. He once wrote of this event, "I'll never forget the first time I walked into the club and lay down on the floor with you [the hippies] in my broken sandals, ragged old jacket, lengthening hair and graying beard, and one of you lying next to me spoke up with the cheery greeting of welcome, 'Hi, Dad! What's your trip?' " ("Our Shepherd, Moses David" 351:29).

His trip was the supposed revolution for Jesus, and within months a handful of the searching young people who had become disillusioned with the world began following his teachings. Known as "Uncle David" then, he opened his home, or rather his mother's home, to them, and so began the model of communal living that he believed the Bible taught.

From a pragmatic point of view, Berg just happened to be in the right place at the right time. The California flower-power scene had attracted not only drug users and freedom seekers, but also the dropouts from staid academic institutions, including some of the cream of America's upper society crop. When the adult children of wealthy families joined, these rich kids gave all their possessions and money to the group, and Mo had the financial means to live incognito for the rest of his life. He started to go underground, and his whereabouts were known only to a faithful few.

Knowing none of this when I joined the Children of God, I was told that Mo was the end-time prophet spoken about in the Bible, which said "Afterward shall the children of Israel return, and seek the Lord their God and David their king; and shall fear the Lord and His goodness in the latter days" (Hosea 3:5). Mo was a charismatic leader, but most of his followers, including me, never even saw him in person. Whenever doubts entered my mind about following a "personality," I reminded myself that it was the *ideal* I was following, not the person who expressed it. I never met Mo and did not desire to meet him, but I thought the ideals he preached could change the world.

Our so-called prophet wrote hundreds of letters to us over the years, which were eventually published in eight volumes. Mo's control over our minds and bodies developed through a gradual process. In the beginning, I was allowed to hear only certain letters, which taught me his "revolutionary rules" such as: attend all classes, study the Bible, go witnessing; do not leave to go anywhere without permission; absence without leave will be considered desertion; no dating, no smoking, no smooching; obey leadership absolutely!

It was very difficult living in such a suppressive environment, but for idealistic reasons, I accepted it. By the end of my first week, however, I was looking forward to going out on a witnessing trip to

New York City. But when the weekend arrived, Praise informed me I should stay at the camp and "get into the Word."

Getting into the Word meant reading my Bible and memorizing scriptures. I was given an old King James Bible, and my New Testament was now in the Forsake All room. Classes on the Bible were held every day. A "set card," which contained over one hundred verses that should be memorized by every new disciple, was given to me with instructions that I should learn at least two verses a day.

One morning, as I sat memorizing, a sister whom I had been told was my "tribe leader" came and gave me a piece of paper. She was the only girl in the camp whom I did not like. A few years older than I, she was always rushing around like she had more important things to do than the rest of us.

"This is your new name," she said curtly. "I got it for you in prayer this morning."

Quoting the now familiar verse "old things are passed away and all things are become new," she explained that each of the disciples took a new name from the Bible when they joined. I was thinking of a pretty name, like Crystal, from the Book of Revelations, or Joy, mentioned throughout the Bible, not realizing that my name would be picked for me.

I opened the folded paper she had given me and read, "Jeshanah."

"Where is Jeshanah in the Bible?" I asked.

She told me some chapter in Chronicles, but I did not write it down, and I was too intimidated by her to ever ask again. So I was called Jeshanah for years without ever knowing where it came from. Much later I found out it was the name of a town.

Daisy was given a name from the New Testament, Berea, which I thought was much prettier. However, she did not like the fact that she could not choose her own name; nor did she like not being able to sing and play guitar at the nightly inspiration. According to people whom we found out were the "leaders," new disciples must "prove" themselves before they played at inspiration. The songs of the group were inspired by God, and they didn't want any "worldly music" around.

"Music is the language of this generation, and we speak it" ("London" 58:33), Mo wrote. "Our music is the miracle that attracts so many to our message about the Man. It's the magic that heals their souls and wounded spirits and proves our messiahship, that we are their saviors" ("Thanks and Comment" 157:6). For idealists who were disillusioned with the sex, drugs, and rock and roll that hippie-dom offered, the fresh and hopeful sounds of the group's music was a definite attraction. Mo's early disciples each played a musical instrument, usually guitar, and many were accomplished musicians and songwriters before they became his disciples. Hard-beating contemporary melodies were accompanied by catchy, meaningful verses such as the following, written by a young man who joined when he was fourteen years old:

> *Life is a lonely highway with no reason to travel on,*
> *And you don't know where you're headed, but you know you've got to go on,*
> *And you don't want to walk alone, but you're seeking a better home,*
> *Oh, Lord, how long will this search go on?*

Since I had already been initiated to the dangers of worldly music by the Jesus People, I did not find this so difficult to accept. Daisy, however, missed playing her songs, which she claimed were not worldly.

Inspiration time started after dinner and lasted late into the night. Since I did not have a watch, and there were few clocks around, I never knew what time it was, but I suspect that we stayed up in inspiration until past midnight, and sometimes until two or three in the morning.

Inspiration started with a prayer, like everything else we did. The room seemed to shake, with two to three hundred people gathered tightly and praising the Lord for up to an hour, depending on who was leading the inspiration. When the praises slowed down, someone started a prayer, then another and another. Finally, one of the leaders plucked a tune on a guitar, which was a sign to start the music, and everyone who was allowed to be an "inspirationalist" would grab a guitar and join in the singing. Most of the songs told tales of being lost, or lonely, or searching for the truth, finding it in Jesus, and now happily serving the Lord. Some songs were apocalyptic, about an end-time that was fast approaching, and warned people to turn to the Lord. Many of the songs had lively Gypsy tunes, and we danced holding hands, going around in a circle, and kicking up our feet in what we thought was a traditional Jewish dance. When this lively activity became too hectic, we divided into groups of two and danced with partners, always holding hands and swinging around in a circle. There was no slow dancing and no touching body-to-body. It was very innocent and extremely exhilarating.

Often these meetings were led by a visitor, whom I later learned was a traveling leader. That person, male or female, eventually took over the inspiration by giving a talk, leading a Bible class, or reading a letter from Moses David.

I was not interested in who Moses was at that time. I was more interested in how to contact my mother. I had lost track of time, but it must have been a week since I had left Lancaster. My mother knew that Berea and I had gone to New York City, but I told her I would call collect in a few days. I knew she would be worried by now. In addition, our family, like most, were always together for Christmas, but for reasons explained emphatically to me, the COG leaders did not want me to go home for Christmas. They explained that Christmas was a "systemite" (meaning worldly) idea, and that to partake of the Christmas holiday spirit was almost like worshiping the devil. Actually, I could not find any verses in the Bible encouraging believers to celebrate Christmas, so there was little I could say to counter their argument. However, I did want to call my mother and tell her where I was. It was difficult to find someone among all those people who knew how I could make a phone call, even though there was a phone booth in the hallway of the main building. Since I was never alone, and had no money, I could not simply make a call.

The day I decided to confront one of the leaders with my request I became violently sick. After vomiting all morning, I went to the bathroom every five minutes with diarrhea. At mealtime I could not even look at food, but since the bunkrooms were so cold, I came over to the dining room anyway, went through the food line, and gave my food to some boys. Everyone was very concerned about me, which they showed by constantly laying hands on me and praying that I would be shown why I was sick and "get the victory." Praise suspected that I was sick because I wanted to call my mother, and she frequently showed me Bible verses that said I should forsake my family.

"And a man's foes shall be they of his own household. He that loveth father or mother more than me is not worthy of me: and he that loveth son or daughter more than me is not worthy of me" (Matthew 10:36–37).

"And everyone that hath forsaken houses, or brethren, or sisters, or father, or mother, or wife, or children, or lands, for my name's sake, shall receive an hundredfold, and shall inherit everlasting life" (Matthew 19:29).

By now I had decided that I wanted to serve the Lord, and it was becoming clear that included giving up my past life and starting anew. I could hardly believe it meant leaving my family, but there it was— written in the Bible. I cried for days, and I remembered when I was younger and had told my mother that I wanted to be a missionary when I grew up, she had cried and said, "Don't do that, I'll never see you again." Although it made me very sad, this seemed to be my fate. Everywhere I went, I was crying, and my new brothers and sisters prayed for me. This was normal, they explained. "No victory without a battle."

One evening, as I was sitting in the hallway with my full plate of food beside me on the floor untouched, a young man came and sat next to me. I knew he was an "older brother," meaning he had been in the group for at least a few months, but he looked to be not much older than twenty. I was considered a "babe," a new disciple. I had also noticed him because I thought he was cute, but those thoughts were supposed to be prayed out of my mind.

"What's the matter?" he said in a kind voice, noticing I did not have a smile on my face like everyone else in the camp.

Like a volcano erupting, I blurted out all my complaints. "I can't stand this anymore," I whined. "I have no time to myself. I can't read anything but the Bible. I don't wear clothes I want, or talk about things I like, or even to the people I want to talk to. And this food. It's horrible. I can't eat. I probably got food poisoning from it."

I felt terrible for being so ungrateful after all they had done for me, and I stopped as mixed emotions of shame and anger filled my eyes with tears.

He put his arm around me, which even in my emotional state I knew was not allowed. He was unusually tender and caring.

"Hey, I didn't like this food either, but you get used to it. And it isn't always like this. We're just in a big colony here, but when I was up in the home in Boston, we ate some real nice food. You know, when I first came here, I used to steal yogurt from the refrigerator when no one was looking."

"There's yogurt in the refrigerator?" I asked, surprised, since yogurt was my favorite treat and I had not seen any since I'd been here.

"Yeah, sometimes. They buy it for the pregnant mothers upstairs. So, it really is a sin to take it. But hey, I know Jesus loves me, and he's forgiven me for more than that."

He went on to tell me that he used to be part of the Mafia in New York City and had committed terrible crimes. He used to take drugs and sell drugs and worse. But now, with this Family and God's help, he was a changed person. And so what if he could not eat everything he wanted? He could help people like me find a new life.

I found it humorous that he talked about food. Maybe he was always hungry like most of the boys here.

"Do you want my food?" I said. "I'm not hungry."

He took it and ate while telling me more of his past life as a sinner.

"Do you have a mother?" I asked, tears again forming in my eyes.

"Sure I do."

"Do you ever get to talk to her?'

"Yeah. I write to her, and I call when I go to New York."

"Well, I haven't talked to my mother since I came here," I cried. "And I don't even know what day it is. Has Christmas passed yet?"

"You mean you haven't called your mother for Christmas and you're a babe? Babes are supposed to call their parents. Who is your tribe leader anyway? She's supposed to take care of that."

He got up and walked down the hall and up those forbidden steps to the second floor. In about ten minutes a leader whom I knew as Hosea came down and talked with me. He and his wife were about my age, but they dressed and looked like corporate managers. I learned later that they did our public relations work. He told me that his wife was coming down so I could call my mother, and if I wanted to, we could go visit her. It turned out that Christmas had passed two days earlier.

This calculated act of apparent kindness probably kept me in the Children of God. I was ready to leave and forget about serving the Lord, even if I was a "chosen one," as they said. At that time, I did not realize they were allowing me to do something that was my right to do all along, and pathetically, I was touched by their love and concern for me. In addition, I ashamedly felt that this longing to return to my "flesh family," as they called it, was really a selfish desire for clean sheets, healthy food, and more sleep. The lessons they had been teaching me, such as to beware of natural inclinations, to rebuke the devil, and to seek godly counsel, became clearer.

Hosea and his wife drove me home the next day as promised. My mother had been terribly worried about me, but fortunately, Daisy had called her mother, so she knew that I was living somewhere in upstate New York. My whole family was amazed that I was quitting college to join a commune, since I had been talking about school as long as they could remember. However, as usual, my mother let me do what I wanted, even though she tried to discourage me. She really didn't know what this group was about, but she seemed relieved that they were at least "Christian." My father was not around at that time, and I never knew what he thought since I had absolutely no communication with him.

My older brother, Steve, was home when we arrived in Lancaster. Hosea witnessed to him about Jesus, and when we left the next day, Steve decided to come with us. I also packed up everything from my personal possessions that Hosea thought the Family could use.

When we stopped for gas on the way up, Steve got out of the car to smoke a cigarette. Hosea stopped him.

"If you want to come with us, Steve, you need to stop smoking, drinking, and drugs, right now."

I watched the interaction intensely. I knew Steve had been smoking for years, and he probably was hooked on a few drugs.

"Okay," he said, and threw the pack of cigarettes into the trash.

Steve was separated into the boys' area when we got to the camp, and I hardly spoke with him after that. I heard that he was "growing in the Spirit" and had already memorized about half of the set card. By New Year's Eve, he was chosen, along with me, to go on a trip to New York City to witness and recruit new disciples.

We were taught witnessing tips on the way down by one of the leaders at the camp. James looked to be in his late twenties, a handsome man who was originally from New York. While he instructed us on the best places to witness and what areas to stay away from, he opened a gallon bottle of wine, and we all received about half a cup to warm us up. I learned that there is nothing wrong with drinking wine, as long as you don't drink too much. After all, Jesus' first miracle was to turn water into wine. I didn't have to worry about getting too much. This was my first and last half-cup until I got married, six months later.

I liked James. He was not as strict as the other leaders, and he did not praise the Lord as long as everyone else did, going on and on indefinitely. When we said our prayers before leaving the bus, he said a short prayer and let us out.

I was paired with an older sister while Steve went with an older brother. This was my first time outside the camp other than the trip home. My older sister was relatively lenient, and she did not want to stand out in the cold as much I did not want to, so we spent a lot of time walking in the hotels. I went to the bathroom once and stuffed a half-used roll of tissue into my bag. It would be used later to supplement the three sheets of toilet paper we were allowed to have when we went to the bathroom at the colony. All the time I was out, I wondered if my brother would come back to the bus.

Due to the extreme confusion caused by the celebrating crowds around Times Square that night, it was ridiculous to try to witness, which consisted of talking to isolated people about Jesus. Returning to the bus early, I waited anxiously for Steve to come back. Finally, he got on the bus, wearing a Cheshire cat grin.

"Hey, man, this stuff is real." he said. "Man, I was tempted at every corner to split. I mean, I know plenty of places in New York to score drugs, but, man, I couldn't do it."

I was so happy. Seeing my brother free of drugs was worth any sacrifice on my part.

Living in the COG during those early days was like learning a whole new way of life. I was eventually told the story of how Moses David formed the group from a band of Jesus People in California in 1968. By the time I joined in 1971, there were COG communities all over the United States, the largest ones being the Texas Soul Clinic, which I had seen on the documentary film, and the one in Ellenville where I was now living. A few months before, Moses' natural children had taken over a large Jesus People commune in Georgia, called the House of Judah. Most of the people who joined with that community were now leaders at different colonies. We had a few of them in New York, but most of our leaders were *the* original members, who had now been with the Family, as it was called by initiates, for three or four years. Therefore, I was able to meet many of the top leaders when I was still a babe, although the value of this privilege escaped me at that time.

Sometime in January 1972 a group of the most dedicated babes were chosen to go to a special training camp in Montreal. My brother, Steve, Berea (old Daisy), and I were among those chosen. Steve had already memorized the whole set card of about a hundred verses, which took most babes at least six months; therefore, the leaders thought he was destined to be a great teacher. We crossed the Canadian border by pretending we were a church group on a day visit to a Canadian youth meeting. One of our leaders even dressed in the traditional Episcopalian black with white collar. This ruse enabled us to slip across the border without everyone on the bus being checked.

Steve felt obliged to inform the leader that he was actually on probation in the state of Pennsylvania, having just come out of prison. Fearing any legal repercussions, they promptly sent him back. I learned months later that he had returned to Lancaster to start a new colony, but he eventually slipped back to his old ways with his criminal friends. It would be ten years before I saw him again.

Meanwhile, Berea, my only other contact from the outside world, was having problems. She thought she might be pregnant from her old boyfriend back home, and whether it was an excuse or not, she slipped away one night into the cold Canadian winter, and never returned. I stayed through babes' training camp, during an intensely cold winter in Montreal, and then returned to Ellenville in the spring.

By now I was an older sister, having been in the group for six months. Since I had no inclination or desire to be a tribe leader, or to do anything in a leadership capacity, I volunteered to work in the nursery. Ellenville now had a population of nearly three hundred disciples and had become the home for quite a few mothers and children, now that spring had warmed the old camp to a tolerable degree. The camp now made use of all five buildings: the main house where meetings were held, food was served, and leaders lived; the boys' dorm; the girls' dorm; and a couple of small bungalows for married couples. A nursery was established in the main building and soon expanded out into the girls' dorm. Regardless of how crowded or uncomfortable the other rooms were, the nursery was always clean and well furnished. I liked being in a place that felt more like a "home."

Leaders and their wives were coming through on their way to Europe, following Moses David's directives to go into all the world and witness. With all these leaders and wannabe leaders around, I felt nice and safe in the nursery where I knew what to expect—doo-doo-filled diapers and babies burping and drooling. Since I had helped to raise four younger sisters, I seemed to have more experience and general know-how concerning babies than most of the newer sisters. Leaders did not work in the nursery. In fact, I was not sure what work they did, other than read the Bible and lead inspiration. By now I was aware that not everyone in this group was idealistic or self-sacrificial, but I wasn't going to let this affect my own spiritual condition. I remained faithful to the ideal of community as set down in the Bible.

Working in the nursery, I became friends with another Family misfit named Salome, a young woman of Jewish heritage. Salome, who was witty and bright, revealed her secret rebelliousness to me as we would sit in the nursery and make fun of the leaders, which was almost blasphemous for mere disciples.

Other than Salome, only Ben, who did night guard duty at the camp, talked with me on a regular basis. Also of Jewish descent, Ben was a tall, dark, and intelligent person who had been in the Family a short enough time to still know how to indulge in interesting conversation. Since I had to bring babies to nurse with their mothers in the middle of the night, I would often stop and talk with Ben while waiting for the mothers to finish nursing. I liked Ben quite a lot, and I entertained the idea of one day marrying him. I had heard that marriages in the group were usually arranged by leaders, and I thought I could jump the gun by picking a husband first. It was a futile idea, since Ben was soon moved to another colony.

Marriage was a big concern for everyone, since no physical contact was allowed between boys and girls unless they were married to each other. As far as I knew, no one was allowed to even kiss before marriage. What made this situation even worse was that, after the leader, your husband was the unquestioned head of the union, and he usually spoke on your behalf to the leaders, who I guess spoke to God. I couldn't imagine having to spend the rest of my life with someone who acted like a lord over me, so I didn't think about it. I trusted in the Lord, as I had learned to do in response to every other fear that had arisen since I had joined this group. Surely if I was making all this sacrifice for God, He would not lead me astray.

Courtship was a quick affair. Many of the couples who had been married recently had been told the night before whom they would be marrying the next day. Ruth was one of them. She had joined at the Jesus People house in Georgia, and she was a typical southern belle. Soft-spoken, petite, and beautiful, Ruth seemed terribly mismatched with a loud and boisterous Italian American. Sometimes when I used to go into the kitchen for baby supplies, I would find them arguing in a corner of the kitchen where they thought no one could see or hear them. Ruth appeared to be very unhappy, and I hoped that my marriage would not be so badly arranged.

There was never a dull moment in the camp, although sometimes I wished there would be. Whenever a new leader came through, we would have all-night inspiration. Now we had a whole band playing every night, and often the best teachers in the Family would lead us through amazing interpretations of the end-time prophecies in Daniel, Ezekiel, and Revelations. We thought we were privy to information no one else in the whole world knew. The most direct revelations from God, however, came through our own end-time prophet, the leader himself, Moses David. His words, through the Mo letters, were distributed to all the colonies and were soon on equal authority to the Bible.

By now, reading Mo letters was a daily requirement, along with reading the Bible and memorizing verses. The letters contained mainly simple, sermonlike platitudes, but sometimes they were more radical. According to the letters, the United States was headed for an Armageddon; therefore, all the Children of God were told to gather funds from various sources and go overseas. The Family spoke often of the end-time prophecy, and whether you believed it or not, speaking about the soon-to-be end of the world became a habit. It seemed to me that we might have only a few years left, and actually, I was rather relieved. I did not know how long I could last with this sacrificial lifestyle.

Although we did not work at "system" jobs, most of us worked very hard just to keep the camp going. We had what we called "provisioners," who were teams of beggars going out every day to grocery stores, food markets, and fast-food chains to scrounge for any food that they would give us. We had witnessers taking weekly trips to New York and surrounding cities, telling about Jesus and trying to recruit new disciples. As far as I knew, our only income came from the "forsake all" of the new disciples; and since most of them were like me, poor college students or travelers, I did not think we had much money. Personally, I never saw any money for years, since regular disciples never handled finances.

Toward the summer of 1972, the Family band led by Jeremy Spencer had come to Ellenville. Jeremy had been the slide guitar player for Fleetwood Mac, the popular rock band from England, and when he joined our group, it made the national papers. Now he had started his own band in the COG, and they had received a contract from a major recording company to make an album. The band enjoyed more privacy and freedom within the Family than even the big leaders did. They all lived in one of the bungalows that was set off by itself. All of the band members except for the drummer were already married. Word had spread that the band would be renting an apartment in Boston in order to work at a professional studio there. With the Spartan conditions we were living in at the camp, an apartment away from the constant surveillance of leaders and older brothers seemed like a mansion in heaven to me.

Due to the number of babies that had recently come into the nursery, I did not have much time to go to inspiration and listen to the band play. We had between six and ten babies ranging from newborns to age two being watched in the two nursery rooms. Mothers were encouraged to leave babies at the nursery all day and night, since we were supposed to be one big family and their children were everybody's children. Only the nursery workers cared for them, however, and since there were few nursery workers, I was often up day and night. Therefore, it took me by surprise when Jeremy came into the nursery to see me. I had only seen him before from a distance, and I was surprised at how short and frail he was. He had brown curly hair that hung lightly on his neck and friendly-looking eyes that were almost merry. I had not seen such a cheery look for a long time, since humor was discouraged at the camp.

"Hi. You're Jeshanah, right?" he asked in his strong English accent.

"Yes. That's me."

"Would you like to help us in a skit tonight? We have this little play planned, and we need a sister. You seem to be right for the part."

"Oh, I never acted in a skit before," I protested. Surely there were dozens of girls better suited for acting than myself, I thought.

"No, no. You are just right for the part."

"Well, do I have to come and rehearse?"

"Just ad-lib as the skit goes along. You'll pick it up, I'm sure."

Jeremy left me wondering what I was to do, but a crying baby interrupted my thoughts.

That evening, my tribe leader made sure I went to inspiration. She personally found another girl to stay in the nursery. I felt honored to be able to participate in a skit with the band. They were always treated as special, and I was somewhat in awe of their talent and fame. Now here I was in front of the entire colony, acting in a skit in which I did not even know the story line. However, it soon became apparent that the skit was about the drummer, Cal, marrying me. It depicted his life history, from a lost hippie to a drug addict in New York, then hitching out to California and meeting the COG, and finally becoming part of Jeremy's band and marrying a sister in Ellenville. My face turned bright red, and I could hardly look Caleb in the eyes. Did he know about this, or was he in the dark too?

Later in the evening we had some time to ourselves, and he informed me that he had requested me to be his mate. How did I feel about that?

A new letter had just come out from Mo saying that couples were being married too quickly, and they should be given three to six months courtship time. I asked if that would apply to us.

"I don't know," he said hesitantly, his blue eyes shining like sapphires on his handsome face. "You see, we have to go to Boston soon, and I would really like you to come with me."

I thought about living in Boston, in an apartment away from the colony. No more babies. No more big leaders. It seemed too good to be true. Serving the Lord would be so easy, I might start feeling guilty.

"Yes, I would like that." I said, thinking more of the apartment and freedom than getting married.

Caleb and I were allowed to spend some time together every day for the next couple of weeks. He was the first boy I had come to know emotionally since I had joined six months ago. Cal, as most of us called Caleb, was only twenty, a year older than myself, but he had already been in the Family for over a year, so he was definitely an older brother to me. It took awhile not to relate to him with the shyness and deference reserved for older brothers, but Cal was very easygoing, and he did not demand respect. I grew to like him very much. His long blond hair hung loosely to his shoulders, which reinforced the impression that he was an independent and unrestrained musician. Most of the boys who joined the group had to have their long hair cut, but musicians were usually exempt from this outward proof of commitment. Cal not only represented freedom, but he was also a basically nice guy.

Before the required three months of courtship were finished, we were married in a Family ceremony performed by a leader before the entire colony. Because of lack of space, most married couples, except for the leaders, had to share bedrooms; however we were allowed use of a couples' cabin alone for three nights. On the first night, Cal was euphoric. I was scared. This was marriage! What the hell did marriage mean in this group? We lived communally. Nothing belonged to us privately. Marriage usually entailed making a home and family—starting a life together. However, when I joined the Children of God, I relinquished my right to have my own home, and my family included anyone else who gave up worldly goals and possessions to follow God in this group. Even though I had been living this life for a relatively short time, I knew that everything was temporary. Perhaps marriage was also.

Cal seemed to understand the significance of marriage—having access to sex. I guess that was explanation enough for him, but not for me. That night, after we had made love a few times, I could not sleep. There was enough light from the moon shining through the curtainless lone window for me to see my honeymoon environment. The cabin was empty except for a mattress on the floor and a wooden box next to the bed, which held a small lamp and the two wineglasses, now empty. Cal's and my small suitcases, holding all of our personal belongings, were lying open on the floor in a corner. It was a sparse room, and the moonlight only accentuated the fact that my wedding night was far from idyllic. I lay awake most of the night wondering what I had done and why. Cal was a very nice person, much better looking and better groomed than most of the boys at the camp, but I did not think I loved him. Romantic love was one of the lies of the devil, I had been told by an older sister. God will give you love for him. Well, I didn't feel it yet, and I didn't feel like making love again. I got up early in the morning and dressed in my nursery work-clothes quietly, trying not to wake Cal.

"Where are you going?" asked Cal, waking up as I opened the door.

"To the nursery. That's where I work."

"No you don't. You don't have to work for three days. We have off, and I'm going to use those three days to stay in bed with you," he said with a sleepy smile.

He pulled me back into bed. My new husband might be kind, gentle, and loving, but he did not understand me. I felt as if I had just wounded my inner emotional being past repair. I had married someone without first consulting myself.

Having been indoctrinated by Mo's teaching that whatever is within us is evil and should be rejected, and that the truth is out there somewhere—always beyond my reach—in a perfect unity with a transcendent God, I did not even try to understand my feelings. Not being able to explore this terrible emptiness that I felt inside me, how could I explain it to Cal or anyone else? I knew only one thing—there was no turning back.

4

○ ○ ○

Sharing "One Wife"

I had been cutting vegetables for the chef salad all afternoon, but at least it gave me relief from watching the children. In the kitchen I could have time to think, which was something we were not supposed to do. Mo wrote in one of his letters that if you thought too much, it was like inviting little devils in for tea in your mind. "You pull up a chair and invite them over and start agreeing with them . . . it's 'cause you get your eyes on yourself instead of the Lord—introspection instead of heaven-spection" ("Dumps" 33:3). Therefore, I felt like I had to be involved in some sort of action constantly, or I might be accused of thinking.

"You're not supposed to cut the vegetables so small," yelled Martha from behind, startling me. I dropped my thoughts and imagined they had broken into pieces as if they were precious china. Looking up into the cherublike face of Martha, I wondered if she could see the pieces of my thoughts scattered on the floor as well as I could.

"I told you that when I gave you the instructions for chef salad. Stay in tune with the Spirit, Jeshanah."

Martha was the wife of the lead guitar player in the band, and she liked to consider herself the lead singer also. However, like all the wives, she also must have a house duty, and she chose to be in charge of the kitchen. She planned the meals, went shopping, and made sure someone else cooked and cleaned. Our band colony, in the suburbs of Boston, had only a dozen members. We each took turns with these chores; however, Jeremy and most of the band were usually relieved of their duties because of practice. They also began playing at local clubs, "to keep in with the music scene" we were told.

The band members looked and acted like the stereotypical musicians of the time. Any Fleetwood Mac fan would recognize Jeremy onstage, with his short stature and curly brown hair, delighting the audience with his Elvis Presley impersonations. The bass player, Sam, a tall nineteen-year-old Californian with dark, ethnic coloring, was distinguished by a gap in his smile where his front tooth had been knocked out. The rhythm guitar player, Enoch, was a tall young man in his early twenties whom we jokingly called "the Pope," since he encouraged everyone to be religious. Martha was a chubby girl with an angelic face; however, she was as tough as the devil on me. I had become the gofer of the home, since everyone else was busy in their calling.

Jeremy's wife, Emma, often could not work in the kitchen because she was caring for her newborn, and Bart, our leader, and his wife, Tirzah, would only cook or clean when they felt like it. That left only the wife of the bass player, who had a baby to care for, our single brother, Abashai, the roadie who did most of the driving, and me. My main job was to help Emma with her children, but I often helped Abashai do all the practical and dirty work of keeping a home running. Abashai was also our provisioner, the person who visited stores and factories asking for free stuff.

Even though Jeremy and the band had received a lot of money to make the album, Bart, who held the highest position in our band colony and was manager of the band, thought we should live as much as possible like other COG homes. I was never informed where the money went at that time, but I was aware that we were living relatively better than other homes in the group.

From what I heard from my husband, the drummer of the band, they had signed a contract with Columbia Records for $50,000. Most of the advance went into buying new instruments and equipment for the band and paying for the recording at a studio in Marlborough, Massachusetts. The rest of the money was used for living expenses for the band families while they were recording, but the upgrade in our living conditions was relative to normal COG standards. No one had personal bank accounts, and I never even bought any clothes but continued to wear hand-me-downs.

We had rented two attached apartments in Sudbury, a suburb of Boston. There were a total of five rooms, two kitchens, and two bathrooms for the twelve adults and six children. Bart and his wife and child took the whole apartment upstairs; Jeremy and his family of five lived in the master bedroom downstairs; Martha and her husband, Obadiah, and their baby were in the other bedroom; and Cal and I shared the living room with Sam, his wife, and their baby. Abashai and Enoch, the rhythm guitarist, whose wife was in England, stayed in the garage, where the band also practiced. In our room we divided the space with a sheet. After spending my first months of marriage with other married couples in the crowded couples' dorm back at Ellenville, I was grateful to have this private area. Always self-conscious of noises made while engaged in sex, I had learned to muffle any sounds.

Having lived with two to three hundred people for the past six months, I felt like this living situation was luxury. In addition, the food was much better, since we actually bought most of it, and I could leave the home on trips to the stores with Abashai to shop and provision, which I really enjoyed. I should have been very happy about my fortunate position; however, my marriage with Cal was terrible. Even worse, it was my fault. Cal loved me. He was proud to be my husband. He treated me nicely, and even tried to make sure I was not overworked, a common dilemma for those on the bottom of the COG hierarchy, such as I was in that colony.

But I knew it was all so wrong. Nothing had changed since the first night I spent with my husband. At that time, I thought that Cal and I were just not meant for each other, but in retrospect, I believe I was not capable of loving a man as a husband. In the Family, love for your "mate" was supposed to be a gift from God; however, there was no special loving feeling in my heart for Cal. Jesus said we should love everyone. Loving "everyone" was easy for me; it was loving my husband that was so hard. Having no clue as to why I could not love the man I had agreed to marry, I thought that maybe that happened to everyone. Maybe love would eventually grow. I did not take this situation lightly, and every day I would invent new causes, reasons, and excuses for not loving Cal as I should.

Mo wrote that he wanted all the complaints about marriage to stop. In a letter called "Get It Together," he told husbands to be nice to their wives (which Cal was), but he also wrote:

> The next time I hear of a wife that is not willing to submit to her husband—after being admonished in the presence of a few witnesses— we'll take her in front of the whole congregation and make her submit to her husband . . . if you won't do it in the privacy of your own bedroom, you will do it in front of us! . . . Do you believe in the Bible? Then why don't you do it? You're breaking the commandment of God every time you refuse! You don't have to feel like it. . . . How are we going to have a Revolution for Jesus if you can't even love your husband or wife, your brothers or sisters, whom you have seen? [123:17–20]

In other words, how could I be a missionary—my one single goal in life?

Mo often denied that he had ever encouraged anyone to marry, and for many years I believed it was only a few of the top leaders, who were eventually demoted, who indiscriminately practiced pairing couples. However, years later I heard the tearful story of Rose, a sister who was present at a mass marriage performed by Mo and his personal secretary, Maria. After Mo had just betrothed a couple, he asked if anyone else wanted to get married. A brother, who liked Rose, stood up and tapped her on the shoulder. Rose knew Mo and Maria personally, and she looked to them for help. Instead, she was told by Maria that Mo thought it was the Lord's Will she marry this brother. They were betrothed in a few weeks, at which time, she later told me, she felt like her life had ended. Not all couples were so badly mismatched, but the majority of us were told that God's Love can extend to anyone. In reality, couples that actually did love each other romantically were usually separated by leaders.

I was still young enough in the Family to believe that my feelings about my marriage might be taken into account by my leaders. I went to Bart and Tirzah to ask for a separation from Cal. I thought that four months of trying was enough. My caring leaders were absorbed in their own private matters. Bart was checking out the latest electronic toy he had bought, some recording device, and Tirzah was fashioning a new dress for Martha, which, I noticed nostalgically, included a lace bodice from one of the dresses I had forsaken when I joined the Family. I stammered out my feelings, hopes, and disappointments about marriage and my request for a separation. They would not even discuss the matter with me, and basically I was told to get into the Word more. However, they did talk to Cal.

"Maybe we need to have a baby," suggested my husband. "You have always been caring for other people's babies; don't you want one for yourself?"

I thought this was an odd statement, considering the fact that the children were supposed to belong to us all, but Cal always had a way of remaining personal in a very impersonal environment.

"Well, yes, but we have been together for four months already, and I didn't get pregnant yet," I replied, somewhat surprised by his statement. Actually, we had not been legally married yet, since most of us did not obtain a marriage certificate unless a child was expected. So what Cal was really saying was that if we had a baby, we would become legally married. I did not consider the added incentive Cal might have had at the time for me to get pregnant, and I think Cal was only repeating what the leaders had told him to say. He probably thought it would be good for both of us, but having a baby made it almost impossible to break a marriage. In those early days, Mo taught that a baby was God's stamp of approval on a marriage.

Cal's question, however, did prompt me to consider having a baby as a solution to my marriage problem. Before I joined the Family, I would have laughed at such a simplistic idea, but after living in a closed society for such a long time, with traditional, and often oppressive, perspectives reinforced constantly by everyone around me, my critical thinking capabilities were extremely weakened. The Bible did say, "Be fruitful and multiply." If God was the one who gave babies, it made sense to ask Him for one. The more I prayed for a child, the more I felt that a baby was what I really wanted in my life.

Ironically, I was still aware enough to know that a child in the Family ideally belonged to everyone. It wouldn't necessarily be "mine." Sitting in the bathroom, the only room that gave me complete privacy with my thoughts since our bedroom was converted back into the living room every morning, I pondered the imagined happiness of holding my *own* baby in my arms and the very real threat of having that baby taken away from me and cared for by others. In order to prevent that from happening, I reasoned, I would make sure that I was always in the "child-care ministry." I even justified my thought processes, which were definitely selfish according to Family ideals. My mother had given me the name "Miriam." In the Bible story, Miriam was the sister of Moses who watched her baby brother in the river and suggested to the Egyptian queen who found Moses that she would get a nursemaid—her own mother. In this way, Moses, although destined by God to live in the royal Egyptian palace, was actually raised by his own Hebrew mother. I reasoned that I could be like Miriam and cunningly make sure I would always care for my own child. Few sisters desired to stay in child-care work for long, so I did not foresee a problem keeping a spot. Curiously, I never noticed at that time how I had to work my way around Family policy. The thought of leaving the Family rarely occurred to me in those early years.

Cal and I tried harder to conceive, and as nature would have it, I became pregnant the next month. The nine months of carrying a child was one of the most joyful times of my life. In my idealistic and naive state, I thought that now I would be fulfilled. Being a mother in the COG carried a certain amount of respect at that time, and extra attention was paid to both mothers' and children's needs. I was given a quart of milk a day, as well as extra fruit and vegetables. I could have time to take a nap and could go to bed early. Life was full of comforts now, and I enjoyed it to the fullest, knowing this would not last.

It was planned that I should have the baby in Troy, New York. All COG girls were encouraged to have their babies at home, and midwives were trained among our group to perform the delivery. There were no midwives among us in the Boston area, but Troy had one sister, Sheriah, who had assisted at a birth. That was good enough training for us.

We calculated the birth date, and I was sent to the Troy home about two weeks ahead of time. Cal was supposed to come down when labor started, and before leaving, I married Cal in front of a justice of the peace.

In Troy, I practiced the Lamaze breathing method, as outlined in advice we received from our child-care leaders, to help during labor. The Troy home was kept very clean, and since I had been assigned to work in the kitchen, I needed to mop the floor every night. After mopping one night on my hands and knees, I felt the labor pains start around nine o'clock. I went to bed, knowing that the first labor usually takes awhile, and some labor pains could be a false alarm. At midnight, I was sure this was the real thing, so I woke up Sheriah. She began preparing the labor room, while I called Cal and started my Lamaze exercises. They put me on the table about three in the morning. Sheriah began prepping me by stretching the skin around the opening, but the labor pains were so strong I had to push her away frequently.

"I don't think that Cal will make it," she said. "Your contractions are coming pretty fast and regular. How do they feel?"

"Hard, very hard," I said between puffing.

Another sister who was pregnant came to see my delivery. She was at my side stuffing my mouth with crushed ice in between my contractions. I chewed on the ice and savored the cool, fresh liquid quickly before returning to heavy breathing.

Cal arrived about 6 A.M. By this time, I could tell that Sheriah was worried. Cal's first sight when he came in the door of the delivery room was the view of my legs wide open, a gaping, bloody birth canal, and me huffing and puffing in between contractions that were less than a minute apart.

Sheriah called him outside.

"I think something is wrong," she said. "I want you to pray about it, but I am going to call for Mary. She is in New York, and she has had more experience than me with complications."

Mary arrived a few hours later and took over for flustered and exhausted Sheriah. Twelve hours had passed since I had first told Sheriah I was in labor, and she had missed a whole night's sleep. Mary continued the job of stretching me with a renewed vigor, but I was so tired, and the pain was so intense that I could not feel the stretching. After each contraction, which now came only a minute apart while I was breathing hard and heavily, I asked for crushed ice. No one told me what time it was, but I noticed the light coming in through the window, so I knew it had been a long time. I also knew that we were not supposed to scream. Childbirth, we were told, was a natural function of the body and should not cause excess pain. If I screamed, it would be a sign of lack of faith in the Word. The Bible, I had learned, said that it is God who delivers babies, so what was I worried about?

But I could not bear the pain any longer. I took my last rhythmic breath and screamed for as loud and long as I wanted. I no longer cared what Mary or Sheriah or Cal, or anyone, would think.

"The head—it's here. Push! Push," cried Mary!

I took a breath and screamed through another push.

"It's a redhead! Push again!"

Were they crazy? I didn't have any strength left to push. I could not do it.

"Push! Push!"

The undeniable urge to push came again, and I pushed while a full body plopped out covered in mucus and blood. Mary held up a baby boy for me to see, and then she cut the umbilical cord and gave him to Sheriah to wash.

I was ecstatic, but the work was not finished. Mary, who was very knowledgeable about childbirth, told me to stand up and squat so the afterbirth could come out. Then she washed me and helped me onto a clean, soft bed that had been prepared. Finally, they brought in the baby.

He was a beautiful nine-pound infant. His perfectly rounded head was covered with bright red hair. Cal had been given a dream in which the baby had red hair and he wanted to name him after the Norse god of thunder. The day he had the dream, he had read a verse in the Bible about James and John being the "sons of thunder." Although only Bible names were the rule in the Family, we named him Thor. As I adored him lying in the softness of my rounded arm and sucking firmly at my nipple, I thought that never again in my life would I be sad. The moment should have been eternal, but it was snatched away all too soon by Sheriah.

"You have to get up and get dressed," she barked. "You ripped pretty badly, and you will have to go to a doctor."

As she said the word "doctor," I shuddered. We all knew that one went to a doctor only because of lack of faith. We had read about the sister who was in labor for three days, and when she finally went to the doctor, Mo said, she developed a spiritual problem. What was my problem? Oh, who cared? My baby was fine and healthy. That was all that mattered.

Cal helped me to get dressed, and one of the brothers drove us to the nearest hospital. I sat in the emergency room for over an hour while Cal talked to the nurse.

"They won't take you," he reported when he finally came back. "They said you are too much of a risk since you did not have the baby here in the hospital."

I felt weak and was shivering. I was continuing to lose blood, and I had no idea how big was this rip that needed to be sewn.

The brother suggested we try another hospital, which was farther away. By the time we arrived, I was holding on to both of them for support. Cal went to talk to the nurse again, but no one would believe that I had just had a baby until they came and saw me.

"Bring her in here," they said. Within an hour I had been sewn by a kind young intern who later advised us to go to an obstetrician, but I never went to one.

I went back to the Troy home and spent the rest of the night admiring my sleeping baby who lay snuggled in my arms. Early the next morning, I had a message to see Sheriah. She was the colony leader's wife in addition to being midwife.

"My husband has already talked to Cal," she said sharply. "We have prayed about this, and we believe that you two must seek the Lord for an answer."

"An answer to what?" I asked.

"Well, as to why the delivery went so badly," she retorted, looking surprised that I would not know. "I want you to pray about this and write me a report today."

I was left speechless. The absolutely most beautiful memory that a woman can have in her lifetime, that of giving birth to her firstborn, had been splattered with this acid of someone else's cruel reality. Now every time I recalled that wonderful experience, I would remember that I had somehow failed.

Returning to Boston in a week, I was grateful to be back. The Family life in a "regular" home was so disciplined, and the leaders seemed to be very harsh. After my experience in Troy, I appreciated the colony in Boston where musicians could still joke and laugh about the idiosyncrasies of life. Jeremy was always a great one for seeing humor in everything, and he was an inspiration to me because he had given up fame and riches to follow the Lord. Although he was respected by most leaders with a kind of man-worship attitude, which placed the "great Jeremy Spencer from Fleetwood Mac" slightly above others, he still lived pretty much like the rest of us, with one memorable exception.

One day, some FBI agents showed up at our apartment looking for the English rock musician who probably had visa problems and found Jeremy in the backyard on "kitchen duty" splitting beans for dinner. Everyone acted completely calm, and the FBI seemed perturbed by our lack of anxiety. Little did they realize that we "knew" everything was in God's hands, so we had nothing to fear from man's laws and activities.

I was not aware of the details of this incident. In fact, it was only years later that my husband told me it was the FBI who had come to our home. However, my husband said that this visit from the FBI was why Jeremy and his family left our home to go to a COG colony in Europe.

Jeremy, behaving in his typical ingenuous manner toward these men who seemed to be important in the world, made me laugh, and I realized after my first day back that I had not laughed during my entire four-week stay in Troy. I decided to work harder and never complain again about being in the band home.

However, life in the Boston home had changed since I had been gone. There had been some trouble at Columbia Records involving scandals in their business, which had nothing to do with us, but for some reason, the band took all of the money that was owed them and left Columbia Records. In any case, the album did not become the big hit we expected it to be. We heard that Mo was not happy with the hard rock album that Jeremy and the band recorded. In a letter titled "Conferences, Colonies, Bands, and Buses," dated July 15, 1973, after the album *Jeremy and the Children* had been released, Mo wrote:

> Those poor band groups have been in pretty bad shape for a long time ever since they got this big-band spirit when the System took them over! But they disobeyed and didn't do what we told them to do. . . . I think these band people have got what they wanted: They wanted a band and they wanted a record—But they failed to be a success or hit because they didn't do it God's way. . . . Maybe we should make such folks an associate colony, if they're not interested in following our authority and obeying only us. [253:10–11]

Since Mo did not mention the name of the band he was talking about, although we were the only ones in the group who made a record at that time, we never were sure whether he meant us. Mo was often vague in naming offenders in his specific judgments, but the result was that none of us wanted to be considered an "associate," which in COG terminology meant a second-rate disciple. We decided to split up and go to homes in Europe—the new mission field. That would be a big change for everyone, but for me it did not matter, since I believed that the life of a revolutionary was always changing, always growing, and always moving forward. The money we had was used for plane tickets, and anything left over was given to other families who wanted to leave for Europe. Most of the band members decided to go to Italy or France. Because I had a German mother, Cal and I decided to go to Germany with our son Thor.

We planned to fly out of New York in the fall of 1973, when Thor was barely three months old. Again, I never saw any money or even documents, unless I had to sign something. Cal and the leaders took care of the paperwork, and I just followed the instructions like a good soldier. We were asked to obtain as much money and goods as we could from our relatives before leaving. I had stayed in contact with my mother through frequent letters and less frequent phone calls; such communication was being encouraged by our leaders now because Mo had recently advised disciples to write their parents and relatives. I believe it was suggested because of the persecution and investigation that had followed when irate parents and relatives went to the authorities seeking to learn the whereabouts of their children. In my case, until I lived in the band colony, I never opened a letter from my mother without a leader looking over my shoulder. If she sent any money, I was urged to give it to the leader right away, to be put to use in God's work. What good would money do for me anyway—I could not go out and spend it. I soon learned that most disciples asked their parents for *things*, like clothes and pens and paper. Cal had learned to increase his few personal belongings with help from his parents, and before we had our baby, they had supplied us with all the baby clothes we needed and a beautiful handmade cradle. Since Cal's parents lived relatively close by, in upstate New York, we visited them before we left for Europe. Having an upper-middle-class income, they could afford to buy us new clothes and camping gear. They also paid for our visits to a dentist; it was my first visit since I had joined the COG. While we were at Cal's parents' house, one of my sisters, Marlene, and her husband and new baby brought my mother to see me before I left. I had not seen my mother since I had "forsaken all" in 1971. It was now 1973, but I was not nostalgic. By now my natural feelings had been buried so deep, I could think only about witnessing to them. My sister asked Jesus into her heart and told me about the difficulties of parenthood and work. I told her, "That's life in the system." Unfortunately, I showed barely any affection to the sister closest to me, less than two years younger in age, and the one who had gone to the peace march in Washington with me. She was only eighteen, and before she reached her twenty-first birthday, she died in a car accident. I never saw her after this day in New York.

Cal told me that we had been given enough money to get through the borders in Europe and three-month visas. We landed in Amsterdam and had to race for a train to Germany, arriving in Essen on a wet, cold evening. No one had come to pick us up as planned, and after hours of waiting and many phone calls, we finally arrived at the Essen colony. Essen, a large industrial city in northern Germany, is not known for its scenic beauty. It is a factory-fueled city, and in the middle of the winter, the gray from the smokestacks was lost in the gray of the skies. What I remember most about the German houses is the stark white lace curtains in every window. I thought there must have been a law in Essen that everyone must have lace curtains, but I later saw them all over Germany. They looked pretty, and for some reason the curtains made the gloomy feeling I felt, living the winter in Essen, a little more bearable.

Our new home turned out to be an old three-story schoolhouse inhabited by over a hundred disciples. Mo had written a letter about letting the nationals take over the leadership of the homes in Europe, since they knew the culture and language of the land. Therefore, power-hungry older brothers were quickly marrying national sisters, usually barely three months in the Family, so they could keep their leadership positions. That seemed to be the case in Germany anyway.

The colony leaders were Samson and Naomi, who together ruled the home with Gestapo-like authority. Naomi was a pretty German girl whose father had helped the Family when the group first arrived in Essen. Wealthy or influential friends of the Family were called "kings," and Naomi's father, a respected Christian businessman, saw our group as dedicated young Christians. He later changed his attitude about us, as most of our kings did. Samson, a suave, clean-cut-looking young man, was one of the early pioneers from America, and he savored his leadership power. Everything ran like clockwork in the large home; the disciples were kept constantly busy cleaning it, begging for food and supplies, or going out onto the streets witnessing.

The nursery was located in one of the larger classrooms on the second floor, near the girls' bathroom, and I was immediately put to work. There were already a dozen small babies in the house and a dozen more on the way. Since we were forbidden to use any form of birth control, and babies were considered God's blessing, they kept coming. Anyone who knew about child care could be sure of a twenty-four-hour job.

Naomi had never been trained properly in child care; in fact she was not trained in anything, which left her with a huge complex to overcome. Most leaders' wives had been in the Family longer than Naomi, and had received some form of training from elder sisters in areas of office work, kitchen supervision, housecleaning, or child care. However, Naomi had joined the home as a sort of "princess," her father being a king of course, and she had received the typical pampered treatment allotted those who were somehow special. That really rubbed my communistic ideals the wrong way, but as always, I knew there was a lesson for me to learn here. Maybe I needed to be more humble. Maybe I would learn to love Cal here in Essen.

Naomi suggested that Cal and I sleep in the nursery, which meant being awakened all through the night. Furthermore, she did not relieve Cal of any work or witnessing responsibilities, and I had to participate in other work duties as well, which contributed to a chronic feeling of tiredness.

The German home existed mainly from the donations it collected on the street and by "litnessing," now the most popular method of raising money in the Family. It involved "selling" our *Family News* and Mo letters on the streets. I had been out litnessing a few times in the United States, but since we had kept some of the money the band earned playing at clubs, I was never pressured to bring in a certain amount. Here in Germany, I learned that everyone had a quota of literature to hand out, and of donation money they were expected to bring in. The literature was translated into the language of the land, and in this way, these pieces of paper became the witness. Mo had been writing a series of letters on how to witness with his "wonder-working words" and recently he suggested that all the disciples "sell" them to people on the streets, in airports, shopping centers, or wherever else they could get people to stop for a minute. Ideally, the method included witnessing about Jesus to anyone who looked interested, but many times we were so busy trying to get money, we did not have time.

The German leadership had set quotas for literature that had to be sold by each disciple every day. The quotas were determined by the amount of time that the leaders thought a disciple could devote to this method of witnessing. For example, the lowly disciple who worked in the kitchen early morning and late evening supposedly had all day to spend on the streets litnessing, so his quota would be high, maybe a hundred letters a day. However, the leaders, who had to spend many hours reading the Word, praying, and making important decisions about colony life, would usually have a low quota, or no quota at all. Cal and I fell somewhere in the middle.

Since Cal was a musician, he thought he could use his talent in the colony band, but music was not highly valued in the German home, so Cal was given no practice time and a pretty high quota. Since I was a nursing mother, and spent many hours day and night in the nursery, my quota was lower. Still, it was never easy to make.

"What do I say?" I asked a sister as I stepped out the door on my first day carrying a pack of lit, Thor tucked snugly into a Cadillac of a baby buggy, bundled in everything I could find to keep out the cold north German winter.

"Just hand them a pamphlet and say, 'Können sie bitte eine spende geben?'" answered the American girl, who had been here for three months. "It means, 'Can you give a donation, please?' "

"Won't they ask what this is, and why I want a donation?"

"It's better if you don't know what to say. These German businesspeople will just argue with you anyway. So just say, "Nicht verstehe," and move on if they don't reach for their pocket. Believe me, it's not worth trying to talk with them."

"What if I find someone sheepy? Do you know enough German to witness?"

"No, I never learned much more than to ask for a donation. You don't have to. If they are sheepy, they'll probably know English. All the young people here know English."

She was right in her assessment. Businessmen either gave a dona-tion right away, or started yelling something like *"Arbeite, arbeite!"* which meant "Go work!" The young people knew English very well, and they were the only ones who were interested in talking with me. I never learned more German than how to ask for a donation.

Even though it was cold and very difficult to make a quota in that tough and dreary city, I loved to go out litnessing. It meant being away from the nursery, away from the colony, and most of all, away from Naomi. I had the distinct impression that she did not like me, but perhaps everyone felt that way about her. She always had some command for me whenever she abruptly entered the nursery.

"Don't you think the babies should be patted to sleep?" she snapped one day when she found me sitting down reading the Bible while a few babies were stirring before taking their naps.

From then on, we had to pat babies to sleep, which was not a good habit to encourage when there are twelve babies and only two adult patters.

"Why don't you write verses on this big chalkboard," she ques-tioned on another day. "Then you can memorize out loud while you are working with the babies. I am sure it will help them in the Spirit to hear the Word."

After that, we always had verses written across the huge black-boards, which had to be changed daily, of course.

Still, I felt fortunate to be working in the nursery instead of in the kitchen or office, where Naomi made many more demands on the poor workers. Cal would often come up from the kitchen in a rage over the stupid suggestions made by Naomi.

"And it's not like you can talk to her about anything," he com-plained. "She won't allow anyone to question her suggestions."

It was evident that Cal wanted to leave the country, but it was hard to get out. In the band colony in Boston, Cal always was allowed to keep a little spending money, maybe twenty dollars or so, but here in Germany, every mark was handed in, and if it looked like you did not make enough, you might be accused of holding some money back. The story in the Bible of Ananias and Sapphira, found in Acts, Chap-ter 5, was constantly held over our heads in the typical Big Brother fashion. I heard this story when I had my first "forsake all" doubts. It seems two of the early disciples did not hand in to Peter all the money they had earned from land they had sold, and they were immediately struck down dead by God as a warning to all. I really doubted that God would do that for a few bucks, but even so, where could we go if we had money to get there? To live at another home anywhere in the world, one needed clearance first, which involved a series of letters to the colony leaders and recommendations from your present colony leader. It was like getting a job. And I suspected that Naomi would not want me going anywhere since I had become her only stable nursery worker. She thought I was dedicated to the work, but actually, I just wanted to stay near my son as much as possible, and my plan worked. As a musician, Cal had no talent to offer the litnessing colony in Germany. To make matters worse, he was used to the musician's life with a less disciplined structure. The tension of hating where he was and being incapable of changing his situation weighed heavily on his mind, body, and spirit.

Our bedroom area in the nursery was situated in a loft overlooking the cribs full of babies. We had a mattress on the floor, but, being in the nursery, it was one of the warmest spots in the cold, drafty building. Interrupted often by the babies' cries, Cal never could sleep very well, and his lack of sleep, combined with the stress he was experiencing, caused him to become physically weak. One day he could not get out of bed. He had developed a terrible case of dysentery, and I began to take care of him, as well as the babies. Sometimes, I had to wash sheets that he had soiled because he could not make it to the bathroom, which was located far down the hall. Caring for Cal brought me closer to him in an emotional way, but I don't think he recognized this at the time. His single-minded intention was to get out of that colony in any way he could. Hardships are said to often bring a family closer, and the unhappiness we both felt living in Essen made me feel a sense of camaraderie with Cal. It was short-lived.

The chance for Cal to escape from his less than joyful situation came when he heard that Jeremy was in Paris starting up another band. Cal sent him a letter, and our leaders received word from Hopie, who was Mo's daughter, that Cal should be sent to Paris immediately. Although there was not room for me and our baby, Cal accepted the invitation and was gone within days. He was told that he might be staying in Paris for a short time only, but that if he stayed longer, he would do what he could to get us there quickly. I was truly happy for Cal, and I did not think much about our separation. Also, I knew that he had a better chance of getting me out of here from Paris than he did in Essen.

Weeks passed, and there seemed to be little he could do to bring his family to France. I received a few letters from Cal saying that Paris was a wonderful place, the home was totally different from any he had been in, and the band was probably going to go into the recording studio soon. I'm sure he missed us, but I think he was so excited about his new start in Paris, he did not spend much time thinking about how his wife and child would get there. We were trained to trust the Lord. Cal wrote that the home in Paris was made up mostly of musicians, singers, and their wives. They lived in a converted stable, and there was no room for children.

It seemed that Cal was incapable of arranging for me to get to Paris, for whatever the reasons, and there was little for me to do but pray. Naomi would be of no help, and without the leader's permission, I would not be accepted in any colony, let alone have the money to get there. A few months after Cal left Germany, a visiting leader came by our colony who gave me a ray of hope.

Bithia, a tall, lanky young woman, was the wife of a top leader from London. She and her husband were not only nationals, they were from high society, which appeared to have status value even in the COG. Having had an elitist upbringing, Bithia was used to doing just what she wanted, and she could not be told by any leader, let alone a domineering Naomi, what to do. Bithia had three small children, who were born before she joined the COG. She was used to buying whatever she wanted for them, and although she was trying to live communally, like others in the Family, she often wrote her parents for extra money to buy the kids something, which she did not turn over to the leaders. Since her youngest child slept in the nursery, Bithia hung around and talked with me. We recognized our kindred rebellious spirits.

"This is really a rigid colony here, isn't it?" she commented one day. She had just set her baby on the rug and lounged back in a way that suggested she had always lived a life of ease.

"What do you mean?" I responded, carefully watching that her baby would not poke my son with the pencil that he had grabbed from Bithia's open bag.

"I mean, Naomi, and her husband; they run this place like a prison. It isn't like this in England. And, boy, you should see Paris!" she said with a smile on her face.

"Were you in the Paris colony?"

"Yeah, I just came from there. It's pretty. . . . You know Hopie is there, and being Mo's daughter, she gets all Mo's letters before they come to us. The Paris home is practicing what we haven't even heard about yet."

"Like what?"

Bithia studied me for a moment, and decided she could be open.

"Well, have you heard about 'sharing'?"

"In what way?"

She divulged what she knew about "sharing," a new outlook on communal sexuality, but she did not completely reveal what was going on in Paris.

Bithia often took me with her on shopping excursions in Essen, even though Naomi would insist that Bithia take a sister who could speak German.

"No, I want someone who can help me with the kids," she said, and, as always, she did want she wanted.

One day while shopping, she asked about my husband.

"So, are you and Cal breaking up?"

"No, I don't think so. He said he was trying to get me to Paris."

"He did?" she laughed. "Well, I would say he probably is too busy in Paris to worry about a wife and son."

"What do you mean?"

"Well, Paris has a lot of men away from their wives, and single girls are ready and willing to serve them."

"Are you saying that Cal shares sexually?"

"I am not saying anything. I don't know what anyone does in the bedroom. I am saying that I would not leave a husband alone in Paris very long."

"Well, what can I do about it? Naomi will never give me permission to go to Paris." Actually, I was more concerned about getting out of Germany than about what my husband might be doing.

"I'll see what I can do for you," said Bithia. "I have a direct contact with Hopie."

The next day, Bithia came excitedly into the nursery.

"I talked to Hopie last night," she exclaimed. "She's such an angel.

It seems that they want to start a nursery in Paris, and they need workers, so she is going to send a letter to Naomi about you coming there."

"Oh, Bithia, you are wonderful!" I cried, giving her a hug.

"But, look, Jeshanah, you have to keep on top of this. I will be leaving in a few days, and I will do what I can from London. However, Hopie is a bit spacy, you know, and she might forget."

Bithia did leave in a few days, and she left the Family before our paths ever crossed again. Since I did not have any kind of communication with Hopie, there was little to do but pray. A couple of days later Naomi said that Hopie would be calling me on the phone that night, at eight o'clock sharp.

I waited by the phone anxiously. The call came in around nine-thirty.

"Hello. Is this Jeshanah?" piped a sweet, high voice on the other end of the line.

"Yes, this is me."

"Praise the Lord. It is wonderful to hear you, sweetie. Your husband is such a dear, and he talks of you all the time."

"Well, thank you. I hear so many wonderful things about you too."

"Well, it is only the Lord, sweetie. Anything good about us is only the Lord. Isn't He so loving?"

"Yes, praise the Lord!"

"Hallelujah! So, Bithia tells me you are great with kids. Bithia is a dear, you know, and so discerning. I trust her completely."

"I have been working with babies since Ellenville."

"Well, honey, we don't have a nursery set up here, you know. It is very primitive. The conditions are extremely crowded, and we have only one bathroom for everyone. Sometimes we have over a hundred people here, but we are trying to keep that down now."

"Oh, I could set up a nursery. That would not be a problem."

"Well, we can see about that later. But I want you to know, this is no place for a baby. You might have to sleep on the floor. And we all eat the same food. We don't have a special fridge for moms and babies here."

"Oh, that is fine. I will take care of the food. My son is strong and healthy." By now, I had been living by faith for so long, I believed the Lord would protect me from anything, especially if I was in the presence of Hopie. Mo's youngest daughter was like a role model for me. Youthful, energetic, and spontaneous, she often got in trouble with the more organizational-type leaders, but that just made her seem more saintlike in my eyes. Hopie was only a few years older than I; yet I knew she had already pioneered most of the European homes. Mo sent his singing daughter and a team of musicians into every country first, and after she made a few contacts with established nationals, setting up a base to start with, more of our disciples would stream into the country. I was proud to be part of her team.

"Well, praise the Lord, dear. It seems you have a lot of faith. Okay. I'm going to tell Naomi to send you over. Hallelujah! Does that make you happy, sweetie?"

"Oh, yes," I exclaimed, not knowing how much enthusiasm I should express to leave Essen, with Naomi standing right next to me. I decided to show my true feelings. "Hopie, I want to be there with you and the band and my husband. Bithia told me that the Spirit is really moving in Paris, and I want to be part of it and help in any way I can."

"Praise the Lord, honey, you will. Now give me Naomi and I will talk to her."

Naomi took the phone in her normal stern manner and motioned for me to leave. I walked away on a cloud and went back up to the dirty diapers, warm milk bottles, and crying babies. They were like heaven to me now.

It took about two weeks to arrange for me to leave, and to find a replacement for me in the nursery; then, carrying Thor, and all my possessions in two bags, I took the train to France. The leadership provided me with the necessary paperwork to make the journey.

◐

Paris was another world for me. Not only did what was happening in Paris represent a turning point in COG history, but Paris was the prototype of things to come. Bithia and Hopie had been truthful about the conditions; they were primitive and physically difficult. We lived in what had been an actual stable, when horses were still used in Paris, in a part of the city called Port de Pantin. The stables had been converted quickly and shabbily to provide the basic necessities of living, such as running water and gas for cooking. There was a large all-purpose room where we ate and had our meetings and inspiration.

In the back was a small kitchen, and there were a few rooms that had been hastily constructed in various corners so that some of the married couples could have privacy. Cal and I were given one of those rooms, which was large enough for a twin mattress and our suitcases on the side. The mattress covered most of the cement floor, so each morning I arranged our suitcases in such a way that Thor could crawl about without scraping his knees on the rough cement. Actually, he never crawled much; he started to walk at ten months. I have always wondered if it was due to his having had so little crawling space.

Upstairs was a communal bathroom with only a curtain hung up for privacy. Next door was the girls' dorm. The boys all slept downstairs in the main room. Leaders had two rooms built on the side of the girls' dorm. The population of the colony varied daily, as visiting leaders and disciples came and went; the permanent population was around fifty. A married couple who acted as "shepherds" for the home, and Hopie and her husband, Joab, the top leaders, lived somewhere else. Only the leaders in this colony had their wives with them, since the married musicians had left their wives back in London, or wherever they had last been. It was a miracle that they had allowed me to come.

Obviously, taking care of one's daily hygienic needs was a problem. Everyone was advised to use the bathrooms in cafés or restaurants whenever they were out litnessing. All showers were taken at the local public baths.

There was no regular schedule for eating. Breakfast usually consisted of oatmeal soaked in milk overnight, with raisins, nuts, or whatever dried fruit was available. Since this concoction, which we called muesli, was prepared the night before and put in the refrigerator, everyone ate whenever they were ready; however, the table was cleared by noon. I remember developing a tremendous liking for this cereal mixture, and although we ate muesli every morning, I never grew tired of it. Unlike in the Essen home, if people were hungry, they could ask the head cook for food. Since the head cook changed every few days, there was no one to blame if all the food ran out. However, as soon as we had a steady person in charge of the kitchen, free access to the refrigerator stopped. Almost everyone not in the band was supposed to be out on the streets selling literature or collecting donated food by noon. There was only one other mother besides myself, and we could arrange our own schedules. I had learned in Essen not to ask for anything, but to pray for it. So unless the other mother, who was only passing through, requested special privileges for us, I usually just followed along with the normal witnessers. All the band, musicians and singers, had a schedule of their own, led by Hopie and her husband, Joab, and I saw Cal only at night.

Despite the harsh living conditions, I was euphoric about being in Paris. The city was a treasure to explore, and I had no leadership keeping tabs on me. After a few days, I understood that whatever one was lacking in physical necessities—food, clothes, personal items—could be bought from litnessing money. As long as I showed up for inspiration in the evening, I could do pretty much what I wanted. This schedule created chaos organizationally, but it was a haven for independent-minded disciples like myself. Of course, I didn't have any money with which to buy extra food, but I quickly solved that problem.

After learning how to ask for a donation in French, I began partnering with Elam, whom I had recognized as a good litnesser. Elam had been in Europe ever since Mo first allowed disciples who were not leaders to come over. He already spoke three languages, and with his dashing good looks, he concentrated his witnessing on women. I soon learned that in gay Paris, the relationship between men and women, even complete strangers, quickly takes on a romantic flavor. I watched Elam as he charmed a Parisian beauty, and within five minutes came back with ten francs. The French were typically rather snobby, unless one knew the power of charm. Luckily for me, Elam taught me this without saying a word; I picked it up intuitively, but I think living in Paris had something to do with it.

The first time we went out together to litness, I had Thor with me in a foldable stroller, and I carried all the changes of clothes, diapers, jars of food, cookies, and Mo letters in a big bag on my shoulder. We had a late start because I had to prepare the baby, but Elam did not mind. Everyone was given a metro ticket to start the day. Elam started passing out letters on the metro platform and asking for donations. By the time we left the metro station, he had some money.

"Let's get something to eat," he suggested. He stopped at a cheese store and bought a piece of Gruyère. Then we went into a bakery and asked for a hot baguette (a long, thin loaf of French bread).

"Here," he said, handing me the bread and a piece of cheese, "put this in the bread and let it melt. It's delicious."

I did as he said. It was one of the most memorable meals I ever had. The warm bread had melted the cheese to a soft, sensuous consistency, and the freshly baked bread held a fragrance I could never forget. We stood on the side of the busy Boulevard St.-Michel, eating with gusto. It was the first time since I had come to Europe that I bought food in a store on my own. In Germany we had not been allowed to spend any of the money we made, and we had to take food from the colony, if it was provided. Elam sensed that I was enjoying his humble gift of food. There were some moments during life in the Family when communion between the right combination of people in the most simple and human situations made the harsh realities of communal life seem like a stepping-stone to an eternal connection with the universal soul. Of course, at that time, I could never describe these moments as such, but I knew they were special. This was one of them.

"Hey, did you ever have a Greek pastry?" he asked.

"No, what is it?"

"Wait, let me get some money."

Elam stopped a few people and sold a few more letters. I followed him to another store, where he bought something called a baklava.

"This is marvelous," I said, my mouth full of exotic tastes of sesame and honey.

He also bought a drink called Orangina, which was a bubbly orange juice. It became my favorite French soft drink.

Thor was about a year old then, and he had started to eat adult food cut up in small pieces. I gave him some of the pastry, which he seemed to enjoy, and he picked the sticky crust from his fingers.

By now it was night, but the streets of the Latin Quarter seemed busier than before. I was worried that we should start litnessing so we could get home with some money before inspiration. Elam smiled knowingly, and I felt so dependent on him at that moment.

"Don't worry," he said, "we don't have quotas here like they do in other colonies. This is the freest place you will ever find in the Family. Enjoy it while you can. Besides, if you don't make anything, I will give you half of mine."

Elam was right about the Paris home. Unfortunately, it did not stay like that forever, but while we had freedom, I enjoyed it immensely.

One night Joab read us a new Mo letter titled "One Wife." Joab was a big, hairy man, at least ten years older than his wife, Hopie, but although I never talked with him very much, I knew he was a gentle man despite his rough appearance. He had kept us excited by this new letter for days, dropping hints that "this was a bomb," and "the revolution will never be the same." Joab had been one of the first to join the Family, when it was still called the Revolution, and his favorite antic was to stop in mid-sentence and scream, "It's a Revolution," to which all fifty-odd of us would scream back, "For Jesus!" That night he stopped to scream about every two minutes.

"Are you ready, brothers?" he asked, his dark eyes grinning with excitement. "This letter will divide the sheep from the goats."

"One Wife" talked about everyone being married to everyone else, and not having selfish little marriage units.

> God's in the business of breaking up little selfish private worldly families to make of their yielded broken pieces a larger unit—one Family.
> He's in the business of destroying the relationships of many wives in order to make them One Wife—God's Wife—the Bride of Christ! . . .
> In other words, partiality toward your own wife or husband or children strikes at the very foundation of communal living. [249:9,12]

Since I always thought we were all spiritually married to everyone else in the Family, I did not find the message of this letter particularly shocking. However, it turned out to be one of the significant letters of our history, starting us down the road to threesome marriages and group sex.

Other letters came out around the same time with new revelations about the freedom we were given in the Family: "Revolutionary Women," "Revolutionary Sex," "Lovelight," "Jealousy," "Women in Love." Most of this freedom centered around sex; in fact, sexual liberation seemed to be the pathway to spiritual growth, as laid out in the new letters. Women were told to dress and act sexier, to attract and keep the attention of men. Couples were told that jealousy is pride and "the selfishness of private property." A wife was reprimanded for not "sharing" her husband with another woman. With the average age of COG members between eighteen and twenty-five at that time, any new liberties in this area were welcomed. We had been under traditional moral guidelines since the Family's beginning, and these new freedoms in the area of sex were exciting and desirable. They didn't seem perverted, in fact, every new revelation about sex was supported with Bible verses or Bible stories. There is much in the Song of Solomon about lovemaking, and a few of the Old Testament patriarchs often seemed more immoral than some of our contemporary television evangelists. I would venture to say that the modern Moral Majority would not approve of King David dancing naked in the streets, or of his taking other men's wives to bed, stories that can be found in the Bible. Any new revelation for which a Bible reference could not be found was covered by Jesus' words: "I have yet many things to say unto you, but ye cannot bear them now" (John 16:12). The implication was that we were now ready for what Jesus did not tell his disciples, and Mo was revealing these things to us. In addition, the sexual sharing at this time involved only those who had obtained a position of leadership. I had heard of and tried the "free love" philosophy before when I was a hippie, and it didn't seem to bring any greater community; perhaps this was only for the more spiritually advanced, such as our leaders. Although I was always curious by nature, I was not very enthusiastic about sharing sexually with just any brother. However, I was interested in the concept laid out in "Flirty Little Fishy," which explained how Maria, Mo's mistress, lured men to Jesus by using her flirtatious powers as a woman. Although it was written in January 1974, it would be a year before we tried this method of witnessing, but I was inexplicably intrigued by the metaphor of "catching fish" (men) with the bait (women) on a hook (the love of God), cast by a fisherman (Mo or other male leader). Why did this prick my interest? Why was I fascinated by a woman being used by a man to lure other men? The image was a classic pimp-prostitute model, but I did not recognize it. Even if I had, we had already learned that God can use anything the devil uses for His own glory. Mo taught us that the devil had a monopoly on sex, and we were going to bring it back into God's realm.

Strangely, although many of us had been sexually liberated before we joined, those who had come from the more religious fundamentalist backgrounds took this new license to the furthest extremes. As sex became more and more prevalent in our lifestyle, I noticed that the most insistent to follow the letters were those men and women who had been good church-raised Christians and had never gone "astray" as I had. For instance, Mo's own permanent lover, Maria, had been a very strict churchgoer before she joined the Family, and Mo was her first sexual partner. Most of the girls I knew who became lovers of leaders, and even those who went to Mo's house, were former churchy "saints." I don't know if they actually enjoyed the sexual freedom, or if they were just oriented to obedience! I followed these letters in part because I had always been rebellious to authority, and I was therefore now trying to prove I was a good disciple. And since, for some unknown reason, I seemed to be resigned to a life of sexually "giving" to men, the new concepts on sex and sharing did not bother me. In fact, it was easier to follow than trying to sell Mo letters on the street.

My husband was more intrigued by these new letters than I was. Since we did not have our own individual copies of the letters at that time, Cal tried to obtain copies to read over and over. He informed me, as if he were letting me in on a closely guarded secret, that there was quite a bit of hanky-panky going on among the leaders here in the Paris home. In particular, Hopie, Mo's own daughter, and Joab, her husband, each had started intimate relationships with single brothers and sisters. Since this was closer to home, my interest was further piqued. I realized that Beth, a young single woman who had joined the Family in Scandinavia, wasn't sleeping in the dorm. She had her own bedroom in a small area behind the leaders' office. I knew that there were quite a few married men who were living in Paris without their wives, and I began to wonder how much "one wife" principles were being followed in the area of sexual sharing here in our colony. I wondered if I would be sharing Cal with anyone soon, and I truthfully did not feel jealousy or experience any anxiety over this thought. At twenty-one years of age, I was interested in whom I might be able to share with, mostly out of curiosity. Sadly, this should have been the time of my life when I would seriously be looking for a lifelong partner, but one had already been chosen for me.

Since I rarely had the chance to become friends with a brother, I understood how sexual sharing could allow deeper relationships to develop. Our life was so busy—everyone spent most of their time either working in the home, witnessing, or attending meetings—that we rarely had time to nurture friendships. Sharing sexually certainly seemed like a way to promote deeper friendships as well as the essential feeling of unity with one another. I did not have a sexual desire or an emotional longing to become close to another man, and I don't remember having a physical attraction to anyone at that time either. But I would have liked someone to talk to. However, these were nothing more than fantasies, since at this point, the sharing concept was the privilege of leaders only. In fact, I learned later that only in the Paris colony, the London homes, and the big colony in Italy where the leaders congregated was sexual experimentation actually being practiced. Cal expressed conflicting hopes and worries about sharing. I think he liked the idea for himself, but he wasn't too keen on letting someone else make love to me. However, with our busy schedules, Cal practicing all day with the band, and myself exploring Paris and raising Thor as a gypsy, we were too absorbed to worry about it for long.

My Paris days were exploding with exciting sensations of life. I was learning French. I was also becoming cultured, which was an adventure for a young, inquisitive American girl. I had little time or money for the relatively expensive museums, but the Paris streets alone are full of culture. Every day I was eager to go out into the colorful city that I was beginning to love. I took Thor to every park in the city, and his first pony ride was in the famed Jardin des Tuileries. I delighted sipping a milk with strawberry syrup, a drink I could share with Thor, while sitting on a crowded café patio, imagining that the lone person beside me was a starving artist waiting for his work to be discovered.

I always dashed away these fantasies, since witnessing was my primary concern. On the street, I considered myself a better witnesser than litnesser, which meant I could talk to someone about spirituality more successfully than I could sell Mo letters. Essentially, I thought of myself as some type of angel, rescuing lost souls from the devil's clutch. For instance, while I was waiting for a metro train one evening, I saw a young man pacing up and down the platform and felt an urge to talk with him. As I got closer, I saw a troubled look on his face, but the desire to speak to him became even stronger. I approached with a smile, and he seemed to back away in apprehension. After hearing my noticeably American accent, he relaxed, and eventually we sat on the bench, along with my witnessing partner, as I spent hours telling him about Jesus. We learned that because of insurmountable personal problems, he had decided to jump in front of a train and end his life, not an uncommon event in the Parisian underground. He was nervously pacing closer and closer to the edge, waiting to jump in front of the next train, when I had approached. Of course, our conversation put a stop, or at least a hold, on his immediate intentions, and he asked Jesus into his heart and came to our home for visits quite a few times afterward.

Caroline, a young, pretty French woman, was another person whom I witnessed to at a time when she needed help. With a young child and an abusive boyfriend, she had used up all the reserves of hope that she had stored up for emergencies and hard times. I met her on a corner of the Rue Montmartre and talked to her about God. She took my witnessing partner and myself to her tiny apartment, where we talked for hours. Her little girl's father was in jail, and her present boyfriend was treating her roughly and not helping her meet her financial needs. She wanted a good home for her daughter, and she wanted to know more about God and His Will for her life. Within a few days, Caroline had left her job, left her boyfriend, and with her daughter moved in with us.

This was our purpose in the world, to tell errant people what God's Will was for them. This was the type of work that drew me to the Family, and since I was still able to help people in a very tangible way, the apparent idiosyncrasies of the COG seemed superfluous.

Living in the Paris home, with the pampered musicians and our most radical leaders, I was again protected from the mundane chore of bringing in funds from selling literature. Sure, we had quotas, which were a set amount of money to bring back, or a certain number of pieces of literature that had to be sold each day; however, with brothers like Jeremy in our colony, who stood on a street corner for four hours and sold only two Mo letters, we felt comically relieved of quota stress. I did not realize it, or even think about it then, but wherever there were really big leaders, like Mo's sons or daughters, or one of his queens, there was always enough money in the home to survive. They obviously had a cash flow that the rest of us did not. Perhaps our best asset was that we had Hopie as the top leader of the Paris home.

Moses David's youngest daughter was one of the unexplainable phenomena I found in the COG. In my naive state of wonderment at all that seemed true and beautiful, Hopie was the purest embodiment of it all for me, representing selfless love in human form. Her wispy blond hair softened the angular lines of her face, and she looked like the good girl next door no matter what age she was or what problems she had. Throughout the many years I was in close contact with her, I can only remember kind words accompanied by a smile and loving look whenever I was in her presence.

As one of Mo's children, Hopie was considered "royal family." Recently, Mo had inaugurated his oldest daughter, Esther, as Queen of the Family. The whole story of the real-life inauguration came out in a letter, and more "queens" were added later. Mo's three other children, Hopie, Benjamin, and Joshua, were also considered part of the royal family, and therefore top leaders, along with their wives and husbands. Since many of the royal family now had mistresses or lovers, they too were classified as some form of royalty.

Actually, the added titles did not mean much to the rest of the Family, since Mo's adult children had always been in the leadership circle. Mo's own mistress, Maria, who was the age of his daughter, was his constant companion; whereas his legal wife, and the mother of his royal children, whom we affectionately called Mother Eve, now traveled the colonies with a young consort. Instead of considering these relationships ungodly, I thought they were enlightening, although I considered the titles to be foolish. I knew that there must be a cache of money somewhere, since the royalty and the leaders traveled so much and always had what they needed, but I could not imagine that it was very much. We didn't make that much litnessing, so where could all this money be coming from? I knew that quite a few very wealthy people had joined the Family, and maybe they had given all their money to the group. I knew that Jeremy Spencer, who had been relatively wealthy at one time, had given everything he owned to the Lord's work, a fact that reassured me. Jeremy now lived in the same home that I did, and he went out on the streets just as I did. If he could live like this, with all the money he had forsaken, why should I worry about who controlled the money? All that I had given the group was an old guitar and a few vintage clothes. However, any doubts about money and who had it were canceled after meeting Hopie. I perceived her to be a spiritual princess, and I was honored to be in her presence. Hopie was the one responsible for bringing me to Paris.

By the mid-1970s, the COG were beginning to set up discos in the larger cities in Europe, wherever we had colonies and musicians. Initially called the Poor Boy Clubs, these weekend discos attracted youth and young adults by providing music and a place to dance. Since the Family had musicians, the entertainment cost us nothing, and there wasn't much financing involved. We rented a hall in a less expensive area of town, sent our litnessers out with flyers advertising the club, and charged a small admission at the door. It soon became the main event of the week, and with all the free manpower and womanpower at our disposal, our discos become regular happenings for the Parisian teenyboppers.

Cal was now the drummer for the disco band in Paris. Since some of the leaders in London told us that including go-go girls drew a bigger crowd, Hopie suggested I be a go-go girl, which meant wearing a skimpy outfit and dancing on stage. Not only did this new role come easy to me; it also meant I would be free of the normal quotas for litnessing, since I now had to practice with the band. It was a wonderful outlet for me, and it became a training ground that led to my professional dancing career. I usually brought Thor with me to practice and let another sister watch him during the disco nights.

As important as dancing became, my primary concern was the nursery. With more women having children in the Paris home, babies were becoming a problem. Fortunately, we never had a major illness or accident among the children in Paris while I lived there, and I attributed this to God's protection. France, like most of Europe, had a free health system, and if any of our members did not have the faith to heal themselves, they could always go to the doctor. I did not then understand why we qualified for this service, or France's laws concerning it, but I know that many of our mothers made use of France's medical hospitality. In addition, France had very strict vaccination laws, and to avoid legal trouble, we all had our babies, Thor included, vaccinated at the local clinics. However, the first step toward making the Paris stables into a home that could accommodate children came with the arrival of Rahab.

A tall, pretty woman who had been in the Family more years than many, Rahab had been married to Benjamin, the son and heir apparent of Moses David. Ben had recently fallen off a mountain in Switzerland while on a walk and died. Mo explained in a letter to us that his son had been too good for the world and had gone to join forces with the spiritual realm. Nasty rumor had it that he had committed suicide. Rahab was in Paris with another mate and a small baby, and since Rahab was semiroyalty, having been the wife of Mo's son, she had to be given a leadership position. Hopie put her in charge of setting up a nursery and child-care department in Paris. The problem was, Rahab had little child-care training; she seemed to have no sense of organization or scheduling, both of which were important parts of any effective child-care program. Joab recognized this lack of practicality, and he suggested I work closely with her. After a few days of meetings, I decided that Paris must be the place they sent those leaders who were too spiritual to do any earthly good.

Rahab and I set up a nursery in the small room next to the girls' dorm. It doubled as a bedroom for Cal and me, which did not make him too happy; but since he was away all day practicing, it only interfered with his sleep. The nursery consisted of single mattresses on the floor along one wall, a soft rug in the middle, and two changing tables with covered trash containers for disposable diapers. It had a softwood floor, so it was safe for babies taking their first steps. Thor was the oldest at a little over a year, and the other two babies, Rahab's and another woman's, usually slept with their mother. The children usually followed the adult schedule, with a little earlier bedtime, and single sisters took turns volunteering to read the babies scriptures as they fell asleep.

Officially, the nursery could be used twenty-four hours a day, but only visiting leaders and disciples made use of it at night. Since it was right across from the only bathroom, we brought water into the nursery to bathe the children, and used a large tub to clean baby materials and wash clothes. We could not afford the expensive Montessori equipment, which was used for the children in the bigger, well-stocked Family nurseries, so we brought various pots and pans, plastic dishes, and spoons from the kitchen, and odd-shaped cardboard boxes for the babies to play with.

Rahab spent many hours in my nursery/bedroom, revealing to me the "new" spiritual growth of the family. She spiritualized everything, and I wondered if she had always been like this or if she had learned it from her deceased husband, whom I had met in Canada and remembered as an ethereal person. Everything from the stain on the babies' bib to the recent death of the French politician Georges Pompidou had a deep spiritual significance to Rahab. Little child care was discussed. Since Rahab came from the London home, where the organizational heads and Mo were, she knew a few royal secrets.

"Do you know who Esther is sleeping with now?" she quipped,

while I patted the last baby to sleep as he lay on the extra blankets we had arranged on the floor. Recently, a few mothers had come from colonies outside Paris for meetings, and our nursery was a little crowded during the day. I was worried if they planned on letting the babies stay here all night, but Rahab evidently was too spiritual to worry.

"Well, I suppose her husband, Jacob," I replied, knowing she would soon fill me in on royal gossip.

"Oh, no. Jacob is living with Enoch's first wife, Pearl. That was really a terrible thing to do to Enoch, you know. I mean, he always suspected that Pearl was more than Jacob's secretary, but until Mo came out and explained about the royal family having consorts and concubines, he really did not know, did he? So Pearl is now Jacob's second wife, and she's having a baby. And Jacob's wife, Esther, is traveling with Hosanna. From what I hear, she is pregnant again, but of course, no one is sure who the father could be."

Even for the Paris home, this was radical information that I was hearing. I tried to change the subject, knowing that, since I was not a member of the royal family, or even a mistress, I should probably not be privy to what went on in their personal relationships. I had heard that the London home was even more on the libertine cutting-edge than the home in Paris, but I was dedicated to our pioneer effort here and didn't care about London's elite or what they did. I usually had the attitude that others could do as they liked as long as it didn't interfere with me or my son. But what I did not understand was that no woman is an island—especially not one living in a commune.

"Do you think we could request funds for a crib in here?" I asked, trying to change the topic. "The babies should really be up off the floor, and it would certainly be safer to have them in a crib, rather than on the bed."

"Okay, I'll talk to Joab about that. Well, you know, of course, that Joab made Beth pregnant. I wonder what Hopie is going to do about that. Oh well, I guess I won't be involved in their stories anymore, now that Benjamin is gone. Mother Eve is coming through here soon. She and I get along marvelously. I think I'll ask her to take me with her."

"What about the child-care program here?" I asked.

"Oh, you'll do fine. I really don't enjoy child care. They just put me here to give me something to do, you know. Well, I hope you never get stuck with Esther. She is a tyrant to work with."

I had already worked with a tyrant in Germany, and I had no desire to be near another one. Esther, however, was our Queen, and somehow I knew that with Paris gaining the Family's attention, we would be graced with a royal visit soon.

Mo's original wife came first. Although she was Mo's first wife—and I don't think they ever divorced—she was never called a queen, just Mother Eve. She was a kind-looking lady in her fifties who traveled with a young man about twenty-five years old. Like her daughter Hopie, she always wore a smile, and always had some words of encouragement. Now that I had learned to read people a little better, she did not seem old, but forgotten. She did not keep herself as attractively attired as the sexy French women of her age. I knew from the letters that she had been raised in the church and had married Mo when he was a budding preacher. I saw pictures of her in the Family history letters in which she was playing a piano in church, and I wondered how this fundamentalist Christian lady could ever be traveling and having sex with a man so young while her husband lived with another woman. I had been socially prepared for this by hippie ideals, but she was more radical than I. How did this poor lady do it? She must really have believed that this was God's true work. She had followed Mo across America while he searched for a "ministry," and had borne him four children. When he'd finally found his calling with the youth of California, the beginnings of the Children of God, her children were all teenagers and witnessed with their father to the lost hippies. I don't think Mother Eve ever shared the limelight during those days, but she certainly made up for it now. Wherever she went, she held meetings and talked for hours. We never knew what to think of her. I had been told that Mo referred to her as the "the old church" and to Maria as "the new church" in his first circulated letter of 1969, titled "A Prophecy of God on the Old Church and the New Church." But he told us to respect her as a Mother and he even published her talks, called Mother Eve letters. At other times we were warned that Mother and her consort were not obeying the rules laid out in the letters and should be banned from fellowship. At this point in Paris she was still respected.

"Come here, honey. You look pretty today. Are you married, dear?" she said to me when we first met.

"Yes, I am married to Cal."

"Oh, he's the drummer, isn't he? Well, honey, you better keep your eyes on him. He's a handsome young man, you know. Are you happy, honey?"

I really did not think much about happiness. I felt I was doing God's Will, so I guess I should be happy. She noticed that I hesitated.

"Well, don't worry, dearie. God never takes anything away without giving you something better," she informed me in an apocalyptic tone. The realization came to me that she had borne all Mo's children and then been cast aside, and maybe she was not happy. I hid this fact from my rational thought processes, a mental action that had become ingrained.

Whenever a leader came through Paris, Hopie and Joab would throw a big party and everyone enjoyed the royal festivities. There would be music and dancing until late into the night, and being in France, wine flowed freely. Every leader in the Family wanted to come through Paris, since we were beginning to have good contacts with music and television producers. A well-known French singer and his producer had seen some of us performing on the streets and were seriously interested in promoting us as a music group. In the small French entertainment world, their influence meant success. We had already made a recording of our theme song "You Gotta Be a Baby," and we had appeared on a few TV and radio shows. Hopie had always been wonderful at making contacts and establishing a good public relations image, but paperwork and legal matters were not something she could be trusted with. Her husband Joab, a Vietnam veteran, was more of an inspirationalist than a manager, so we knew our so-called organizational geniuses, Esther and her husband Jacob, would be sent our way soon.

Esther came like the Queen of Hearts, yelling "off with their heads." I heard rumors that Mo had sent Esther to Paris to put our home in order. Whatever the reason, a pall settled over Paris after Esther arrived. She was a small lady whose physically fragile appearance gave little clue of the tremendous power she held as Queen of the Family. Having known the loving, free, and easygoing Hopie, I was not prepared for the Queen's wrath. She had been given complete authority over all practical matters in the Family, which was now centered in Europe. Esther came to our home with her last baby and a child-care helper in tow. Her older children were all taken care of in the large Italian child-care center that she had personally set up a year earlier. Her positions on how children should be taken care of were full of contradictions. Even so, Esther was in charge of setting up huge nurseries and schools where many of the children were sent. I knew from the Family testimonies that these nurseries were clean and well organized, that children were taught in Montessori-style classes from the age of two, and that our nurseries and schools were on a par with the best the system had to offer. In comparison, here in Paris we did not have a great practical setup, but at least the babies slept with their mothers at night—they had to since we had no cribs. I remembered watching babies all night in the nursery in Ellenville, and trying to understand how a mother could be sleeping over in the married couple's rooms or in the leaders' house, and not be worried that her baby was crying somewhere far away. I didn't want Thor crying in the middle of the night only to have him be held by some passing nursery worker. As far as I could see, big, organized nurseries meant separation of mother and baby, and, consciously or subconsciously, I did not want this to happen to me. Up until now, I had kept Thor with me night and day, but Esther's appearance in Paris marked the beginning of the end for my close relationship with Thor.

Esther held a major meeting with leaders in Paris in which she ranted about the deplorable conditions in the nursery, attacking especially the lack of structured schedules; of cribs, beds, and playpens; and of Montessori equipment or even educational toys. In addition, she sent a letter to all the other Family homes, citing the Paris nursery as an example of what not to do.

I remember when she finally came into the nursery to chastise its nursery workers. "I cannot believe that you girls actually let the babies sleep on the floor here. Do you think that is a good way to take care of God's children, or any children for that matter? How in the world were you girls raised anyway?" she fumed.

There were only two of us present, myself and another young mother. Rahab had conveniently had herself transferred to another home soon after Esther's arrival. I was upset at her for leaving me alone, but many years later I learned why Rahab had been so eager to escape Esther's presence. It seems that Esther, her own sister-in-law, had taken Rahab's first baby from her and given her to another woman to raise. No complaints were ever voiced since Esther was our Queen.

"Jeshanah, I heard you were trained in Ellenville. Well, I know Ellenville had a very good nursery. Pearl herself went through there on the way to London, and she was very impressed. Surely, you know better. Why don't you have access to hot water in here? Why don't you have a refrigerator just for the children's food? And never again do I want to hear of a home anywhere in our Family where the babies sleep on the floor. Do you understand?"

She spoke to me as if I had it within my power to do something about the conditions of our nursery. Surely she must know that the humble servants did only what they were told to do. If the leader of the home told me that babies sleep on the floor, I put them to sleep on the floor. (It wasn't actually the floor; there were clean mattresses and sheets.) One of them was my own son, who'd had a handmade cradle when he was born. Of course, I did not like him to sleep on the floor, but he was a "revolutionary baby," and in the Family we did it the revolutionary way. Which meant, do what your leaders say, and don't ask questions. Maybe she did not know how the proletariat lived, having never been anything but a leader.

"I wouldn't even let my baby in your nursery. I went out immediately and bought a foldaway crib when I knew I would be traveling," she added. "What do you girls have to say for yourselves?"

I was literally biting my tongue to keep from responding. I could not tell her that we simple servants did not have money in our pocket, or in the bank, or under the bed, or anywhere else, to go out and buy a crib. I could not even buy baby clothes with money my mother sent specifically for the baby unless I got permission first.

"I am just going to have to write the world about this," she said, meaning the Family around the world. "I want everyone to know that this should not happen again." She left our wonderful Paris home to bring her baby back to the safety of the Italian child-care center, and she wrote her letter, mentioning the lack of cribs. I took comfort in thinking that anyone in the Family with half a brain would realize that mere nursery workers could not go out and buy cribs. It was like saying, "Let them eat cake!"

But there were deeper worries about why I did not like a fully equipped nursery. Esther had only brought her youngest baby with her, but she had four or five others who had been left back in Italy as she traveled around Europe. I could foresee a time when I would have to leave Thor behind in an institutionalized children's home, and my fears were realized. Within a year, Esther's trained child-care workers had come to Paris and set up nurseries and schools, and from the time he was eighteen months old, I had to leave Thor at the school located about twenty miles outside of Paris. He cried every time he had to return, and I tried to be "revolutionary" about our separation. Thor was allowed to stay with me on weekends only, and as I became more involved in the music world, many of my weekends were taken up with activity. I consoled myself that now Thor at least had a bed, although in a room with a dozen other toddlers; he had a regular schedule, unfortunately enforced by spankings and other disciplinary measures; and he had Montessori classes. But he didn't have me to hug him when he fell and cut his lip; to praise him when he used the potty; or to acknowledge his genius when he surprised the "teachers" by adding numbers before they taught him how. I wanted to be there for every new piece of life he discovered, in pain or in joy, but after Esther's visit, I was temporarily banned from child care. My plan of staying in the nursery to be with my son had failed. I now fit the archetype of the "bitter" Miriam instead of the skillful baby-watcher. Life was not offering me easy problems with easy solutions.

Hopie came by to see us after Esther left and explained that she also got a good going over.

"Don't worry, honey, God only dishes it out to those He knows can take it. You are a strong sister, and the Lord is going to use you mightily."

I was encouraged by these words from the Bible, even though I knew they were used repeatedly in any situation where a disillusioned brother or sister needed uplifting.

In the end, the cribs were never bought, since our finance brother said we could not afford them. Therefore, I was given a provisioner and a few quota-free days to go out and try to get some free baby cribs.

With Esther gone, the Paris home returned to its old joyful ways. The musicians and singers had two fairly successful records, though none of us knew where the money went. Our leaders were busy working out contracts with the system producers, and meanwhile, all the Show Group, as we were called, were told to go on litnessing and making quotas like normal disciples. That must have been another organizational decision initiated by Esther. We spent our days practicing, and then ventured out on litnessing sprees with big quotas to make.

Lately, we had begun using the method called "busking" to make our quotas. In pairs, with one singer and one collector, we performed uninvited at outdoor cafés. Stationing ourselves in front of our unwittingly captive audience, we played a few songs on the guitar, and then the collector went around the tables with a hat to collect money and hand out Mo letters. On a good day, we could make our 100-franc quota easily in a few hours. I often brought Thor with me in a stroller, especially before the schools were set up. Of course, that was a problem when it rained, or when we got out of the home too late, which is what happened on the eventful night when we started singing inside the metro trains.

Cal and I asked Nahum, our lead guitarist, to go busking with us. He was a dark-haired, broody fellow, who played great guitar. I had brought Thor along that evening since it was a weekend and the nursery was closed. Not only did we start an hour after the good busking times, but it was raining and cold. None of us wanted to litness the old way, by going up to people and asking for a donation while forcing our Mo letters on them. We tried singing inside the metro station corridors, like the traveling hippies we saw, but few people would stop, and even fewer left a donation. Sitting on the bench while waiting for the next metro car to take us to the Champs-Elysées, where we thought we might find some people in the cafés under the awnings, Cal had a bright idea.

"Why don't we sing inside the cars," he said. "The people are stuck in there and they can't get away."

"I think it's a great idea!" I said encouragingly. "I'll collect, and Cal can hold the stroller.

We all had a quota to make, so it was worth the try. We entered a car half-filled with sleepy, unsuspecting riders. Standing together at the front of the car, Nahum strummed a note, Cal held on to Thor's stroller so it would not move, and I called across the car, *"Bonjour. Nous avons quelques chansons pour vous"* ("Hello, we have a few songs for you") by way of introduction. After three songs, in which we all sang and Nahum held the passengers captive with his guitar, I aggressively invaded the privacy of every rider on the metro car by holding my basket under their nose and offering a piece of unsolicited literature. Asking for a donation, I smiled and gave the letters out to everyone. The whole procedure took about five metro stops. When we were finished, I said, *"Merci,"* and we moved on to the next car.

"How did it go?" asked Cal anxiously, as we sat on the bench to wait for the next car.

I surrendered the basket to him, and he counted over 20 francs.

"Wow," said Nahum. "That only took about ten minutes. We can get our quota in an hour." Indeed, in less than an hour we had collected 176 francs. Each car seemed to get better. God was blessing us!

After our last car, we got off the train and sat on the metro station bench in a state of exhilaration.

"What are we going to do about this?" asked Nahum. He was already thinking that we should keep this a secret for ourselves. Cal was a little more magnanimous.

"I think we should tell our leaders about this and let them decide. It would be nice if the metro cars could be the exclusive territory for the band members, since we have so little time for litnessing."

All of the Paris Family homes lived by selling letters on the streets or singing at cafés, but since there were now so many of us—over five hundred during the peak time of 1974 to 1976—the best litnessing and singing spots were becoming saturated. Before we discovered metro singing, the whole Paris turf had to be divided, with each home vying for the best busking areas. At one time we had three separate Show Group homes in Paris and a few regular homes, which I never visited. Since most Family members learned to sing and play basic guitar, the method of making one's quota on metro cars was certain to become popular.

"I think mothers should be included," I said. Even though I was considered part of the band, through my dancing, I knew how hard it was for mothers to make their half quotas, and I saw this as a great opportunity to ease their added burdens.

We told our house leader Micah what had happened, but word got out and within a month all the Family members in Paris were singing on the metro cars. Depending on who was the top leader in Paris at the time, different rules were made about who could go on the metros. During the "band only" rule, a lot of unbrotherly feelings arose among the regular Family members. Of course, all of this planning was made without ever consulting the metro authorities. For years we played cat and mouse with them, always on the lookout for the metro police. Many times, we would be taken to their station and told we were not allowed to sing in the cars, only in the corridors between the metro stations. All this did was waste our time. The metros were too lucrative to give up. By the time I left Paris, we were singing on the brand-new RER, which ran to the suburbs in twenty-minute stops.

We always turned in our money every night, along with the literature count, but everyone knew we only gave out literature to fill up the statistics on our reports. If we did not make our quota, we were not supposed to come home; however, this rule was usually not obeyed. Instead, privileges were taken from us. For instance, once Cal did not make his quota on time and he was told he could not go on a planned trip to Mont-St.-Michel, so another couple in the band, Breeze and Abraham, went out that night to make it for him. Cal and Nahum, who often sang together on the metro, were also the only brothers to be picked up by police and taken to the police station. When the authorities found out that their visas were long overdue, they were going to be sent out of the country. However, since they were important members of the band, our producers stepped in and obtained proper visas for all of us.

I was not aware of what our producers, who were not in the Family, did or did not do for us financially; however, when we all went on the road, we usually stayed in cheap campgrounds, while our leaders and the producers stayed at fancy hotels.

The Spirit was moving in the music direction, and we landed our first big contract to produce an album. Our Show Group name was Les Enfants de Dieu, which means "The Children of God." Our first album and the singles "My Love Is Love" and "Liberty" became big hits with the French teenagers, and through contacts that our producer had, we were asked to perform at radio shows, on French television, and to join the famous Europe One tour of France as performers. In 1976 we toured Spain, Holland, Belgium, Germany, and England.

The French have a fascination with live spectacles, called the "gala," which is a cross between a Las Vegas show and a music concert. Many French performers spend the winter in Paris, performing on TV or radio or at local theaters, and then go on the road with a gala in the summer. These shows require musicians, vocalists, sound technicians, lighting technicians, and, usually, dancers. With the amount of talent and personnel available through our Family, putting together a gala was a piece of cake. Our galas were really a fancy inspiration time for us, something we had been practicing for years. Everyone in the Paris Family wanted to be involved, and when word got to Italy and England about our shows, performers were sent to Paris. Sure enough, Queen Esther soon wanted to leave her real-life castle in Italy, the home of a duke whom one of our women had married, and she returned to the Paris home to be in on the act.

When the Show Group first started, I stayed with nursery work. Many of the female singers had children, and I was needed more than ever to take care of babies. In addition, Thor was now a little over a year old, a very cute age, and I enjoyed staying with him as much as I could. We were now living in a seven-story building where we were "squatting" in the Bourse area of Paris, the equivalent of New York's Wall Street financial district. A nursery was set up on the top floor by the sisters who had been trained under Esther. The nursery overseer begged me to stay in the nursery, and I did so happily. However, when Hopie heard that they needed dancers, she sent for me. I became the only nonsinger in the group, since all the other girls doubled as backup chorus and dancers.

The producer liked my dancing style and put me in the front line, next to the lead singer. When Esther arrived, she moved me to the back of the line, and put herself in my place. I did not mind, since I had never had formal dance training, and I was sure it would be noticed by the professionals we were soon to work with. They would find out what amateurs we were, Esther included.

Our little makeshift show was fine for the little radio programs and small theaters, but when the producers told us we were to go on national TV, they suggested we get a choreographer. My old nursery friend from Ellenville, Salome, who had been a professional dance instructor before she joined the Family, was sent from Italy.

I was overjoyed to see Salome, but she had changed quite a bit. Working in Italy for two years now under top leadership, she had lost some of her rebelliousness. She had also gained a considerable amount of weight, and although she was by far the best dancer among us, the producers usually kept her off stage. Salome was a wonderful and sensitive teacher. She knew I had no training, and so she took me aside and developed the natural talent I had for dancing. I always thought of her as my miracle worker. We learned a little jazz and a little modern dancing; we did stretching and other exercises and practiced routines for six to eight hours a day. Of course, Esther rarely showed up for practice, and I knew she would be in trouble on stage.

During our first stage rehearsal for the Guy Lux show, the most popular variety show in France—the equivalent to our Ed Sullivan show of the 1960s—the TV producer made Esther leave the front line and brought me from the back to take her place. It was obvious she could not dance, even the simple little two-step we did. He, of course, had no idea that she was our Queen. Ever since that day, I was always in the front line, even when the former professional dancers came to join our group. The number in the Show Group fluctuated between two dozen to thirty, including singers, musicians, dancers, technicians, managers, and leaders. Singers competed to get the spotlight, of course, but the worst fighting was between the leaders.

Esther finally maneuvered the control of the Paris Show Group out of her sister Hopie's hands. Hopie gave up the reins willingly, explaining that she was a pioneer, and she departed to start a new work in some unfamiliar Arab land. Esther was now with us constantly. She left most of her five children in Italy at the school, but she brought her baby and a personal nursery worker with her. Even with the fine nursery established by her own trained people, she did not leave her baby with regular child-care workers. Later, as we got more popular, Esther brought her oldest daughter, who was still a pre-teen, to sing in the show.

Because I was spending so much time away from Thor in those early days, I finally tried to leave the Show Group, saying that I needed to help out in the nursery. That resulted in my being given nursery duty in addition to show practices. I was usually relieved of making my quota on practice days, during the week; however, I had to make it during any weekend we stayed home, and that meant bringing Thor with me. My little boy learned busking before he was two years old.

The fun and glamour of being involved in TV, live shows, and recording were somewhat diminished by the constant surveillance of the Family leadership. One was never quite certain how to act, since we lived like "normal" COG, but we had to behave like some special stars in public. I still never had my own money with which to buy clothes. All our clothes were either bought by Esther or made by a seamstress with Salome, who designed the costumes. We were supposed to look nice, but I was never sure what nice meant when one had no money to buy anything. One day, as we were loading the bus to go on tour, Esther was standing in the front of the bus giving her usual speech on how to act. Being the last one on the bus, I had to pass her. We were going to be in southern France for almost a month, and I did not want to be away from my two-year-old for so long; however, staying home was out of the question. I was told that there were other mothers on this tour, Queen Esther included, and if they could make the sacrifice of being away from their children, so could I.

Esther looked at my legs as I walked down the aisle. "Jeshanah, do you have nylons on?" she asked in front of the whole group waiting on the bus.

"No," I said, thinking it was an honest question requiring a simple answer.

"I can't believe that you are not wearing anything on your legs. Proper girls do not go around with bare legs, Jeshanah." She embarked on a ten-minute speech about how she never again wanted to see any girl in the Show Group representing God's Family with nothing on their legs. If she ever saw it again, that person would be out of the Show Group fast.

I wanted to stand up and leave the bus. I did not care if I was in or out of the Show Group. In fact, at that moment, I would rather have been back in my bed waiting for my sleeping son to wake up. But most of all, I wanted to raise my hand and pose what seemed to me an obvious question: "Excuse me, but where do we get money to buy nylons?" It was the second time that Esther had publicly degraded me for not having something that I had no money to buy. The last pair of nylons that I had been given had half a dozen runs in them now, and no one had replaced them. Besides, I never read any rule that said we had to wear nylons. I didn't say anything. Why start a scene? I suspected that Esther was waging her own futile battle over my being in the front row, but she knew as well as I did that the producers would not let me go now. My face was on all the publicity photos that they had paid for, so I had to be in the show. Still, she liked to pretend she had the power to kick someone out.

Compared with Esther's verbal abuse, the letters that Mo was writing at that time seemed innocuous. While the Paris Show Group was becoming famous in France as a clean-cut singing group comparable to the *Sound of Music* family, Mo had taken a harem of buxom beauties to an island near Spain to pioneer a *new method* of witnessing. He shared with the Family his enlightening experiences through a series of letters that emerged slowly and eased us into the radical new way of witnessing. I was so engrossed in dancing and show business at that time, I hardly realized what had happened. The whole sexual revolution was going on around me while I spent half my days stretching and learning new steps, and the other half trying to catch up with my son's growth. I knew that there was something called "flirty fishing" being developed in London and Spain, but I was too busy to wonder about it. When we received the letters called "Flirty Little Fishy," "Look of Love," and "Lovelight," I read them with detached interest, but basically they seemed to be a rewording of what I had been doing all the time, winning people with love—"God's Love," of course. It was only later, when we got the King Arthur series of letters, that it dawned on me where Mo was really going with this new method.

These dark, shameful letters would soon become the guiding light of my life as I surrendered my *body* to God's supposedly highest calling. But before that would happen, I needed to feel that I had at least a voice inside my soul. For the next three years, I struggled to identify my voice in this strange life I had chosen, and although all I found was a feeble cry from a deep abyss somewhere within, it was enough to keep me connected to myself. I would not explore the depths to locate the origins of this cry for many years. For the time being, I concentrated on the surface crevices. There were cracks in my own psyche and I thought I would block them up—fill them in with something, never imagining that they would merely get larger and deeper. One crevice was caused by my loveless relationship with Cal, which was emotionally stressful for both of us, and it was beginning to affect all facets of my life. Perhaps if I had looked within myself at that time, listened to the feeble voice that was hardly distinguishable then, I could have found creative self-solutions, but instead, I looked to the Family for direction.

5

○ ○ ○

"God's Whores"

"I want to get out of the Show Group!" I lamented to Micah, the leader who had been sent to Paris to help Esther manage our entourage. Micah had been through many emotional and spiritual trials since joining the Family. We knew from gossip that his wife, whom he had married when marriages were still a personal choice, had been taken from him and given to a man Mo was recruiting into the family. Micah's two young children were now with his ex-wife and her new husband, and he rarely saw them since they lived in London.

Micah was, nevertheless, always cheerful as he struggled to portray a positive spirit. A well-built, handsome young man of Mexican heritage, he was also a talented musician and songwriter, and perfect to help organize the unruly Show Group. He had established an empathetic relationship with those who came to him for counsel, and because of his reputation as a balanced and just leader, I felt safe approaching him with my problems.

Micah had recently married a former nightclub singer who joined the Family and was now in the Show Group. Talitha was something of a prima donna, until Salome encouraged her to share her large and luxurious array of lingerie among all the showgirls. Since I was her size, I acquired the nicest intimate apparel I ever owned. I actually felt that this was a blessing. I had never been allowed to go out and buy my own lingerie, and the underwear we obtained free from stores and factories, or which our leaders bought for us, was very plain.

When I told Micah that I wanted out of the Show Group and my marriage, he replied that this was out of his realm of decision-making power, so he sent me to a higher authority, to Esther's first husband, Jacob, who, of course, was Mo's son-in-law. Jacob had a large office in the building we occupied in the Bourse area of Paris, although he did not actually live with us. He had been one of the first disciples, so he was in his thirties, about ten years older than I, as evidenced by his thinning hair and protruding belly. He looked rather like a worldly businessman, but we knew better. Jacob was third-in-command in the Family at that time.

"I don't have a good relationship with Cal," I explained to him. "We argue constantly, and I know it's mostly my fault but I just can't get the victory over this. Also, I don't like being away from my son so much. With all these practices, shows, and witnessing on top of it, I have hardly any time with him." Most of the leaders had changed mates at least once, I thought to myself, so why couldn't I get away from mine?

Jacob listened intently.

"Why are you so sad?" he asked, in a way that made me think that I was special. I burst into tears. I was really sad, and perhaps I did not have a good reason to be.

"I don't know," I mumbled.

"Well . . . what would make you happy?"

I thought for a moment. "I think I would like to be full-time with the children," I murmured hesitantly, knowing his wife had taken me out of child care.

Child care had grown to a respectable position in Paris. The top floor of our Bourse building had been converted into a nursery for younger babies, but by now Thor was away all week at the school in the country. Since I had a show on weekends, I hardly ever saw him, usually only when I visited the school during the week. I longed to be with my son, and working in child care would give me that opportunity.

"I can understand that you want to spend more time with your son," he said. "I think that is reasonable."

It amazed me to hear him say this. Not even his wife, Esther, spent as much time visiting her children as I did. Since I was usually reprimanded for being overly concerned about Thor, I thought Jacob would rebuke me for being so selfish and unsacrificial, but instead he seemed to sympathize with my plight. It was the first time I heard a leader entertain such a bourgeois sentiment as wanting to spend more time with your child. He was a father. Maybe he could understand the confusing emotions that I was experiencing. I was touched by this man's empathy for my dilemma.

"What if you had some sort of project involved with the children's department? It doesn't mean that you can stop participating in the Show Group, but you will be exempt from witnessing. Would you like that?" he posed.

I thought it was a start. Any project with children would give me more time to see Thor. "Yes, that sounds wonderful."

"Okay, come and see Pearl tomorrow. I'll let her know what you need to do."

Pearl, who was Jacob's second "wife," was in charge of all child care in Paris, which had grown to huge proportions. She came from a wealthy background, and when she joined the Family, her parents became very involved in anti–Children of God activity. The story I had heard about her parents was that they visited a few of our homes in the States with police escorts, but since Pearl was no longer a minor, they were required to go through a long legal process to get her out of the Family against her will. With their money and influence, they were about to cause serious trouble for us in America. I had been told that New York State had started investigating us due to her parents' insistence. Therefore, Pearl was whisked off to a secret home in Europe, leaving her new husband, Enoch, in our band home in Boston. We later found out that she had become Jacob's second wife while in London. With her model's face and well-kept hair and skin, her beauty was awesome, and I respected the high status she had achieved in the Family, now being mated to Jacob. She was cold and distant, as I had expected, and from her clothes and makeup, I knew that she enjoyed privileges that the rest of us did not.

When I went to see her the next day, she said, "Jacob informed me that I should give you a project with the children. Do you know what he had in mind?"

I had no idea what Jacob intended, so I told her what I had been mulling over. "Well, I think it would be useful for mothers to have their own Montessori kits. This way they can teach their own children at home when the kids are with them on the weekends. I also think it would be very useful for the mothers out on the mission field, whose children do not come to the school."

Pearl looked at me with a hint of surprise and hostility. "Okay. Can you give me a plan tomorrow of what you want to do, and I will look it over. If Jacob said you were to have a project in child care, I guess you will have to!" she sighed.

I stayed up all night writing a proposal for my project, and I handed it in the next day. It included a design for a wooden container, about the size of a shoebox, that could hold learning tools for preschool-age children, such as counting rods, sandpaper letters and numbers, adding cubes, dressing frames, and anything else useful in learning how to dress oneself.

Jacob called me to his office a few days later. "Did Pearl give you something you like?" he asked.

"Well, I gave her a plan, and she said she would get back to me."

"She will, soon. Meanwhile, I'd like to talk to you about the other problem you are having. Why don't we go out for dinner and discuss this?"

I had never considered going "out to dinner" to discuss a problem with a leader. Normally if we discussed something over dinner, it would be in the Family dining room or in the leader's private office. This was different. Jacob took me to a good French restaurant, and told me to order anything I liked. Since I had never been to a restaurant of this category, I hardly knew what the menu meant, so he ordered for me with a self-satisfied sigh.

We talked over dinner about why I was unhappy in my marriage. One evening out led to another, and finally he invited me to his apartment. I did not realize that leaders had their own apartments. I thought they all lived in another colony somewhere. By this time, I was beginning to suspect that Jacob had designs of his own on me; however, we had been taught that "God works in mysterious ways" and not to question how God does something—just accept it. I had prayed for a change in my life, and perhaps this was how God would answer my prayer. Therefore, I followed Jacob's lead, and instead of questioning why he was doing this, I reverted to my natural tendency to consider everything a grand adventure. He showed me into a small one-bedroom apartment with a cozy sitting room.

"Would you like a drink?" he asked.

"I'm not sure. Whatever you suggest."

He gave me a vodka with orange juice. It was the first time I had had hard liquor since joining the Family. His tongue loosened with each drink. He was having his own problems with his wives, he told me. Esther, it was obvious, was no longer interested in him and had a young consort traveling with her. He thought Pearl had married him for his position. He seemed to be saying that he needed a sweet, tender woman who cared about him. I could not imagine why he thought of me as a sweet, tender woman. After all, I was trying to leave my husband.

"You know, Mo has every leader in this Family with new mates. It will probably be going around the whole Family soon, but he wants us to experiment with this 'one wife' idea first. It is not as easy as you think to be in the royal family."

I could not believe he was talking so disrespectfully about our leader and prophet. It was scary and exciting. The alcohol had begun to numb my revolutionary training.

"Jeshanah, I am going to take care of you," he said, kissing my neck awkwardly. "You won't have to worry about anything in the Family again."

Though I was secretly repulsed and felt no desire for Jacob whatsoever, I let him lead me to the bedroom and have sex. The whole time, all I could think of was getting home to my safe colony. I felt ashamed and humiliated, but I could not understand why.

True to his word, Jacob gave me a big project in child care. Pearl was not happy about allotting one of the Show Group dancers such a responsibility, but she did what she was told. The project kept me busy and content. I felt useful now that I was doing something productive. With the carpenter, I designed and put together a dozen Montessori kits for mothers in the field. Typical of communist bureaucracy, by the time news of the kits got out, the leaders' wives wanted them. They ended up in the leaders' hands, and few actually were given out to the mothers who really needed them.

To clean up my other problem, Jacob met with Cal and talked to him about having a trial separation from me. I don't know what was discussed or how Cal initially reacted, but Cal began to stay in the main Show Group home located in Colombes, in northern Paris, and I moved to the home in Sceaux, a southern suburb of Paris. Thor began spending one weekend with me, and one with Cal.

Jacob took me to his apartment regularly, usually without the dinner prelude. I also began drinking periodically, and hoped that no one would find out about me and Jacob. But of course, everyone knew, even Cal. He bore the hurt and shame heroically, just as Micah and others had done before him. They all obeyed leadership like good revolutionaries. I am sure that Cal, like myself, took his grievances to the Lord. He could have complained, but against a leader as high as Jacob, it was almost useless. He could have left the group too, but I know he would never have left our son. I was ashamed of myself, but I could not see clearly what to do. I had started this, and I would have to see it through to its conclusion. Perhaps it was better to stumble ahead blindly than stop on a dark and unfamiliar road.

After the Montessori project was finished, I started writing. I had an idea to put some of the easy Mo letters in children's story form. I thought that the children needed Family stories written especially for kids, so I made up a series of fantasy animal stories based on morals in the Mo letters. I did not talk about this project with anyone, but it kept me distracted from the more stressful areas of my life, such as my deepening relationship with Jacob.

I also stayed awake at night reviewing my life and actions in my mind. Cal was definitely not a bad husband. He had always been kind and considerate, never having that demanding attitude that some of our men had with their wives. Since we were taught that husbands rule over their wives in the privacy of their "home" (we never had our own home, so this meant bedroom to me), he could have been a lot more demanding. However, he wasn't, and therefore I had felt more *compelled* to give him the sex he wanted. I didn't want to discuss this with him, since it would hurt his feelings, and yet I was hurting him a lot more now.

One day, Jacob picked me up at Sceaux in his car. Only leaders were allowed private use of our cars, and the one Jacob drove was a modest vehicle I had seen before in our Family.

"I'm going to Switzerland for a few days," he said. "When I come back, I'd like you to start living with me."

I had just finished my first children's story, and I was feeling good about myself. I was as free and independent as one could be in the Family. I was able to be involved in child care, and I saw a future for myself there. I had open access to visiting my son at school during the week, thanks to Jacob's influence. I was feeling a newfound *joie de vivre*. Why would I want to live with Jacob? He already had two wives. Why did he need me? And why would I again allow myself to be joined to a man I did not love?

"I don't want to do that," I blurted out, without considering what his reaction would be.

For a moment, he looked totally devastated. Then he quickly regained his composure.

"Jeshanah, you don't have much choice. You either live with me, or you go back to Cal. I'll be gone for about a week, but when I come back, I want your answer."

He dropped me off near the house without giving me time to think about what he said.

"Do you have ten francs?" I asked.

He smiled and reached in his pocket, perversely happy to grant my request.

I got out of the car and went to a local grocery store to buy a bottle of wine. There was a small park near our home, and since we never witnessed anywhere near where we lived, I could safely get drunk without worrying that I would be seen by someone who knew me. I had never done this before, but being with Jacob often, I had developed a taste for alcohol. Sitting on a park bench, I opened the bottle and started to drink away every thought that I had stored in my mind's closet. I took out each feeling of guilt and every self-condemning accusation, and shook it like the rumpled piece of old cloth it represented. I had left my husband, a major sin in anyone's religion. I had allowed myself to become involved in an adulterous relationship, one of the worst sins of all. Then I remembered that Jesus had prevented the crowd from stoning an adulterous woman. I wondered if that woman had also been obeying leadership and Jesus knew that? In my stupor, I cast my thoughts aside with the privilege enjoyed by those drunken individuals who claim that "nothing matters anymore."

Since I drank a whole bottle of wine on an empty stomach, I felt sick when I stood up to walk home. Entering our house while everyone was around the dinner table, I passed by quickly, went to the bathroom, and threw up.

After cleaning out my conscience closet, I spent the rest of the week singing on the metro and visiting Thor. When Jacob returned, he called a meeting at the Colombes home. He had news from Esther concerning the Show Group; she had been in a hospital in Switzerland, deathly sick with a disease supposedly brought on by working too hard. We were all to have a prayer and fast for her, and try to get back into God's Word more. Every time a big leader got sick, especially if it was Mo himself, part of the cause usually lay with the followers.

Jacob was waiting at the door when I came in the Colombes house. "Well, what's your decision?" he asked.

"I can't do it," I answered, and followed the others into the meeting room without looking him in the eye. I had hidden that dilemma in the back room of my mind along with other unanswerable questions, and my response had come straight from my heart. Later, Cal and I were called into Jacob's temporary office upstairs.

Cal knew what had been going on, but like a loyal revolutionary, he was trying to take it as a test from the Lord.

"Cal, I want to apologize," said Jacob, without glancing at me. "Like you, I thought I could help Jeshanah, but it seems she does not want my help either. I want you to take her back. She's yours. Take good care of her. She needs a strong husband."

Cal looked tentatively my way, trying to catch my eye. Jacob had offered no clue that he was going to give me back so heartlessly. I had no choice in a matter that concerned with whom to share my life. I stared at the floor while anger, shame, and confusion played havoc with my heart. I could say nothing. Only large, uncontrollable sobs were piling up at the back of my throat, like a huge tidal wave waiting to flood everything in its path.

"Well, I will leave you two here to talk this over. Cal, you can move to Sceaux, or Jeshanah can move here, whatever you like." Jacob got up and left the room.

"Why don't you love me?" asked Cal, clearing his throat. "I think I loved you."

"I don't know," I cried, letting the torments of my soul transform into tears. "I don't think I know what love is. I hate myself, and I hate what I have become."

I returned to the meeting with a tear-stained face. It seemed to me that everyone must know what had happened because no one asked me anything. Maybe they were just better revolutionaries than I was.

Cal moved to Sceaux. We set up a room in the basement of the home, and I spent many hours downstairs by myself, reading letters or writing new stories. Cal tried to get to know me, but I was a closed person. I had too many questions and not enough answers, and nobody I talked to could supply any. Cal had secretly brought a copy of *Watership Down*, by Richard Adams, into our room, and I read it like a soul starving for food. When I asked him where he got it, he replied, "I got contacts, baby," imitating James Cagney. I would have liked to read more, but since we were really not allowed to have books in the home, Cal did not bring any more.

A few weeks after Cal and I were reunited, our home leader asked to speak with us. From the look on his face, I could see that I was in trouble.

"Jeshanah, we just got this new letter from Mo, and you're mentioned in it."

By the tone of his voice, I knew that this was not an honor.

"Do you want me to leave?" asked Cal.

"No, I think Jeshanah is going to need all the help she can get for this one. I am going to leave this letter here for you to read. When you are finished, please bring it to me, Cal. I need to read it with the whole colony."

We sat down, heavy in silent apprehension. Cal read the new Mo letter called "The Uneager Beaver" out loud. It was about the children's story I had written. In the story a beaver, looking for a name, learns a lesson on moderation. It seems that the editors at our publication unit had liked it so much, they gave it to their best artists to illustrate. They created a large coloring book for children, and then sent it to Mo as a surprise, for his approval. Mo sent them back this letter, which he also sent to the worldwide Family.

The editors were berated for spending so much of God's time and money on such a worthless story. They were fired from their special positions and sent to some obscure country to be missionaries, supposedly to learn discernment. Then Mo publicly humiliated me in the letter. He said I was foolish, a bad writer, and probably plagiarized the whole story. He said that I must not be in the Word to write such nonsense; that I probably had been overly influenced by ungodly fairy tales as a child; that my story had nothing to do with his Mo

letters, and I did not understand the spiritual message of his revelations. He suggested that the whole Show Group get back into the
Word and spend less time practicing and singing and dancing.

I could tell it was hard for Cal to read this to me. He knew that
I had written a pretty good story, so good that our editors made it
into a bigger production than anything they had ever done with a
Mo letter. That had been their mistake. They offended Mo by taking
someone else's writing and making a larger, more detailed publication.
Ironically, they thought that Mo would be impressed; after all, the
story was supposed to be based on one of his letters. However, he
was furious, and the whole worldwide Family now knew never to put
anybody's writings above Mo's.

I accepted this humiliation as punishment for all the horrible things
I knew I had done, which Mo did not mention. Mo was a figure as distant and all-encompassing as God himself; and just as I have never seen
God, I had never seen Mo. In the beginning I thought I might like to
meet him sometime, but as he wrote more and more letters rebuking
the faults of everyone near him, of anyone who got in his way, I thought
that I'd just as soon be out-of-sight, out-of-mind. Of course, since he
was a God figure in our group, any big mistakes would surely reach his
attention and be dealt with severely. Just like God does! It's all there in
the Bible. I sent a long letter of apology to Mo, and he personally replied, writing "Amen" in red ink at the parts of my letter he evidently
agreed with and then adding a few words at the end. These were the
parts of the letter to which he wrote "Amen":

> I am very sorry for writing that story about the beaver and I ask that
> you and the Lord forgive me. . . . I was really influenced throughout
> my childhood by silly storybooks and fairy tales, however to the best
> of my knowledge, I don't remember reading a story exactly like that
> one. . . . I really pray for any children who have read this story, that
> God will set their hearts and minds right. . . . I know it will only be
> by the fresh water of His Words that these impurities can be washed
> away. . . . Along with your forgiveness, I would like to sincerely ask
> you to say a little prayer for me.

Mo wrote in red ink on my letter:

> We do and have prayed for you a lot . . . We really love you and are
> so sorry we had to spank you—But it was needed. Now let me love

you up real good—Be my Valentine—And *His* Seven hugs and kisses and lovins and one great <u>BIG ONE</u>—all the way—Dad 31/1/76

Time healed the wound, but I was always known as the "Uneager Beaver" girl after that letter. Mo, whom some of us had started calling Dad, now sent personal messages to me through leaders. If he had not heard about me before, he had now.

However, my notoriety was quickly forgotten. The group of letters known as the King Arthur series were finally being distributed to the Family, and members were struggling to find out what this would mean in their situations.

The King Arthur letters explained a new method of proselytizing, called "flirty fishing," or "FFing" for short. In this series of letters Mo laid out in detail the new doctrines that changed the Family permanently from a radical Jesus People commune into a sacred sex cult. Mo's secretary, traveling companion, and lover, Maria, became our first woman to try out this new method of recruiting men to the Lord. I never met her, but from the eyewitness accounts of those who knew her, she was not a pretty woman. Mo himself had written that Maria used to be a quiet, homely girl, with buckteeth and a very bad complexion. He beautified her by putting her on a strict diet, telling her what to wear and how to do her hair, and giving her such love that her face literally beamed. She smiled a lot and was no longer shy. With Maria in tow, Mo went to dance classes and ballroom dancing establishments in order to recruit new members into the Family. They finally met Arthur, a rather hapless man. Maria took him to bed on Mo's advice, and she hooked him on God's Love.

How this actually transpired was detailed in the King Arthur letters. Mo sent Maria in to seduce Arthur through sex. The metaphor of fishing was loosely taken from Jesus' instructions in the Bible to become "fishers of men." Arthur was hooked. Since Mo was not about to give up his beloved Maria for the man, he instead took Micah's wife, the beautiful Beth, and introduced her to Arthur. Beth, after giving Arthur all the sex he wanted, convinced him to join the Family. Arthur became known as a "king," since he was "fished in" personally by Mo.

Of course, mixing sex with religion was sure to cause a scandal, but it wasn't until Mo took a flock of sexy young women to Tenerife, an island off the coast of Africa, to practice and preach this method openly, that the press began taking a serious interest. Eventually, popular magazines, such as the German *Stern*, sent reporters and photographers to the small island, and Mo's first public photo appeared depicting him as an old religious guru with a bevy of women. Dressed in a long black robe with Maria beside him, and surrounded by women with low necklines, Mo quickly became the scandal of the town. Besieged by reporters and police, he had to flee the island, but not before he laid a curse on the place. Uncannily, the island had a major airplane crash the day he left it for good.

Although I was wondering how "flirty fishing" would affect me, I soon became distracted because my real sister Ruby, eight years younger than I and now almost sixteen years old, was coming to spend the summer with me. I had stayed in contact with my mother over the years through letters and convinced her that Cal and I were not the crazy, perverted people that she had read about in the anti-COG articles put out by the churches. My mother believed, or wanted to believe, that we behaved like good Christians. So when Ruby asked if she could visit me in Paris for the summer, my mother agreed.

Ruby had always been a bit rebellious and—somewhat like me— did not seem to fit into any groups at school. She also had a beautiful voice, and we soon had her singing on the metro with us. She enjoyed communal life, and after a month she told me she wanted to join the Family. I discussed it with my home leaders, and for some reason, they thought she should go to the colony we had set up in Holland for new disciples. I think they wanted to get her away from her big sister's sheltering arms.

While in Amsterdam, Ruby was taught about our new recruiting practices, although she was too new in the Family to do it herself. Meanwhile, all the letters about "flirty fishing" had been leaked to the American press, and the churches were notifying everybody about our evil ways. My mother immediately called my house and wanted Ruby home. Since my sister was not there, it was all I could do to calm my mother down, ensuring her that Ruby would be sent back soon. My mother was terribly angry, and we had Ruby returned to Paris and then sent her back home. I think my little sister had not really understood all that was going on in the Family, but she knew enough, and it was to haunt her the rest of her life. Like myself, it would take her years to figure out concepts like right and wrong, and she returned to America promising to join the Family when she was of legal age. She never did. Needless to say, this episode made my relations with my relatives rather strained for years to come.

My robotic obedience to the Family was soon tested to its limit. At our house in Paris we heard that wealthy Italians were coming to see our Show Group. Since these were men from the upper class who held positions of influence in their country, we were told to please them in any way they wanted, with whomever they wanted. One of them, Flavio, was called a "king," indicating that he must have given us some financial support already. Actually, the title was now being used loosely, and many "kings" were just men who never joined our group but whom we wanted to keep as friends.

After Flavio saw one of our shows in the Paris area, a manager named Ben came to see me in the dressing room.

"Flavio wants you to come to the club with us," he informed me.

"Have you asked Cal?"

"We said we would have you home tonight, and Magdalene would spend the night with Flavio."

By now I had become accustomed to just obeying orders, having learned that I was going to have to obey or leave the Family in the end. Also, we all knew that fishing was under way in Paris, and although I was never asked to participate, I was sure it was just a matter of time. I had decided to belong to a social experiment called the Family, and this was just another variable; no one was twisting my arm. And, how would we ever start a new society if everyone balked at each new experience? Sure, it seemed strange and deviant, but that is what living over the edge is about. Accepting Family ideology by faith, I gave my body much as a soldier is taught to give his or her life. And truthfully, Flavio was not so bad. He was a sweet, charming Italian, and I had enjoyed talking to him at the party where we first met. I was not in love with my husband, and Cal knew this was coming as much as I did, although we had never talked about it.

I went to the club, and Flavio danced only with me. It was clear Flavio wanted to spend the night with me. Ben was sent to Sceaux to get Cal's permission and I was told by another brother that my husband had agreed.

I was taken to the Colombes home in a car, and Flavio and I went to the blue room, which had already been prepared. It was my first experience of being offered as live bait to a man. During my experiences with Jacob, I had already crossed the threshold of moral ambiguity, and the detailed instructions in the Mo letters provided me with both a rationalization and a script to follow in sexual encounters. Through letters like "Revolutionary Sex" and "Revolutionary Lovemaking," we had learned anything we did not already know about making love. In the Arthur letters, and later in the letters written from Tenerife, Mo went into detail about how to massage the man, how to give oral sex, and other sexual practices that were pleasurable for a man. However, he steered us away from anal sex or sadomasochism, and I was never afraid of a man becoming violent, although perhaps I should have been. I knew that being a witness to God was my main job, and although the letters told mostly of men who had already been witnessed to, Mo assured us that God's Spirit would shine through us as we made love. I wasn't so sure of that, but I was not afraid or shy that first night.

In fact, I found it easy to perform my role without any emotional attachment or moral dilemma. As always, I did not use any type of birth control, but I was not even worried about becoming pregnant. Flavio evidently had been witnessed to by our women and seemed to know the salvation message; I think he was already saved. That was a relief, because I was too tired to preach to him. Although he was extremely handsome, and had a better physique than any man I had ever seen, I don't remember feeling any pleasure. I did not experience pleasure in sex for many, many years. First it was a duty, then a tool, and finally a burden. But I was very good at faking pleasure. I often had myself convinced.

The next morning I woke up and wondered what I was to do now. Flavio was still sleeping, so I got out of bed before he would wake and ask for me. I knew I had to get back to Cal. He had probably been pacing the floor all night, waiting for me to come back and make love to assure him that I was still his. I dressed quietly and went downstairs, looking for someone to give me some metro tickets. Ben was in the kitchen drinking coffee. He had been up all night.

"Did you hear the commotion last night?" he asked.

"No, what was it?"

"Cal came over and was trying to get upstairs to pull you out of bed. We had to stop him forcibly."

"But he said it was okay."

"Who told you that?"

"Micah did."

"Well, we never got his okay, but we never really needed his okay anyway. Mo has given us ultimate authority," Ben explained to me. "Cal threatened to break down the door. I calmed him down and took him home. Come on, I'll drive you back."

All the way home, Ben advised me to be kind and tender and give Cal anything he wanted, as if it was my fault that this had happened. I had been up half the night already, and now I envisioned another few hours making up to Cal. The physical drain of the last twenty-four hours left me little energy to think about emotional issues. I did what I was told to do. I was being a good soldier of God. But in the back of my mind, I thought, "Hey, it's me that gave my body—I did the work! What's all this fuss about Cal?" Well the truth was, my body belonged first to God, then to the Family, then to my husband. Actually, the God and husband part is in the Bible; we added the Family.

Ben came in with me and promised that from now on Cal could be in charge of my extramarital affairs, especially those with men outside the Family. True to their word, Cal took over as my only fisherman, and he gave me away sparingly at first. Cal became known as the most possessive and jealous husband in the Show Group. Other husbands did not have the problems that Cal did with sharing their wives, as far as I could tell. I say this because most wives began to go out regularly on club excursions with male leaders, but I only went if Cal was along.

Of course, Cal had calmed down considerably by the time I got there in the morning. First, he wanted to make love passionately. Then he wanted me to tell him the whole story, minute by minute, of what had happened. Where did Flavio touch me? Where did I touch him? How many times? And more and more. I made up some parts just because I couldn't remember every detail, even though it was only the night before. It just wasn't that important to me. Now ask me about the details of how my son laughs when I tickle him, or how he climbs up the slide ladder by himself, his strong, solid legs pegging each step like a carpenter's hammer, and that I can tell you. But sex? It was all the same to me.

The word desire was never mentioned. If it had been, I could have honestly told Cal that I did not desire Flavio any more than I desired him. If someone had asked me about desire, I would have realized much earlier that desire was not part of my sexual relationships, and I could have begun to try to understand why it wasn't. As a teenager I had wanted sexual experience primarily because sex was part of the hippie scene; as a wife it was part of the marriage institution; in the Family it was part of witnessing and loving others. I don't think I ever desired sex or felt aroused. I wanted to be touched and hugged— to be cared for—but I had learned that intimate touch invariably meant sex also. If Cal would have asked me these questions, perhaps we could have understood the problem, but Cal wanted to know if I still loved him. I couldn't believe he was asking me. Didn't he re- member that I tried to leave him? Didn't he remember that Jacob forced me to go back with him as a wife? I knew that he wanted to be loved romantically and deeply as a lifetime soul mate, but he knew the rules of the Family as well as I: We loved everybody uncondi- tionally. I answered him in Family jargon.

"Yes, I love you!" I said, hoping he would let me rest for a while before I had to go out witnessing. He took me in his arms, and I felt so very uncomfortable. Who was I anyway? And who was this man holding me in his arms? In many ways, being with a stranger for one night of witnessing was better than feeling like a stranger with your husband every night. I often consoled myself with the thought that the majority of women do not know their husbands, and those ideal stories of romance and love I had heard before I married were just system lies, like almost everything else we had been told. Years later, when well-meaning people asked me, "How could you hurt your hus- band like that?" I would sigh and run through my head all the com- plex questions I needed answered before I could attempt to answer that one. For instance: Define husband for me. Define love. Define hurt. What is the meaning? And so on. Instead, I answered with a simple "We were both in the Family, and it's too long to explain."

After my initiation with Flavio, I had a battle within myself over using sexual favors to lure converts to the Family. Whether I was rationalizing or not, I finally concluded that I was helping the men I loved through a sexual channel. I personally believed in Jesus' salva- tion message, and even if these men had not asked Jesus into their heart, at least they had heard the message. One day they would remember. However, I gradually came to realize that the leaders seemed to be using sex as a tool to gain powerful friends and contacts, and my husband felt that fishing was a last resort for pulling someone into the fellowship of God's family. The purpose of FFing was in continual flux.

6

○ ○ ○

Flirty Fishing in the Kingdom

Sexual favors to strangers was fast becoming our main method of witnessing about the Lord. Even our work on stage took second place to going to the top Parisian nightclubs and picking up men who seemed interested in what we were offering. The showgirls had an easy time meeting the rich and famous, so they began to go out regularly with a fisherman by their side. After Cal grew tired of sitting around in clubs until three in the morning, he started to let me go with a regular fishing team, as long as he could make the final decisions on which men I slept with. If the male leader who was with us thought a man was potentially worthy of our special gift of love, I was instructed to make a date with him, letting him know I would bring my husband along. That sounds odd to Americans, of course, but the French were not as surprised as I had thought they would be. Most of the men I went to bed with while I was married to Cal met my husband first. I truly believe that our motives were generally to be able to reach a stratum of men we would never meet elsewhere. We still went singing to make money, and as far as I know, we did not receive any money from the men we met at the clubs during the early years. Other than the witnessing motivation, we wanted to meet men who were influential and who could help us politically or in our music business.

Sometimes I would pass the fish on to other women in my group, since I had no desire to give sex to all the men drawn to me. That left me free to go on the dance floor. Dancing had become my only personal mode of self-expression, and moving to music had a mantra-like effect on me. I liked dancing alone, and the crowded disco floor offered an absurd opportunity to pretend I was by myself for a few minutes. It was a chance to be free from the Family's constant control and the pressure of perpetual witnessing. To this day, I use dancing as an escape mechanism.

Since we usually went out with groups of four or five girls, and only one fisherman, the brothers had to take turns in the role. Being a fisherman was not necessarily a desirable task. Basically, a fisherman looked like a pimp, coming into a club with a group of girls who immediately went around picking up guys. Cal soon realized that I came to the club because I enjoyed dancing, not to have sex with other men, and I think that made it easier on him. Since we went out at night, while Thor was away at school or in bed watched by a sister, it did not take time away from my son. It was the perfect job for a Family mother. During the day, the women who had gone out the night before were excused from work duties, witnessing, or practice, so I used this free time to take the metro out to the school to see Thor.

During the early days of using sex as a lure, the primary goal was to convince the man to ask Jesus into his heart. That could often be accomplished without going to bed with him, and I knew it well. I only went to bed with those men who were hardened to what we thought of as the *Spirit* of God working through us. Most of them were ready to accept Jesus after a few close dances. I often talked incessantly about Jesus and God's Love while dancing, especially in the early days. If the man asked for a second dance, he knew what we were preaching, so that would establish him as potentially interested in the Lord. During subsequent dances, I talked less and let the man touch me more, and the French men are not shy about touching; neither are French women embarrassed to be touched. I could not help but notice that our French sisters took a lot more men to bed than I did. During the course of an evening, I invited the men to come and sit at our table so I could introduce them to my friends. Sometimes, another woman would take over, especially if a man spoke only French. I preferred letting a French sister witness to him then. On other occasions, the male in our group would engage in a discussion with the man, and often they became friends in one evening. In fact, Cal started a few lasting friendships with men I had lured to our table. Hopefully, by the end of the evening, the man had heard the full salvation message, which is basically the same simple message taught by the evangelical Christian faith: Believe that you are a sinner, that Jesus died for your sins, and that he can give you salvation so you can again be united with God and go to heaven. The proof of one's belief was to verbally ask Jesus into your heart, which was merely an outward sign that you believed. I would venture to say that more than half of the thousands of men we talked to in clubs asked Jesus into their hearts. Of course, whether they really meant anything by repeating this simple prayer is open to debate; however, we were always optimistic.

If a man argued or showed absolute disinterest in this message, we usually let him go at that point and looked for another dance partner. However, many of these same men would come back to our table on a later occasion and would not argue this time; we assumed that they had thought it over and liked our message now.

Actually, giving sex to a man often depended on who the fisherman was at the time. Some of the higher leaders, who had been with Mo at clubs, gave the girls to the men very easily, even if the men already had asked Jesus into their hearts. "Give him a treat," they chuckled. "He deserves it." Or they would say the man needed more proof of God's Love, so go to bed with him. The middle leaders, who were afraid of doing something wrong, were more careful about giving the women away. Mo was very interested in the statistical information on this new method, and the Family began keeping detailed FFing statistics, such as number of fish witnessed to, fish loved, and fish saved. Women had regular reports to fill out at the end of each night, and they were collected, tabulated, and sent in to our headquarters in Switzerland, called World Service. Every month, these report forms were filled out by our home leader and sent along with our tithe (10 percent of all the home's income) and our monetary gifts for the worldwide work. Soon "FF" testimonies from around the world started to appear in the *Family News* magazine. Some told of the "trials and victories" experienced by husbands and wives as they obeyed Mo and started sharing sexually; others told of hardened middle-aged businessmen, a group we had never reached before, who asked Jesus into their hearts and changed their lives, seeming proof that this method worked. Just as any new theory is supported by tangible examples, the idea of recruiting through sex was supported by these testimonies, and within a few years the method had become part of our everyday existence.

Around the time our sexual recruitment practices were evolving in the mid-1970s, Mo wrote a series of letters in which he condemned Israel's position against the Arab nations. Still indignant over the disappointing reception he had received on his visit to Israel in 1971, he told us in a letter titled "Breakdown" that it had been his heart's desire to establish a Christian work there. He wrote us that "after two thousand years of knowledge of Jesus Christ, [Israel] is still in rebellion! If any nation on earth is without excuse—the Jews are. . . . 'Ye do always reject the Holy Ghost' " (66:16). I have since come to believe that this was merely a temper tantrum on Mo's part due to his not being recognized by his formerly beloved Jews, since he claimed to be "a Christian Jew." Irritated by his unsuccessful attempt to establish a colony in Israel, Mo later became enthralled by Muammar Qaddafi, the terrorist leader of Libya. It was a bizarre relationship, which was not understood by many of the group's members with whom I spoke.

Most of us in the Family were far too busy to keep up with Mo's confusing line of political reasoning. We were the peasants, the proletariat too busy supporting the kingdom to spend time in reading, research, and reflection on the Mo letters such as "Israel Invaded," published in 1973. In it, Mo predicted that Israel would be invaded and conquered by the Soviet Union, Libya, and other Arab nations, and he prophesied (supposedly God speaks in King James language): "Therefore I will rise up and destroy thee who calleth thyself Israel, O ye children of the devil, and I will return my land unto them whom I have given it, that they may be forgiven from thee, O ye enemies of the Almighty and ye crucifiers of the Son of God and ye rejecters of thy King!" ("Israel Invaded" 281:63). Mo insisted the message about Israel be distributed on every street in the world, which instantly caused trouble for our homes, especially in Paris. We tried to soften the anti-Semitic overtones by placing the Israel letters beside testimonies about our missionary work in India in the literature we gave out to the public. However, once Mo started on a radical topic, he stayed with it until the message became redundant. Now his new pro-Arab position had reached the most powerful leaders of the Muslim world.

Qaddafi invited Mo and his family to be his guests in Libya. In June of 1975 Mo published a new letter documenting the visit. That signaled the end for Les Enfants de Dieu Show Group. All of our producers were Jewish, and they immediately withdrew support.

Around this time, most of the Show Group felt it was time to go on to other things anyway. We had been singing, dancing, recording, and performing for four years. We had produced a number of records and albums, performed in every major city in France, and appeared on nationwide TV and radio almost weekly. France had heard our message, and besides, due to the Israel letters, our days in France were numbered, so we all began looking for new mission fields. Even though many successful projects we started were destroyed by Mo's letters, we had become accustomed to deceiving ourselves that this meant it was not God's Will to continue there.

During our quiet periods, the leaders sent out teams from the Show Group to sell leftover albums. We went two by two on what we called "faith trips," which meant we were given no money, just fifty to a hundred records to sell. We usually did quite well, since records brought in more funds than Mo letters.

On one of those trips, I went with my dance partner, Jonathan, to the south of France. Jon was one of my all-time favorite brothers. Admitting to homosexual tendencies before he joined the Family, he was now married and had children. Jon was more fun to be with than anyone else I knew. He was clever, witty, not too serious, and best of all, always ready for adventure. A tall, slim, and very refined-looking young man, Jon somehow managed to be dressed in the latest fashion and always looked impeccable, from his well-trimmed hair to manicured hands and pressed shirts. He usually added a long, flowing scarf to his attire for additional flair.

As my dance partner, Jon could invent new steps during a major performance to cover any mistakes I made. Jon always told me to just keep on going, no matter what happens.

When Jon and I took a faith trip to the south of France to sell one hundred records, we planned to go to nightclubs along the Côte d'Azur. If we sold all our records, Jon wanted to go to Rome. I didn't really think we would sell them all. Besides, Thor was at the school during the week and I wanted to be home before the weekend. However, we sold all our records on our first day on the Côte d'Azur.

Jon and I were standing on a deserted St.-Tropez road late at night when he reminded me that I had promised to go to Rome if we sold out. I agreed we'd go if we got a ride there that night. Rome was more than three hundred miles away.

We waited for more than ten minutes for the first vehicle to appear. Finally, a red car came around the corner slowly and stopped for us.

"*Dove vai?*" asked the man behind the wheel of a flashy sports car.

"*Roma*," answered Jon.

"*Si, si.* I too."

The Italian spoke little English, but Jon knew enough Italian to find out that the driver was indeed going straight to Rome, and he would take us.

I squeezed into the tiny backseat and fell asleep before we were out of France. When I woke up, we were in Rome. We stayed at the Family colony, where Jon's old friend lived, for three days, and sold Italian literature on the streets to make money for us to take a train back to Paris, in time for me to see Thor on the weekend.

Back in Paris, I couldn't stop dreaming about the beauty of the Côte d'Azur. Although I never visited art museums, I fell in love with the living, natural art of the sea, the coast, and the lovely Provençal scenery. In a few weeks, I convinced Cal to take another faith trip down there with me.

This time, the trip was not as easy. Cal and I had trouble acquiring a ride out of Paris, and at nightfall we found ourselves in a tiny village near Grenoble with no place to sleep. A large, muscular man with a thick German accent offered to let us stay at his farmhouse in the country.

Cal and I suspected nothing as we rode with the man into an even more deserted area. He pulled up next to a dilapidated and isolated building that looked more like a shed than a farmhouse.

"Let me make you something to eat," he insisted as he led us into a room cluttered with newspapers and articles of clothes. We felt obligated to comply, but both Cal and I were becoming uncertain of the man's motives, especially when he started drinking large quantities of alcohol. We began to suspect he was a madman, and we were no less fearful when he finally told us the story of who he was.

"See all these newspapers around?" he said. "Well, they talk about the terrorist acts that have been happening in Germany. Have you read about it?"

We didn't follow the news very much and responded in the negative.

"Read them," he insisted again. Sure enough, there were articles on terrorism marked in the newspaper.

"That's me they're talking about," he said with pride, fingering the large butcher knife he had been using to cut the sausage and bread.

I felt a shudder go through my body, and Cal began to talk nervously.

"Well, maybe we'll just go now instead of waiting until the morning."

The burly man was plastered by now, and he demanded that we spend the night. Since there was little room to sleep in the small, disordered shed, we convinced him to let us stay in the car.

Neither Cal nor I slept at all, and as soon as the sun came out, we crept silently away and headed toward the road. There were no cars in sight. About half an hour later, we saw a vehicle coming. It stopped and we saw that it was the German. He seemed sober now, and without mentioning the terrorist story, he drove us to the superhighway, where we caught a ride to St.-Tropez. Both of us were more contemplative after this incident, and for some unknown reason, Cal began to offer me to other men with greater ease. Perhaps he felt, as I did, that God had just saved us from a potentially dangerous situation.

As soon as we arrived in the quaint and celebrated village of St.-Tropez, we met a lawyer from America who was vacationing there to visit the nudist camps. A soft-spoken, sedately good-looking man of about forty, he talked with us all day, and he let us stay in his rented bungalow that night. After bunking down on the carpet with our sleeping bags, Cal told me to go to the man's bed and give him oral sex. Probably, Cal was worried about me getting pregnant with another man's baby, since it had been over three years that I had not become pregnant with him, even though we made love frequently.

The lawyer was, needless to say, surprised, but he did not protest. He had already heard about God's Love that day, and I told him that this was just another part of it. Afterward, I went back to make love with Cal, who of course needed emotional comfort. I don't think I ever got emotional comfort from anyone. I had grown accustomed to living without it.

Right after our return from the south, the Family decided to start a home near Monte Carlo, so Cal began making preparations for our move. It entailed getting approvals from our leaders, who were encouraging us to leave Paris. Taking Thor with us, we met the leaders of the Nice home, and they said we could stay with them while we looked for a home to open in nearby Monte Carlo.

Both Cal and I were excited by the move south. Les Enfants de Dieu was definitely finished, and the whole Show Group was splitting up. Most of the people we had lived and worked with for the last four years we would never see again, but that was part of the revolutionary life.

The new home we arrived at in Nice was very small. In an apartment with two bedrooms and one bathroom, there lived a Swedish couple with their baby and a single French sister named Mara. Cal and I had thought that our marriage problems would diminish in a new environment, but instead, working so closely together every day, they intensified. The Swedish couple seemed to be having troubles of their own, and they never became involved with ours; however, Mara confided in me a few weeks after our arrival that the Lord had shown her in a dream she would marry my husband, Cal. It was not such an unusual statement, since threesome marriages were allowed in the Family.

While in Nice, we continued to support ourselves by selling Mo letters on the streets, but in the evening, Mara and I went to the clubs while Cal stayed home with Thor, who was now three years old. We always had our drinks paid for by the men we met, and sometimes I met a man to whom I would witness further. This meant that I would introduce the man to Cal, and if he said yes, I would spend the night with him, usually at his hotel room, since most of these men were tourists. Whenever I had to spend a night away from home, Mara shared sexually with Cal. Eventually, I talked with Cal about a threesome.

"Mara already told me that she believes she will marry you, Cal.

Since she is spending so much time with you, maybe we should include her in our marriage." Threesomes were becoming one of the better options in marriage relationships, and in many of the homes where FFing was practiced, they were common. In our cult, and in many other cults as I found out later, threesome marriages (they were usually two women and one man, but not always) turned out to be a workable solution, perhaps because it supplied more help with women's work and children and more regular sex for the husband.

"I don't know," said Cal. "That's a big responsibility for me."

I knew Cal well enough to understand that he had something else on his mind.

"Don't you like her?" I asked. Mara was a cute, petite Frenchwoman, who was four years younger than I, and many people said we looked like sisters. We both had long blond hair and blue eyes, wore the same size clothes, although I was taller, and we both loved to dance.

"Yes, I do like her very much."

"Well, is it the sex?"

"No, of course, it is different than it is with you. But it's still fine."

"Don't you believe in threesomes?"

"Well, I have been thinking about it too, of course. It would make a lot of sense, especially if we move to Monte Carlo. But . . . I'm concerned about you."

"Oh, I don't mind. Not at all. Don't worry about me. I like Mara very much."

I could see Cal's face flush as I said this.

"So you don't mind sharing me with someone permanently? You know, I am serious about marriage. And if I marry her, it will be for good."

"Oh, I understand. I don't care. I mean, yes, I know you are concerned and will take good care of her."

"I want to take care of you too."

"Don't worry about me. I don't need extra attention. I won't be jealous at all."

"That's what I mean, Jeshanah. I think you don't care at all. Is this a way for you to get further away from me emotionally?"

It was like he had thrown cold water on my face. It woke me up.

I had been so excited about the prospect of Cal having another wife, I had not stopped to ponder why I liked the idea so much. I assumed it was because I was a true revolutionary, but in that moment of truth, I knew that I would be relieved to have someone share the burden of being a mate to Cal. I could never tell him that, however. It would hurt him too much. There were other threesome arrangements in the Family, and the testimonies in our Family mag were full of praise for this new idea. I bought into it, thinking it was a logical alternative for loveless marriages. Unfortunately, Cal seemed to love me in a nonrevolutionary way, so I tried to reassure him.

"Cal, we will always be connected because of Thor."

"You won't try to leave me if I marry her?"

"You know you can't really marry her. That would be illegal."

I laughed, but Cal was still very serious.

"All right, I will talk to the leaders about it."

Mara, of course, said she already knew this would happen. With her on our team, we had enough help to start a new home, so we started living like a separate "home" even while in Nice. Two of us went out witnessing and making money while one stayed home with Thor. We began praying for a small home in Monte Carlo.

During our first excursions to Monte Carlo, Mara and I had met Jean, a native Monegasque who was close to fifty. Both Mara and I were in our early twenties. Jean seemed to like me, but he enjoyed Mara's company more. As I listened to the two of them converse in French, I became acutely aware of my lack of education and culture. Although I had been to college, and Mara had not even finished high school, she knew so much more about literature, history, music, and art than I did. Jean and she discussed topics I could not even enter into. I felt that I would have to educate myself. But how could I do that? We were not supposed to read anything but Mo letters. And after my previous experience as the Uneager Beaver, I surely should not be reading books. Instead, I began to pay more attention to every piece of culture and knowledge I could glean from the people I met. Not only did this increase my own knowledge; it also made me seem more interested in the other person, which was a wonderful asset to my role as a witness.

Our prayers for a home in Monte Carlo were soon answered. Mara knew a young man who owned a basement apartment in Monte Carlo. It was not in very good condition, but he said that if we fixed it up, we could stay there rent-free. We accepted immediately and moved into the exclusive Monaco principality with little more than our suitcases.

Thor was three years old now, and I spent a few hours each day teaching him to read and learn math. Sometimes I took him panhandling and distributing literature with us, but usually he stayed home with Cal. We all enjoyed the wonderful Monaco parks and beaches daily. Everything was within walking distance, which was extremely convenient since we never owned a car. Since Mara had already given herself to a Monegasque taxi driver, we obtained free taxi rides whenever we needed to travel a distance.

Among our first "fish" were an Italian businessman, an American lawyer, and the son of a famous actress. All of them were given sexual love in order to reach them with God's message. None of these early fish ever gave us money, although they often took us out to eat as a family or bought us gifts, such as a bed for Thor, shoes, or groceries. Many of the women in the Family were spending a considerable amount of time with their fish, and so we felt it was a sign of the Lord's blessing when we were given these "gifts."

Since there were only three adults among us, we decided that as long as any two of us agreed, we should go to bed with the man. We were careful to keep clean, and since Mo now told us to go to the doctor to be checked for sexually transmitted diseases, whenever someone had any type of health concern, we took care of it immediately. However, due to prayer or luck, we never got anything serious.

My first experience with the jet-set elite took me by complete surprise. In a club, I had met an interesting American who took my phone number. The next evening, I received a call from him.

"Hello, is this Jeshanah?" asked a voice I remembered from the previous night.

"Yes," I answered.

"Well, you remember me, Tony?"

"Yes, it is nice to hear you again."

"I thought you might like to go to a party tonight. A friend of mine is having a delightful party in Cannes. I could send you a chauffeur and car in one hour."

"Yes, I would like that very much," I said, not knowing if Cal would agree or not. "How should I dress?"

"Wear the best outfit you have. This is a chic affair."

We arranged a time and I gave him my address. Then I went to talk to Cal.

"You should have asked if Mara could come," he reprimanded. "You know I don't like you to go alone on the first date." It was an established rule of the Family. Ever since our first days in the group, we were told to always go out two by two, which was the way Jesus sent his disciples to witness. Also, "since the devil walked around as a roaring lion seeking whom he may devour" (I Peter 5:8), we were told to stay together for spiritual safety and to remind each other about our spiritual mission. Actually, I was never completely alone with anyone outside the Family until I started this new type of ministering with my body. I had my excuses ready.

"Well, Mara met him last night. I thought that would count as a first date."

I did not know why I forgot to ask about Mara. Perhaps I did not want to take her along. Mara made me feel inferior in some way, and she usually pointed out mistakes I made later when we discussed the evening together. Also, I was beginning to enjoy the extra personal freedom I had recently acquired with our move to Monaco.

"What will you wear?" asked Mara, who knew she had better taste in clothes than I did

"I thought I would wear the dress that Jeanie gave me," I answered. Jeanie was a famous singer in France who had been a friend of ours in Paris. She often gave us her "old" performing clothes, which the leaders usually took. However, a long silk dress with a deep slit up the front was given to me since I was tall and thin enough to wear it. I felt very self-conscious in the sexy dress, and I never wore it out to the clubs. Mara thought it was too gaudy and made a face.

"Well, if it was good enough for her as a singer on stage, I'm sure it will do fine," I said. "There is nothing else anyway."

The real problem would be a coat. We settled on a beige raincoat, the newest thing I owned but still vintage. We had group prayer before I left, but I was a little apprehensive. Both Cal and Mara clearly disapproved of me going alone. We did not even know where I was going in Cannes. For the first time I began to worry about safety, but I tried not to show it. After all, it was my idea to go alone.

I bathed, as we always did before a date. My waist-length hair hung straight down my back as usual, but the recent shampoo had added body. I wore a little makeup now: some lipstick, eye shadow, and mascara, and I sprayed on some cologne. The black going-out shoes I always wore matched the dress, but they looked frayed. I wore no jewelry at all except a necklace with a gold heart and a circle inside, a symbol often drawn by Mo on his personal letters of love to us. It had been given to me by a kindhearted female leader in Paris. The only other piece of jewelry I owned was another Family symbol, which we called David's Harp. It had been specially made for me by Cal. I looked in the mirror before leaving and saw how tatty the raincoat looked, so I took it off and held it over my arm.

The chauffeur who picked me up did not speak to me the whole way to Cannes, about a one-hour ride on the lower cornice road. When he pulled onto a small road leading through the woods, I felt uneasy and tried to glean information from him on my whereabouts.

"Whose house is this we are going to?" I asked.

"You will find out," he retorted curtly.

I wondered if I was being kidnapped. Perhaps the driver was part of a pornography ring. I really did not know this Tony guy well, and now that I thought about it, he seemed a little sinister.

After we traveled down a tree-lined private driveway for a few minutes, a huge white mansion appeared in front of us. The driver pulled up to the well-lit veranda accented by impressive Roman columns, and another man, a valet I guessed, opened the car door for me.

Following the sound of other people, I walked into a split-level room which opened to a patio with a pool. There were about five sets of couches and sofas around the plush-carpeted room, and a long oak table set with hors d'oeuvres. Outside, on the upper level, I saw a pool and patio. I looked around for Tony. There were mostly black and Arab-looking men there, as well as young, extremely beautiful women. Everyone was dressed so much more elegantly than I, and their sparkling jewelry reminded me that I had not worn so much as earrings.

"Jeshanah, come over here," called a man who appeared to be Tony. I had only met him the night before in a dark club, and now I noticed his gray hair and age-lined tan face.

I walked self-consciously to the couch he was sitting on.

"Jeshanah, I would like you to meet my wife," he said, as he introduced me to her and a few other people sitting there. This was interesting. I had never met a fish's wife before, but I soon found out that Tony was not a fish.

Tony continued to talk with his group, and I sat down wondering what I was doing here. There was a woman with a Barbie doll face sitting next to me, and I was relieved to hear she was American. She was a model, she later told me, but due to her short stature, she usually modeled only face, hands, and feet.

"You would be surprised how many requests there are for feet," she said. "But I really would like more face shots. If I don't get more work in Paris, I might have to come down here permanently. What do you do?"

"I used to be a dancer," I said, which was my normal explanation for living in France. I was surprised she did not ask me what I was doing now.

A waiter came by and offered us drinks. I declined, but she took another and gave him her empty glass.

I noticed that she kept looking at a large black man standing with another blond woman.

"That is the one I want," she said. "He is the special guest, I heard." She smiled at him coyly.

Even my introduction to wealth and luxury in Paris had not prepared me for this. The house was fancier than the famed Hôtel George V in Paris, which I had been in a few times. The opulence reminded me of a scene from *La Dolce Vita*, but more modern. For the first time, I realized how far removed I was from real life. Not only was I "not of the world," as Jesus had told us to be in the Bible, but I felt more alienated from the world now than ever. It was sometime in the late seventies, and for seven years I had been living a life of almost total social isolation, in contact with those on the outside only through witnessing. I was glad that Mara had not come. It was the first time I was alone among so many outside people, and had she been present, I never would have felt this utter alienation. I never would have forced myself to think seriously about what I was doing there. Whenever I was with another sister, I felt I had to "fill in the gaps" and make sure that God's Will was being accomplished. By myself, I did not feel this pressure to perform for my Family, and since I hardly cared what these people thought of me spiritually, I had no role to fulfill.

At first, I could not quite understand what was happening. Tony was here with his wife, so it seemed to be a real party. But here was this model flirting with what seemed to be an African elite. All the men wore lots of jewelry, huge rings with diamonds and gold chain necklaces. All the women looked like models. Their faces were impeccably made up, their clothes seemed to come straight from the fashion magazines, and each one had a stunning hairstyle. I felt very inadequate, and compared with them, I looked like a little girl who had tried on her mother's clothes. Tony interrupted my thoughts.

"Jeshanah, you are not as animated as you were last night. Here, let me introduce you to Amir."

He led me to the table and I talked with an Arab man from Kuwait. I did not even know where Kuwait was on the map. Luckily, dinner was being served, and I was relieved from having to wonder what to do next, since everyone was eating at a formal setting. I tried to gain some information from Amir, but he was obviously not interested in me. He was busy eyeing a gorgeous redheaded woman who seemed to be over six feet tall. My physical attributes paled in comparison to what these women offered.

In addition, I did not get any sense that these men were interested in a Godly message. As I sat at the table, eating food I couldn't even identify, I searched my mind for a memory, a connection, any information that I had stored away in the back rooms of my head before I had joined the Family that would explain what was happening here. How should I act? What was expected of me? I remembered a sociology class in which we learned that all human interaction is socially defined. We play roles we are taught to play; however, sometimes we can also choose roles. Where did that theory lead? I wished I had learned more. I felt so much like Alice in Wonderland sitting at the Queen's table with a bunch of strange characters. My thoughts were interrupted by the person next to me, a short, balding, fleshy man who asked if I was coming downstairs to dance.

He led me downstairs where there was a club-size discotheque, complete with a deejay. I sat down on a chair on a raised platform on one side of the room, and the man joined a group by the bar. One by one, different women stood up and danced in front of all the seated men. I looked around for the American model I had met, but she was not there. I noticed that the African man she had pointed out was missing also.

Someone called that I should get up and dance. Even though dancing came easily for me, and I knew I could dance better than these women who were wiggling their bodies oddly without following the music, I felt that my dancing would not be appreciated by these men unless I danced like Salome before King Herod. I wasn't ready for that yet. Instead, I remained sitting in my chair. I had been tempted to enter their world, and I understood now that these women were very expensive prostitutes, euphemistically known as high-class call girls. This was not what Mo was talking about in the letters. I could choose not to play this role. Feeling very unsettled, I decided to just sit this evening out and hope no one bothered me until the chauffeur took me home, if he was still around.

While I was pondering my eventual departure, a middle-aged, short and stocky Middle Eastern man came and sat down beside me. He had a wonderful, warm smile that spread across his small, round face like a moonbeam. Somehow, I felt I could trust him.

"What is the matter?" he asked. "You look worried."

"Yes, well, I am not sure what I am doing here."

"These are my friends. Do not worry. They will not harm you."

"You see, I have never been to a party like this. I am usually with some of my own friends."

"Yes, well, maybe someday I will meet your friends also. Now relax. No one will harm you." He patted my knee and got up to go.

Immediately after he left, the tall blonde who had been talking to another man came over to sit next to me.

"I see you know my boyfriend," she said cockily.

"No, I don't know him. Is he your boyfriend? Who is he?" I replied innocently.

"Why, he is the host of this party. He owns this house. Really, don't you know him?"

"No. Tony invited me here, and he didn't tell me whose party this was."

The girl saw that I was obviously not competition.

"Why, that's Adnan Kashoggi," she replied as if I should know him.

"I never heard of him," I said.

She threw back her head and laughed.

"He is just the richest man in the world, that's all. Where are you from anyway? You will surely hear about him if you stay here very long." She left and went over to her "boyfriend," giving him a playful kiss on his bald head.

With relief, I noticed that some people were leaving. I went upstairs and asked for my coat and for the chauffeur, but since I did not know his name, it took a long time to find out who brought me. I was obligated to stand in the hallway in my humble raincoat, while all the other girls were helped into furs.

My chauffeur was finally found, and I was taken back to Monte Carlo in a subdued, but wiser, state of mind.

Cal was excited by my story, since it was the first time we had penetrated elite society, which was our mission in Monte Carlo. I had been pondering the situation all night and concluded that we, the women in the Family, had something much better to offer these men than those beautiful models did, but we had to have better access. We couldn't just go to parties and be picked and paid for like a piece of pretty merchandise. How could we get to meet these people on a more personal level? We discussed this over dinner, like guerrillas plotting a strategy. Cal wanted to write to "World Services," the Family headquarters, and ask for money. Every home sent World Services 10 percent of their income, and that money was used to support top leadership, the publications, and needy mission fields.

"Why would World Services send us any money?" I asked. "We are not a mission field."

"Of course we are," said Cal. "We have to get into these expensive clubs, and I should be going with you, if we are going to meet the right people."

Mara agreed with Cal, and they sent a letter to headquarters. As far as I knew, they never got a reply. I was beginning to worry about how Mara always sided with Cal, however. I was not sure if it was because they actually thought the same way, or if she was trying to get closer to him by standing up for what he said. Since I was basically egalitarian-minded, I didn't like the power imbalance occurring in our little team of three, especially since I was often the odd one out. I talked with her about it, and she told me that I treated Cal disrespectfully. I was not sure what she meant by this, but it started a division between us. I guess I had imagined that we women would stick together, and instead she supported the designated "head of the house." Many years later Mara informed me that when she first joined our marriage, she thought she would like to be part of a threesome. However, when she realized my lack of love for Cal, she began to become more emotionally attached to him.

The apartment we were loaned was completely remodeled after three months of hard work. The young man who had given it to us rent-free liked the new look so much, he decided to move back in. He gave us a month to find someplace else to go. Of course, we could never afford Monte Carlo rents, and even the apartments in the small villages around Monaco were out of our price range. After praying about the situation, we seemed to get an answer from the Lord through a couple who used to work with us in Paris.

Abraham and Breeze were childless, freedom loving, and very talented. They had been friends of ours in Paris, as much as Family members could be friends. Abe never listened to the house rules—he always had a stash of wine and snacks in his room. He also had worldly music, since as a musician and sound technician, he was allowed this privilege. I was afraid to listen to too much worldly music, since I thought it might have undue influence on me, but I often stopped by Abe's room for a chat.

Breeze had come to Paris from Holland after the band did a show there. She wanted to be in the Show Group, and Abe seemed to be a door to that opportunity. As a singer and violinist, she was integrated into the show, and she eventually married Abe. I thought she might be in love with him, but I knew she was secretly having sex with one of the leaders from Italy. It was secret because she did not get approval from Abe first. When she developed a fallopian tube pregnancy and had to be hospitalized, Abe stayed by her every minute, and his love for her was endearing. I concluded that Breeze had been punished for the deceit of engaging in secret sex, just as I had. It seemed that sexual sharing was moral, as long as it was done in the open and all those involved were in agreement.

Abe and Breeze tried to live in a few homes after Les Enfants de Dieu broke up, but as artists they felt uncomfortable with the strict rules. They heard we had opened a home in Monte Carlo and asked if they could come. We welcomed them gladly. With two musicians on our team, we could make enough money to pay rent. The Lord was blessing us, so we must be doing right.

The five of us, along with my son, moved to a three-bedroom home on the beautiful hillside of Eze-sur-Mer in the winter of 1978. We rented a small house, called a villa, which had a much cheaper rent in the winter months. Summer was still six months away, and we thought by then we would find something else.

My experience in Eze was one of beautiful days with my son flawed only by ugly times in argument with Cal and Mara. I seemed to gain strength from the natural charm of the tiny beach and quaint villages along the coast. Taking my son, who was now four years old, for long walks by the seacoast path along St.-Jean-Cap-Ferrat, I became closer to him than I thought possible for two human beings. Unconsciously, he became my reason for living.

Cal and Mara were made "colony shepherds," mainly because they were home most of the time and could devote themselves to reading the Mo letters, filing reports, praying, and other time-consuming activities that home leaders needed to do. They decided all practical matters in the home, such as how to spend money. However, they also decided whom I should go to bed with, and although I never minded that Cal had that authority, it bothered me that Mara was advising him about my sexual relations.

As a threesome, we had slept together in the same bed in Monte Carlo, but now Mara was pregnant and needed more rest. I agreed to move and began to sleep in Thor's bedroom in an extra bed. I always got up early in the mornings to play with him and teach school lessons anyway. Cal wanted me to sleep with him sometimes, but since I went out almost every night, and he was asleep by the time I got home, it just never happened. Although I knew from the Mo letters that sharing sexually was established as a general routine between brothers and sisters in most homes, we did not share here with Abe and Breeze, who had their own bedroom. That was not because we had qualms about adultery. Mo had told us that "the Mosaic Law has been done away with. Whatsoever is in Love, against such there is no Law" ("How to Answer Our Enemies—Preach Sex" 2475:28). I think I was too busy watching Thor, singing and witnessing, "fishing" at the clubs, and sleeping with other men to have time to share.

Abe sometimes went singing with his wife, Breeze, in Nice, but it was apparent that our most lucrative arrangement was for Breeze and me to sing in the elite cáfes along the Côte d'Azur between Nice and Italy. Breeze had a wonderful voice and was an accomplished musician. I had natural, spontaneous energy and a childlike "anything is possible" faith. Together we covered the restaurants and cafés with harmony and love and left with enough funds to meet all our humble expenses.

When we went out fishing for lost souls, the men were invited to the house to meet the family. Even though pregnant women in the Family still went out, and there were many testimonies in our *Family News* about women sharing sexually while pregnant, as Mara's pregnancy proceeded, she often stayed home due to fatigue.

Men were legitimately allowed to sexually recruit women into the Family, and although this happened sometimes, it seemed to be much more time-consuming, and became a rare event. We began calling the babies who resulted from sex with men who never joined the Family "Jesus babies." Ideally, those children were to be loved and treated like all our children, but in reality, they were not, and many Jesus babies grew up to be psychologically disturbed teenagers. As for myself, even though I never practiced birth control, I did not become pregnant again for seven years.

One day traveling on the train, we met a young British student, whom I witnessed to but thought did not need sex. Cal felt otherwise. Our new friend came to our house, and after receiving Bible classes from Cal, and asking Jesus into his heart, decided to stop his travels and stay with us. I knew that he was a virgin, and he was younger than I. I saw no reason why he needed sex; after all, he had already decided to stay. But both Cal and Mara thought he needed physical love, and they thought I should give it to him.

Instinctively, I felt I was violating some natural trust this poor young boy had for me as an older and wiser sister. I knew that I would never marry him, or even become a steady sex partner for him, and I felt that, as the innocent virgin he was, sex would mean something a lot deeper than just "supplying his needs." Reluctantly, I did as I was told. The student seemed infatuated with me, and we had to spend hours teaching him that I was only an expression of God's Love, not his "soul mate." Eventually, he accepted the lesson, and he stayed with us, going on to become one of the leaders in Switzerland. From the perspective of one inside the group, this seemed to prove that the "method" worked.

Meanwhile, I began having open and heated disagreements with Cal. He felt I was pulling away from him more, and I felt he was using me. Mara wanted peace, and when I suggested that I go to Paris for a month or two, she convinced Cal it was a good idea.

I remember well the sad day when I had to leave Thor on the quay of the Nice train station. Cal would absolutely not let me take him, but I was sure that Mara would send him to me after a few weeks. In her frail state, she could never keep up with my energetic boy. So even though I thought I would be separated only for a short time, it was a heart-wrenching good-bye.

"Where are you going with a suitcase, Mommy?" he asked in a tiny, almost fearful voice.

"I'm going to stay in Paris a little while, honey."

"I want to go with you."

"Not this time, sweetheart. Maybe soon," I murmured as my voice cracked, and I kissed him tenderly on his cheeks.

My precarious psychological state left my emotional resources depleted, and I was hoping that in Paris I would have time to think things through. Not only was I painfully aware that I had married a man I did not love, but I also had been giving my body to numerous men whom I did not choose. Living in Eze, as the almost sole provider of the home, yet with the least personal choice, I saw no change in my situation. I had recently received a sweet letter from James, one of the brothers whom I was close to in Paris, and he suggested a little vacation for me. I thought that odd. No one in the Family took vacations, but something about his letter made me feel that he was more liberated from Family rules than anyone else I knew. He now wrote that they had room for me in their small home in Paris. If nothing else, I could have a little reflection time. I had always thought that God would give me Thor—after all, I had done all this for Him!—but I needed to figure out a way to have him for myself.

However, as I entered the train and looked back, I had a premonition that I was leaving Thor for a long time. Cal had his hands tightly on his son's shoulder, but Thor's eyes were with me. I brushed the tears and thoughts away and boarded the train.

James was the same sweet and capable brother I remembered from the Show Group days. He knew a few very rich men in Paris who had already been given numerous women from the Family. When I arrived in Paris, these men wanted me too. Unfortunately, I slept with one of them before we found out that there was a venereal disease going around. When one of the women in our home got it, James took me to a private doctor in one of the fanciest areas of Paris.

I knew this must cost a fortune, and I imagined that one of our clients was paying. When I worked in the Show Group, the family members who were foreigners were issued the *carte de séjour*, which entitled us to free medical and social services. But my *carte de séjour* had not been renewed after the Show Group split up. Many of our foreign members received the *carte de séjour* by marrying French nationals, and all children born in France were given free medical services.

James noticed that I was a little apprehensive. I had not been to a doctor since Thor was born and I had needed stitches. He tried to put me at ease.

"Don't worry," he said. "You can witness to the doctor, you know. He might be a sheep."

The doctor interviewed me extensively. He had already seen a number of us, and he was curious as to what was going on. I explained it all to him.

"You see, we believe that God supplies all the needs a man has. And if we say we love someone, then why should we not give that person sex as an expression of God's Love?"

"But how do you choose to whom to give this sex?"

That was a tricky question for me, since of course, my leaders always chose for me, but I knew I should not reveal this to a stranger.

"Anyone interested in knowing more about God's Love can be shown love through sex," I answered demurely.

"Do you get paid for this?" he asked.

"Oh, no, we never take money."

"But some of the men I treated were obviously very rich men," he said, realizing that he could be honest with me. "Surely, your group must target rich men."

"Not really," I replied, recalling my recent experience with the poor young student. "But often, it is the rich men who are most needy for God's real love. Like the Bible says, it is harder for a rich man to go to heaven than for the camel to pass through the eye of a needle."

For some reason he seemed to accept this as a reasonable answer and nodded in agreement.

"*Alors*. You are in good health. Continue to take these pills, and see my secretary about getting the last appointment next Friday. I will have the rest of the lab reports in by then."

Friday I came after a full day of witnessing on the street selling literature. The lights were low in the waiting room, and there was no secretary. The doctor came out of his office in the back.

"Hello, Jeshanah. My secretary had to go somewhere tonight, so I let her off early. But this should not take long. Come back here."

I followed him to his formal office in the back.

"Well, you don't seem to have anything. You are lucky."

"Thank the Lord," I said automatically.

"I was thinking, though. I am very interested in God, and would like to know more about His Love, as you explained it."

I looked at him for a second with distrust. He was a doctor. Why would he want to have sex with someone who had been to bed recently with men who had VD?

"Oh, who cares," I thought. I had explained to him why we were doing this, and he didn't seem interested in being witnessed to. He was a nice-looking man, and I wondered if he was married. Well, it didn't hurt me to do this. I had recently been with men twice his age and size, and after those experiences, his trim, healthy body was a welcome sight. However, it was my first experience with a "short version" of sexual witnessing. I thought it would be easier to give him oral sex, since we were in the office, and it was over in a few minutes. I left and never saw him again. If nothing else, my trip to Paris had shown me that I could make some of my own decisions.

After eight weeks in Paris, all I could think about was getting back to Thor. I decided to go back to southern France by train. Having become very independent living in James's home, I knew I could make some decisions on my own. I tried calling Cal, but the phone had been disconnected. Thinking they did not have enough money to pay the phone bill, I wrote a letter saying when I would arrive. But when I arrived at the station in Nice, there was no one waiting for me. I tried Cal's number again, but it was still disconnected. I knew he must have received my letter by this time, so I could not imagine why no one would be there to meet me. Finally, I decided to call our leaders in that area, Peter and Sheila.

"Hi, Jeshanah. Praise the Lord! It is good to hear from you. Where are you?" said a sweet voice on the phone.

"Well, I'm at the train station in Nice. I thought Cal would meet me, but no one is here. I guess I'll take a bus to Eze."

"Oh, no, honey," said Peter, who had picked up another phone. "Haven't you heard that they moved?"

I felt like I had just taken a dagger in my heart.

"What do you mean moved? Where is Thor? Why wasn't I told?"

"You wait right there and we will come get you," said Sheila. She sounded truly concerned.

They arrived within half an hour. I then learned that Cal and the whole home had moved to a house in the mountains "somewhere," and he did not want me to know where he was.

"I don't care about Cal," I cried anxiously. "I want to see my son. I haven't been with him for over two months. I want to see him now!"

"Jeshanah, we are going to talk to Cal about this. You can stay with us for now. And we will try to work this out."

"What do you mean try? You are the leaders here. If you say Thor should see me, than Cal has to obey."

"Well, Mo is telling the leaders to try to persuade the disciples now, and not to command them. We are your servants, after all," he replied, repeating by rote the words we had all read in the letters, but which I knew were lies. No leader had ever served me. Being on my own in Paris, with James never telling me what to do, I had regained some of my former independent nature. This is one reason I never thought I was brainwashed. At some points of my life in the Family, I thought clearly, like the autonomous person I had always been. But I know I was manipulated, and these leaders knew exactly how to manipulate me right now through Thor.

"Jeshanah, honey, the Lord will take care of everything in His time," said Sheila in a voice coated with honey. "Let's pray about this together and find out what God's Will is."

I didn't need to find out what His Will was. I wanted to see Thor. It was never part of the agreement that Cal disappear with our son. That was unfair. The Family needed to help me. But I soon understood that they had their own agenda. Like so many times in my life, when I saw my walls of idealism crumbling before my eyes, I bent over to pick up the pieces. There were still the ideals to be upheld, and even if Cal and the leaders were playing against me, I knew in my heart that what I did was for God. Surely, He would not let me down. This was a time to be "wise as a serpent, but harmless as a dove" (Matthew 10:16), so I listened passively while my leaders talked to me. Rather than dealing with my heightened state of desperation to see my son, Peter told me I had been destined for a special mission to head up a home in Monaco.

I was biting my lip not to ask about Thor.

"Peter and I have access to a flat in Monaco for a few days. We thought you could come with us and we can go out together," piped up Sheila excitedly. "Of course, eventually we will try to get visitation privileges for you to see Thor," she said, as if she had read my mind, or maybe she was sensitive enough to see the pain written in my eyes.

"Jeshanah, I want you to realize that God is in control here," added Peter. "This might be a 'hard saying,' but I believe it is the Lord's Will that Thor is away from you right now. This will give you more time for God's work, and at least at the very beginning of this effort, we need you free from child-care responsibilities."

Peter had no idea how many times I had heard that same spiel while I was a dancer. How often had every leader who came through the Show Group in the three years of our heyday told me that I needed to forsake Thor for the work? I had been accused of loving my son more than God many times, and despite my best efforts to do both God's work and be a mother, it seemed that God was still jealous. Like the Bible said, "I, the Lord your God am a jealous God . . . and I will have no other Gods before me." Did He really mean that my son could be a god?

"Remember how the Lord tested Abraham," said Sheila. "He had to forsake Isaac, but he was given back."

I knew that Old Testament story. It was one of the stories I had the most trouble with. Why would a loving God want to test someone to that extent? Should I believe it? What choices do I have?

"I know, Sheila. I am repeatedly put to this test with my son," I responded sadly.

"Well, maybe you haven't gotten the victory yet," replied Peter in his harsh leader-knows-all voice. "Maybe this will keep coming up until you finally forsake him in your heart."

His comment prompted me to see a vision of myself sitting on top of a spiked fence. Sitting on fences was a recurrent vision, since I had so much difficulty choosing. On one side was the land of milk and honey promised by God and the COG, and on the other was the filth and despair of the world. Which side would I jump into? It all depended on which side Thor lived, and *that* was never revealed to me. All I could do was hang on to those pointed slippery spikes until I could see more clearly.

"I know, Peter. Please pray for me," I said, more because I knew that is what they wanted to hear than because I really wanted prayer.

We actually spent the next few days in prayer, which was the usual procedure when a big move or initiative was about to be made. The Children of God, for all their hypocrisy, seriously believed in prayer, and those who made it to the top were often people who publicly spent many hours in prayer. During my hours of silent praying, I would try to hatch a plan to find out where Thor was staying.

I had learned that Cal and the whole colony had moved someplace in the mountains between Nice and Antibes. Breeze and the men had been playing at restaurants along the coast, and Mara was soon due to deliver her baby. Through constant and careful maneuvering, I finally persuaded Sheila to ask Cal to call me. I waited by the phone anxiously the night he was supposed to call. The ring of the phone made my heart pound heavily in my chest.

"Hello," said a distant voice, evidently calling from a badly connected public phone, "is this Jeshanah?"

"Yes, it's me. Cal, is Thor with you? Can I talk to him? Please let me talk to him. Don't do this to me! Please?" I started sobbing uncontrollably, which I had told myself not to do.

I felt that Cal's silence meant he was considering my feelings, but I was wrong.

"No, Jeshanah. Thor is doing very well without you. He doesn't even ask about you anymore. You know it has been over three months now. He calls Mara Mommy."

It was the most hurtful and hateful thing he could have said to me. I could not hold back the sobs, which made me unable to talk any further.

"Well, maybe this wasn't a good idea," said Cal coldly.

"No . . . pleeease don't hang up. Pleeeease, Cal, don't hang up."

"I'll call you tomorrow at the same time. I have to talk to Mara," he said and hung up the phone.

I knew that Sheila was just outside the door, but I could not help myself. I just fell on the bed and cried and cried.

When I finally got back to reality, I wiped my face and went to see Sheila. Despite her years of following Family rules of leadership, which could harden the most tenderhearted people, Sheila still seemed somewhat sympathetic. In any case, she was all I had for a friend at this moment.

"I can't live without at least seeing my son," I explained, trying not be become overly emotional. "I just want to see him. That's all."

Sheila had no children, and it was probably hard for her to understand the deep mother instinct I was feeling.

"But if he is doing fine, and he is in God's hands, taken care of by the Family, why would you have to see him too?" she asked.

Fortunately, I had cried all my tears for the day, or so I told myself, and I was able to answer her dry-eyed.

"I must be weak in this area of my life, Sheila. I can sleep with anyone. I can stay up all night and go out every night and witness; you know that. You know how much I sacrifice; that's why you want me here. I will do anything you ask me to do, I promise! But Sheila, I just need to see Thor, that's all. I can't stay here and do this if I don't see him."

"I'll talk to Peter about it," she replied. "But ultimately, it is Cal's choice. We are not allowed to dictate those things anymore."

I knew that was not the full truth. The only way they could not dictate was if Cal left the Family, and I doubted that he had at that point.

Whether they talked to Cal or not, I did not know. I heard later that Abe had heard me crying over the phone and tried to convince Cal to let me see my son. Mara also told me many years later that it was the leaders who had told Cal and her that I was needed for FFing and that they should keep Thor. The next night Cal called and said I could meet him and Thor at a public park in Nice, but only for one hour.

I will hold every minute of that one hour in my heart for the rest of my life, next to where the minutes of Thor's birth are stored. The meeting was to be at a park near Place Massena, in the center of Nice. It was a sunny day, and I wore a light jacket and a long skirt. On my way to the park, I looked anxiously around, mistaking any little red-haired boy for Thor. He was nearly five years old, and I wondered how much he had grown in three months. I thought that he might not recognize me. I was twenty-five years old and had been told I looked much younger, but I felt like a broken, old woman who had lost her child in the Holocaust and now had heard he was alive. It was melodramatic, but it was real to me.

I saw Thor when I was still a block away. Cal held his hand by the fountain.

"Thor!" I cried, running toward him.

He turned around at the sound of my voice, and letting go of his daddy's hand, he ran toward me.

I fell down to one knee and held my arms open wide while he ran full-force into my embrace. A little taller and more robust, he still had a baby face and was smiling brightly. I had tears in my eyes, but for a few minutes, I was happy.

Cal was touched by our display of raw emotion, and he conceded to allow me periodic visits with Thor. It was a promising start, and I did not see that I had any other recourse but to agree and thank him profusely.

Walking home after that emotionally charged meeting, I felt that God indeed loved me. After spending three days in the belly of the whale, I must have said something that pleased God, because now He let me out of the darkness. I could again enjoy the blue of the sky, the softness of the gentle wind against my cheeks, and the sound of my son's laughter in my ear. God must love me, I thought, and the Family was so good to me. No matter what the sacrifice, I was thankful to be called to do a special service for Him and His work, because I now knew that ultimately, He would give me the desires of my heart, as He had promised in His Word! And if I thought about it honestly, giving God's Love to strangers was certainly not a sacrifice for me. In fact, it was the easiest work I ever did in the Family.

7

○ ○ ○

Casting the Net

Sharon was chosen to join me in Monaco. Recently arriving from Paris, Sharon was just as I remembered, only a little thinner. She had been our lead female vocalist, but she was one of the few performers who never got a big head. Tall, blond, and largely built, she always reminded me of a Valkyrie opera singer when she was onstage. Off-stage, she was shy, insecure, and absolutely loyal to friends and family. The only self-gratifying action that I ever knew her to indulge in was when she had a private affair with one of our songwriters. She was very much in love with him, so it surprised everyone when instead she married Timothy, a skinny, feminine-looking brother years younger than she. I never knew if their marriage had been suggested to them, or if they fell in love, but they were a strange combination in everyone's eyes. Timothy absolutely adored Sharon, and she treated him with love and respect.

Timothy, Sharon, and I got along wonderfully, and within days we were singing in the best restaurants in old Monte Carlo. When we needed more privileged contacts in order to get into Jimmy'z, the fishing hole we had our eye on, Sharon's friend Pierre, a movie producer, helped us out.

"Sure, bring along as many girls as you wish," Pierre said enthusiastically when Sharon queried if I could come along on their evening date. He met us at the Café de Paris dressed in flashy clothes. He was a large, ruggedly handsome, and extremely jovial man, and I could not help but notice what a striking couple he and Sharon made. Sometimes I wondered what she would have done had she not joined the Family. Certainly her strict Catholic upbringing had not prepared her to sleep with French movie producers in order to gain entrance to a private club.

As we stood before the small, dark, almost hidden entrance to Jimmy'z, the guardian of the door peeked through the sliding aperture and gave her decision whether access to the private club would be denied or not. Before it was our turn at the door, a group of colorfully attired "beautiful people" walked right past us, knocked on the door, and were ushered in. I noticed that one of them was Andy Warhol, recognizable by his white and distinctively styled hair. We were next, and although I was beginning to doubt if Pierre could get us in on this evidently superprivileged evening, he gave no sign of concern.

Pierre knocked on the door. The slide was pushed back silently while those now familiar eyes scrutinized our group of three. Pierre said something I could not hear to the guardian and she quickly opened the door and let us pass through. Entering the vestibule, I followed Pierre and Sharon into the next room, looking around at the other tables for any faces I knew, but it seemed that everyone had eyes on us instead. We were led to the VIP tables, which were curved booths that sat directly next to the small dance floor. The lovely lady at the table who greeted Pierre was Catherine Deneuve, the most famous actress in France. We were introduced as we all sat at her table, and I found her more elegant, gracious, and beautiful than could ever be revealed on the screen.

After being seated with the celebrated actress, we were never denied entry to the private club again. With access to Jimmy'z, we decided to get a table for ourselves, since without one we would always be dependent on some man from another table inviting us over. Standing at the bar in Jimmy'z signified a lower status; with our own table, we could pick and choose from our vantage point. We knew what we were doing there, and the fish did not. Using money we had left over from singing, we bought a bottle of vodka and took a table.

It is not possible for me to list all the men that I went to bed with during this time. Much later, when I was out of the Family and trying to get rid of what I thought were ghosts, a Christian pastor told me to name each man I had been with, or visualize him, and then cast him out of me. I found that it was not only impossible, but tiring and depressing, and I abandoned the practice of casting out demons as soon as I arrived at the Monte Carlo days in my mind. I have never regretted the decision to abandon that technique for ridding oneself of recollections, for I found it guilt producing and totally in conflict with what I really felt for these men at the time. They were not demons, or even bad spirits that possessed me; in fact, if I believed in possession at all (which I'm not sure I do), I possessed these men with a good spirit. What I did was *in* love and *for* love, and I think that faith is what protected me from the horrors and degradation that I witnessed in all the high-class call girls whom I met during that period of time.

The Children of God firmly believed that we lived in a different world from anyone else, and we merely stepped into this mundane world of material things and sinful natures in order to save more people from ultimate spiritual death. In fact, death itself was just a stepping-stone to a higher spiritual reality—a doctrine held by many religions. But we believed that dying without accepting Jesus' salvation would mean hell. It's very hard to say how much I really believed this, now that I am so far removed from it, but I know that my motives were not flesh induced or emotionally inspired. For many years, I did not feel physical pleasure during sex or even desire while flirting. I took on the role of a vestal virgin, offering my body as God's gift of love, a perverse combination of the purity of sacred devotion and the intimacy of marriage bonds. Although I eventually came to realize that not all our girls were so innocently naive about sex, I was able to keep my emotions and my mission so carefully separated that I lost the key to romantic/soul-mate love without ever having used it.

The men I was with were not aware of my mission, however, and they each reacted differently. Nevertheless, I could group these men into the following categories: (1) those who simply made use of the free sex (these were the men I have generally forgotten); (2) those who genuinely liked me or who felt a romantic inclination toward me (these are the ones I remember best); (3) those who found my spiritual message sexually stimulating (these were the ones I recall with pity or disappointment); (4) those few who fell sadly in love with me but not the Family. These were the men I did *not* share with sexually, as soon as I found out that their concept of love was not compatible with the one I was preaching. Perhaps these were the men who could have truly helped me, who cared enough about me to want me out of the Family's control, but I was too detached from my emotions to recognize real love.

Within a few months after starting our little "home" of three in Monte Carlo, we found an apartment in the plush, private residential area of Cap Martin. Among the exclusive millionaire mansions that lined the coast of the last French peninsula before Italy, ours was one of the few modest houses, and it had been divided into two apartments. We rented the one downstairs, aided by a large security payment from Timothy's father. Sharon and Tim had a beautiful baby girl now, so Tim's father wanted to see them more settled. The house was in walking distance of a bus stop, which could take us to Monaco, the principality that considered itself separate from France but which was served by French public transportation. Carrying a guitar or two, neatly enclosed in a case, and dressed in stylish clothes that we had collected over the years in Paris, we usually hitchhiked, in order to meet more people. At night, after singing or going to the clubs, we had to ask a man we met to take us home, or use one of the taxi drivers who had been a client.

Since Mo's photo had been taken in Tenerife and published widely throughout Europe, Mo lived completely underground now, but from the speed with which we received his encouraging messages, I suspected he was somewhere nearby. That made me rather nervous. I knew that Mo pulled women out of their homes at will to live in his "harem." I imagined life in his home to be terribly restrictive and embarrassingly open about sexual activity. This sounds sanctimonious, considering what I was doing, but there were a few things happening at his house that I felt were past the limit of what I could do, such as walking around naked in front of all the children who lived there.

Recently, Mo had been sending us letters explicitly describing the sex between himself and every woman in his home. Sometimes, the descriptions were not flattering, especially if the woman did not please Mo in some way. One young woman whom I knew was rebuked in a letter because she preferred to return and live with the father of her baby rather than stay in Mo's house.

By now, I was in a continual state of ambivalence over whether I believed in Mo or detested him. It was as if he had given us all a beautiful way to live and then destroyed it; but we kept hanging on for different reasons. About this time I received a message from one of our leaders through Tim.

"I am asked to remind you that you are the writer of 'The Uneager Beaver,' so we should keep a very close watch over your spiritual growth," said Tim hesitantly one morning.

"But that doesn't mean that you are not doing good right now, Jeshanah. We just want to be sure nothing happens that could hurt the work we are doing here," added Sharon sweetly.

"We thought you should have more time in the Word, you know. You have been going out every night, and you usually miss morning devotions. I think we will switch the morning devotions to noon, and we all should be up by then," said Timothy, seemingly pleased that he had already come up with a workable solution.

"Can I go on a bike ride right now?" I asked, wishing to get away for a few moments. "I will take a Mo book with me and read something in the field down the road."

Sharon spoke up immediately and said that would be a good idea. As I rode through the posh neighborhood, seeing only the large servants' quarters from the streets, I thought about Tim's message. Surely it meant that Mo did not want me too near him or any of his pet projects. That was fine with me, as long as I could stay near my son. What if Mo thought I was too unspiritual to raise a child of God? Why did he keep harping on that story I had written? Did I not already receive forgiveness for that? According to the Bible, that sin should have been washed away.

I parked the bike near a pretty orchard, probably someone's private property, and sat under an olive tree. Opening my booklet to one of the more "milky" Mo letters, I tried to read, but my eyesight was hindered by tears. I closed the book and let myself cry uncontrollably. They were tears of despair and confusion. I grasped for meaning in my life, and I came only to Thor. My son was happy and healthy. I was near him, and I knew that if I was good enough, if I obeyed and sacrificed, repented of sins I didn't even recognize yet, I would get him back one day.

When the sobs subsided, I admired my surroundings of neat fences, manicured pastures, and picturesque olive trees with their gnarly, bumpy trunks suggesting a life of difficulty. After releasing the recurrent pain and replenished by nature, I got on the bike and continued my ride around the Cap.

As I continued along the road, pushing the bike now, I met a woman named Sophia, who was visiting from Provence. She promised to visit the next day and to bring her host with her.

Sharon, Tim, and I were excited about the prospect of meeting someone who actually lived in this exclusive neighborhood, but we were not prepared to meet Charles. We had in mind a stiff, dignified CEO type, or maybe a flashy Hollywood pretender. Instead, Sophia walked in the next day with an unpretentious-looking young man who slightly stuttered at first acquaintances.

Charles was of medium build, slightly taller than average; he wore his straight, brown hair in a conservative short cut, and looked eerily like Anthony Perkins when he wasn't playing a psycho. I thought he was handsome, and his strangeness only made him more appealing. Charles had a look that contained a blend of extreme sensitivity and discernment, a combination that I have found makes normal life more difficult to live. As I grew to know Charles better, I discovered that he overcame this difficulty by considering nothing "normal." But then, he could afford this luxury.

Charles had received a title of nobility and a substantial inheritance from his grandfather, who also provided an intricate royal history. An illegitimate child without formally recognized parentage, he had been adopted by a wealthy Hungarian Jew, himself ennobled by Emperor Franz Josef II of Austria-Hungary. The Hungarian noble's mother was a Hapsburg and his father was rumored to have been Queen Victoria's son, Edward, who became King Edward VII. The queen, by special decree, had granted him the right and privilege to use his foreign title in Britain. But the paternity issue was never finally resolved, and the most likely candidate to be his ancestor was the Austro-Hungarian baron himself.

His grandfather had also passed on to Charles the responsibility for a wildlife foundation, which included a large piece of property and an enormous villa on Cap Martin. It was here that Charles lived and cared for a number of protected animal species, but his mild manner and scruffy attire made it impossible to guess he was a descendant of one of Europe's oldest royal lines.

Charles and I immediately struck up a close friendship. He had been married to the daughter of his grandfather's housekeeper, but their marriage did not last long. It appeared that Sophia, the young lady I talked with on the road, was someone interesting he had met while picking grapes in France, and although he informed me that they'd remained in contact throughout the years, she was gone in a few weeks and I never saw her again. Of course, Charles and I spent more time together after Sophia left, and I remember my first evening visit to his chateau as one of the most mysterious and melodramatic moments in my life.

The huge chateau, set off from the main street by a winding drive, appeared nestled in the wild trees like Dracula's castle when I first saw it in the bluish-purple light of the evening. The gray stones contrasted with the live pink flamingos that populated the small pond in front of the chateau's massive doors. We entered through the back door that led past the servants' kitchen, actually the only kitchen in the house. I imagine that nobles never had to cook for themselves in the days when the castle was built. Charles, however, used the kitchen quite frequently to entertain guests. In fact, most of the ornately decorated rooms with their Baroque, gilded furniture were never used by Charles at all. This night, he led me to the library, which had a small room next to it that he used for his bedroom. Instinctively he felt that the library is where I would want to be, and Charles seemed to want to please me. Lighting a fire in the darkened room, he let me browse through the books. I touched them hesitantly. The Family had been through a number of book burnings, and we were discouraged from reading anything, especially books such as these, that seemed to hold ancient wisdom. I was drawn to one in particular, a book by Chiero on reading palms.

"Are you interested in palm reading?" asked Charles, coming up from behind me so silently that I jumped. "Oh, I'm sorry. I didn't mean to frighten you."

"No, well, yes. I think I am. This looks very intriguing," I said as I thumbed through sketches of the heart line, the fate lines, and others. I was wondering if I should tell him that we really don't believe in anything but what is in the Bible or the Mo letters, but since this was such a rare opportunity to find out something really interesting, I decided to keep that subject for later.

"My sister was into palm reading, among other things. She moved to Greece and opened a bar there with her girlfriend." said Charles quietly.

"Oh? Is she still there? I would love to go to Greece."

"No! She committed suicide a few years ago. In fact, I think this book is hers. Do you want to borrow it?"

Dire thoughts raced through my mind. Tim had warned me that I should not go to Charles's castle alone. Both he and Sharon thought that Charles hid some great secrets in this place. Did he know black magic or something? The eerie shadows made by the fire caused what looked like ghosts to play on the bookshelves. If I took this book, would I be possessed? I looked Charles in the eyes and saw nothing but sincere devotion to a friend, along with a sadness brought on by thoughts of his sister.

"Oh, Charles, that would be lovely. Are you sure you don't mind, this being your sister's book? I'm sure it means something special to you."

"You are special to me too, Jeshanah. You picked up that book, among the hundreds in this room, so I think you should take it."

"Okay, but only to borrow. I'll learn how to read palms, and I'll read yours one day."

I went home that evening with a confusing realization of having found a friend *outside* the Family. That was not supposed to happen.

"I don't know about that book," said Timothy questioningly as we went over the previous evening during our noon devotions. "What if it has a strange spirit attached? You know what Mo said about spirits using things as vehicles."

"Well, we can pray over it and cast out any spirits," replied Sharon. "Mo's own grandmother read palms." I never understood if Sharon was just coming to my rescue as a friend, or if she was just a closet rebellious woman.

"Yeah, and Mo himself had his palm read by Madam M," I added, by now earnestly desiring to read this book.

Although we wanted to keep Charles as a friend, Timothy and Sharon thought it would be unsafe to give him God's Love since he lived so close. They were also concerned about all the questions Charles asked. He was very inquisitive, and living right down the street, he could spy on all our doings. Since the Family was inherently paranoid, living illegally in most countries, having no visible means of support, and not adhering to local laws, such as sending children to school or doctors regularly, the idea of having an outsider know about our daily activities was out of the question.

"Has he made any physical advances towards you, Jeshanah?" inquired Sharon in an excuse-me-for-intruding voice.

"Well, no, not really. We kissed once after the movies, but he was so shy about it, I didn't want to push anything," I answered, remembering the kiss that Charles had given me. His hands shook as he held my hand in the car, and his lips were quivering. I didn't feel that this was someone I should seduce. He seemed so vulnerable.

"Jeshanah, witness to him every time you're alone. Then, if he wants sex, he knows what it's for, and if he doesn't we know why."

"Why?" I asked, wondering what Timothy's train of reasoning could be.

"Why, he's not a sheep then."

Ironically, Timothy's simplistic advice was really the best we could follow. He usually gave the right advice for the wrong reason. If I slept with Charles, I felt, he could be terribly hurt when he found out that I did the same with lots of men. I did not want to hurt my new and only friend, and although I had various degrees of closeness to Charles throughout the years, I never had a sexual relationship with him. He never asked for it either, and we enjoyed a platonic but deep relationship, a rarity it seems between a man and a woman.

By the winter of 1978, Sharon, Timothy, and I had established ourselves in Monte Carlo as an eccentric but accepted singing team. Going out by two, we took turns staying home with the baby. We sang at most of the restaurants near the palace—they all had enough of a clientele to make it worthwhile—and at some of the fancier restaurants down in the Monte Carlo casino area. With Sharon's amazing talent, I did little but collect the money after she sang, make new contacts, and talk to anyone who had questions. After a singing excursion, we usually went to the Café de Paris to sit with a drink and wait until the clubs started to fill up. I was used to drinking nightly now, and although I never became a heavy drinker, I felt that I could witness better after a glass of wine. Often, we met people just sitting in the luxurious and much frequented café. Now I had a new tool for breaking the ice. If I saw someone who looked like a prospect for fishing, I introduced myself by asking if he wanted his palm read.

One evening, as I was drinking my third or fourth kir, I spied the cooler-than-thou crowd hanging out at the back of the room. I got up and walked straight to their table, keeping my eyes on a short, muscular man who I believed was a high-bred noble.

"Do you want your palm read?" I asked, taking his hand and studying it curiously. He looked up with glassy eyes.

"Can you do this?" He responded too simply, caught off guard for a second.

I studied his hand for quite sometime, while the others at the table debated the validity of palm reading. Actually, even though I had digested the Chiero book completely and knew the lines, clever palm reading becomes perfect with practice. Much of it is relying on intuition and feelings. As I held his small, square hand in my long, slender one, I was surprised at the coarseness of this noble hand. His fingers were short and stubby, with flat, square fingernails. I had more than enough material to reveal what I thought of royal titles and elitism based on blood and wealth.

"You have the hands of a peasant," I said, as I kept my eyes intently focused on his palm. I felt him jerk his hand ever so slightly, and then relax.

There was a roar of protest from his friends.

"Some connection you have with God, not to recognize a noble hand," chirped a little pretty thing at the end of the table, obviously having heard about me before.

"This is a work hand," I continued. "In the old days you would have been working in the fields. Today this hand would work in the factories, but it seems you have had some help from fate." I had no idea how accurate I was in accessing his ancestry. Many years later I would find out that his famous family was once known as "the dynasty of the peasants."

This seemed to be enough for him. He pulled his hand away.

The gentleman, whose name was André, bellowed for more drinks.

"What will you have, Jeshanah? Sharon?" he asked kindly. His deeply tanned face showed early signs of age, although he was probably still in his thirties. At twenty-six, I still looked much younger than anyone at the table, probably due to my lack of makeup and unstyled hair. I was beginning to feel sorry for what I had said. It had obviously moved him in some way. When they all decided to continue the party at his house, we were invited.

André lived in one of the swankiest private apartment buildings in Monte Carlo. Situated to have a view of the sea, the mountains, and the best spot to watch the famed Monte Carlo Grand Prix, I knew this apartment cost a fortune. Not only was André a noble; he also had money, which gave him a top position among the young jet-set crowd. This evening he had invited a few models to his home. One of them was a "James Bond girl." Since I did not go to movies very often, I would never have recognized her, but she was introduced as such.

I felt uncomfortable in this crowd, so I suggested that Sharon sing a few songs. I noticed that André listened intently as he tried to figure us out. People were coming and going, and a few times I tried to excuse myself, but André always pulled me back, insisting I stay. Finally, Sharon took me aside.

"André wants to bite," she said, reverting to her leadership role. "I have to go home, but I think you should stay here. He may never have another chance to hear the message like this."

Sharon left with a chauffeur who was called from the casino area. I wondered why André wanted me to stay. He had acted disinterested in me for the last couple of hours. Suddenly he seemed to notice I was there when everyone had left.

"So, tell me about this talent you have for reading palms," he said, seemingly unaffected by the lack of sleep that made it hard for me to keep my eyes open.

"Oh, I just started it. Maybe I read your hand wrong. I know you have some title or something."

"Actually, I am a descendant of Napoleon. Come, let me show you."

He took my hand and led me on a tour of his apartment, showing me all the objects he had inherited from his famous ancestor. I was too tired to show due amazement, and I guess he took this as ignorance or lack of sophistication. We ended up in the bedroom, which sported a tiny, boatlike wooden bed that he claimed had been Napoleon's. It looked like the right size to me, and I was hoping I could lie down in it, mainly because I was thoroughly fatigued. In fact, we did lie down, and in robotlike fashion I told him that we were really messengers from God. I told him that I was God's Love to the lost souls in Monte Carlo. My eyes were closed. I did not know if he heard, or understood, or even cared, but I know I told him, and then we made love.

When I arrived home in the morning, Sharon and Tim were at the kitchen table eating breakfast and feeding their daughter in the highchair. We discussed our evening with the Monte Carlo jet set over croissants and coffee, and we all agreed that they were not the type we should concentrate on. They seemed too rich, young, and beautiful to think about needing God at this point in their lives, and we decided that they were just having fun, while we had a mission.

Soon after, we were told by Mo that the Monte Carlo home should be a secret in the Family. The only trouble was that it was no secret to Cal and Mara, who lived on the other side of Monaco in Cap Ferrat. I used to joke that Thor's parents lived on the two most beautiful and exclusive Caps in the world. My main concern was that Mara and Cal insisted I could only visit Thor at their home and never brought him to my place.

There are no simple explanations of why the situation was like this. Cal claimed that I had deserted Thor, although he knew that I had only gone to Paris temporarily. I knew he was keeping Thor as revenge against me. But I felt guilty for not having been a good wife, so I tried to work out custody of Thor while keeping Cal's feelings a priority. Cal clearly had the cards stacked to his advantage. Not only did he have physical possession of our son, but the leaders also preferred that Thor stay with Cal. They were still saying that God wanted me to put Him first, so right now, as always, all I had for leverage was my body. That is what the leaders wanted—for God's work, of course.

I spent every free day with my son and often spent the night so I could be with him more. I knew that Cal intended to send Thor to French school in the fall, but I kept up with his reading and writing in English and practiced math exercises with him. His chubby little five-year-old body was full of energy. Often we would take long walks around the Cap, stopping to look at fish or discover a turtle. Thor had a great imagination, and he liked to pretend he was a pirate, or a soldier, or a knight. I played all the other parts—the villain, the damsel in distress, the enemy, the poor old lady who needed defending. At night I made up fantastic stories of Thor riding a white horse and flying off to another world to save his princess Chiara, a little girl who was his friend in Paris. We bonded intensely, and for this time I was forever grateful, since we both would need that connection to make it through some very rough years. Still, I was upset that Thor could never stay with me in my home. One morning, sleeping in Thor's room, I woke up early before anyone in Cal's house was stirring. It was still a little dark outside as I shook Thor awake.

"Shh, don't say anything, Thor," I warned him as he opened his eyes and looked at me with a smile.

"We are going on an adventure before anyone else wakes up. Do you want to do that?"

He shook his little red head yes and jumped out of bed rubbing his eyes. I had already prepared a small backpack with some of Thor's clothes, which I put over his shoulders. I didn't want to carry a suitcase and arouse suspicion. We tiptoed through the French doors that opened up into the yard. Thor was very good about being quiet, and I could hear my own heart beat excitedly. I was planning to kidnap Thor back.

I kept looking back over my shoulder while we headed for the road, thinking that surely God would wake up somebody to run after me if this was not His Will. No one came. As soon as we reached the main road, I stuck out my thumb. Most of the light traffic that came down the road to the Cap were domestic workers coming in, not going out.

"Why aren't we taking a bus?" asked Thor.

"Because it is too early, honey. The buses are not running yet. But this is an adventure. You want to do something different, don't you?"

"Yes, but I'm hungry."

"Okay, as soon as we get a ride out of here, we'll stop and get something to eat."

"Can I have a *religeuse*?" he asked, requesting his favorite French pastry.

"You can have as many as you want, honey, as long as you drink it with milk."

I would not be safe until we got a ride out of the Cap. Finally, I saw a gray Mercedes come down the road. I frantically waved him down.

"I have to catch a train," I said. "Can you take us to the train station?"

The driver let us in and dropped us off at the Beaulieu station.

I had decided to take the first train going in either direction. Luckily, the first one was headed for Italy, the direction I needed to go. We got off in the Menton station, and I took the first bus going by Cap Martin.

Timothy and Sharon were just eating breakfast when I arrived with Thor. Sharon took my little boy in her arms while I cried on Timothy's shoulder.

"Oh, Timothy, please let me keep him. I just want to have him for the weekends. Please help me."

"He'll help you," said Sharon from the side. "We'll make sure you can have your son on weekends, Jeshanah. I promise."

Sharon stuck by her promise. Timothy called Peter and Sheila, who came out immediately knowing that Cal would throw a fit. Cal came out to the house and searched, never thinking to go upstairs where Thor and I were hiding in the neighbor's apartment. Peter and Sheila kept telling Cal to quiet down and go home, since they were afraid he might blow our cover. Finally, Peter and Timothy took Cal by force back to his home. Thanks to Cal's display of disobedience to leadership, the leaders were now on my side. They told Cal that unless he agreed to allow Thor to stay with me on weekends, I would keep Thor in an undisclosed location indefinitely. He agreed.

Having Thor on weekends was like heaven on earth for me. Now Breeze and Abraham came over more often, first as liaisons from Cal's home to make sure I didn't keep Thor, and then as regular guests. Breeze was my old singing partner from Eze-sur-Mer, and she started going out to clubs with us more often, which was a relief for Sharon, who was pregnant again. We all suspected that Sharon had become pregnant from a one-night stand. Timothy took this like a real soldier of the Lord. He cared for Sharon, and eventually he treated the new baby as if she were his own.

Breeze had been trained as a violinist, but now she wrote songs, composed music, and played the guitar. She was shorter than I and rounder, but she made the most of her good points. She wore heavy makeup that accented her big brown eyes, and she permed her shoulder-length brown hair so it hung in waves around her face. Her firm, well-endowed breasts were highlighted by the clothes she wore, revealed in a low-cut bodice or tightly wrapped in a clingy material. Breeze knew how to make a man look twice.

Unlike most of the girls in the Family who worked with me, Breeze never seemed bothered by fatuous worries of competition. In fact, seeing my poor knowledge of makeup and clothes, she took it upon herself to give me a makeover. She suggested that my waist-length hair be cut a few inches and curled in spiral waves. An experienced seamstress, she made dresses for me that accented my figure and drew attention to the curve of my derriere. She even encouraged me to wear shorter skirts that flaunted my long legs. I felt safe with Breeze and trusted her opinion almost as much as I trusted Sharon's. More than any other home I had ever been in, I thought that the members of this home embraced the ideal of true brotherly and sisterly love.

With Breeze on our team, I had pink business cards printed that read SONGS OF LOVE, IMPRESARIO: JESHANAH and our phone number printed on the bottom. We now passed as professional singers, which mainly meant that it was easier for me to book us at private parties. I carried these cards with me at all times, handing them out freely, and this became our cover for many activities during our time in Monte Carlo.

While waiting for final approval from Peter and Sheila for Breeze to join our home, I met Salim, a dashing figure, well known in elite European circles. Once I saw a picture of Salim and his wife in a national magazine, accompanying a story about a high-society party in Paris, and only because of this did I know of his privileged status in society. I eventually discovered that he was a financier who was respected and feared as one of the top players in the international finance world, but since wealth and materialism meant little to me at the time, I never inquired into his business or his private life.

As I have already described, Salim was the man who first gave me money for sex. Until that point, if I received any money it was understood beforehand by the man that it would pay for rent, food, or necessities for the Family. I would ask them to take me shopping, and of course some were surprised to find me buying baby clothes, children's shoes, or a blender. This might not seem like an obvious difference, but receiving necessities and other supplies instead of hard money somehow made it seem less of a monetary exchange for sex. However, around the time I met Salim, we began receiving the letters from Mo saying that we should take money for it! "My Lord, you're providing enough FF service and getting laid, it's time you got paid!" ("Make it Pay!" 684:11). Women started to accept money for giving love, then they asked for it, and finally the Family set up its own escort services. Taking the money from Salim was a turning point for me and for our work in Monte Carlo. He was to be my first steady fish in Monte Carlo. I eventually thought of him as a friend who showed his appreciation with gifts, but he also provided introduction to quite a few Middle Eastern billionaires.

As I became more acquainted with Salim and his lifestyle, I was often reminded of the quote attributed to Lord Byron, which Mo had highlighted for us in his letters: "I have drunk every cup of fame and tasted every pleasure, and yet I die of thirst" ("War and Peace" 255: 98). The more I met these men who had all the material wealth they wanted, the more I felt like a true angel of mercy, bringing their wasted and thirsty souls the water of life. I don't know if they shared this sentiment, but I certainly let them know how I felt, especially Salim, who was the recipient of my letters and poems. In fact, I first thought that he truly cared about me when I saw a card I had written to him stuck under the glass top of his desk, in view for all his closest acquaintances to see.

Salim was not the only one I sent poems to; on the contrary, sending notes to the men I met was part of my witnessing procedure. I usually followed a night together with a pretty card I personally selected that reminded me in some way of the man or our experience together. I wrote a verse or a Mo quote that made reference to the salvation message or continuing in God's Love. However, for Salim, due to our lengthy relationship, I began to write personal poems. These were not love poems, in the usual sense, but instead they explained a spiritual love in "higher realms" of eternal life, such as this excerpt taken from one long poem I composed and sent to Salim:

> Then from the view of this great mountain height,
> The world's injustices were plainly in sight,
> If your heart is breaking, then let us cry,
> For the pain, for the suffering, for all those who die,
> For the greed, for the selfishness, for these things not right,
> Our weeping surely may endure for this night.

This was the type of poem I wrote to a millionaire who introduced me to billionaires, some of whom have been accused of making their money by dealing in arms. I believed I was giving them spiritual insight, and I consoled my conscience that I was taking from the rich to give to the poor. Once Salim understood that I used none of the money he gave me for myself, he started to buy me personal presents.

"Do you ever buy yourself a dress with the money I give you?" he asked me one evening as I dressed in his hotel bedroom. I had on what I thought my best dress, which he had probably seen a dozen times now.

"No, I give everything to the Lord's work. You know that."

"But don't you work for the Lord too?" he responded, playing in the fantasy I had shared with him.

"Well, we decide together what is needed. I don't think I need clothes. Did my clothes attract you to me?" I asked with a smile.

Salim allowed himself a rare smile and went into the adjoining sitting room.

"Have you ever been to Yves Saint Laurent?" he asked me when I came into the room, ready to leave. I thought he was talking about a small village nearby, St.-Laurent-du-Var.

"I think I visited there once," I replied.

"I want you to go there tonight and pick out a dress," continued Salim. "I will meet you at Jimmy'z later to see what you have bought. Get whatever you want."

"Isn't that a little far for me to go tonight?" I asked, still thinking he was talking about the village.

"No, it's right across the street. Kahlil will accompany you there," he said with a quizzical look on his face. He was beginning to understand that I didn't know what he was talking about.

Kahlil was Salim's right-hand man. He took me across the street from the Hôtel de Paris to two haute couture boutiques displaying the clothes of Christian Dior and Yves Saint Laurent. I felt foolish when I realized what Salim had been referring to. Mara and I had often looked in these display windows, while she pointed out to me which clothes were tasteful and which were not. I wished she were here with me now to help me choose a dress. I wished somebody were with me besides Kahlil, and I felt awkward asking for his opinion. But since he was the only one, I asked anyway.

We went through half a dozen exotic and colorful dresses, which made me look ridiculous, and Kahlil agreed that they were not for me. Then he suggested that I go next door to the Dior boutique, which had more conservative styles. He helped me choose a few evening dresses, and we finally agreed on a simple black satin dress overlaid with embroidered chiffon and a sheer cape covering spaghetti straps. Kahlil suggested I buy shoes to go with it. Made of a black velvet, with very high heels, they were the most exquisite shoes I ever owned.

Salim looked pleased to see me when I arrived at the club in clothes that made me seem like a different person. That evening he introduced me to the mayor of Nice and his wife, who were sitting at the table. I showed them pictures of my son, which I carried with me at all times. The mayor's wife, who was American, thought this was terribly endearing.

On another occasion, Salim bought me a signed, limited-edition print by a contemporary artist he had discovered in Paris. Salim said that the painting, of a nude, waiflike girl with adolescent-sized breasts, reminded him of me. She had flowers in her long hair and held a folded piece of material around her hips, in which she had collected a bouquet of flowers. A vine was entwined around her slender left arm, and she looked gently at a dove she held in her right hand. The lines of the figure were lightly sketched over a blue background. This print said more about Salim's feelings for me than all the words he could have uttered, but never did.

I often have wondered why it was Salim, and not some fly-by-night client, who first gave me money. Throughout the waves of doubt about the concept of sacred prostitution that I continued to experience during my Monte Carlo days, it was often Salim's special attention and our presumed spiritual connection that caused me to focus on the sacred side, and convinced my tortured mind that I was not a prostitute.

8

○ ○ ○

Sacred Prostitution

By the summer of 1979, we had moved to Beausoleil, the French village that is literally attached to Monaco. In our new home we had more room, a benefit since Peter and Sheila had been sending us sisters to try out as sacred prostitutes in Monte Carlo. One of them was Sheba, an icy beauty who had recently discovered her husband's homosexuality. To everyone's shock, Mo was tentatively condoning homosexual relationships now. Mo had always encouraged lesbian relationships, but he preferred men to be with women. A close relationship with a young man in his own home seemed to have sparked Mo's enlightenment, which he detailed in a letter. Although it was not clear if Mo actually engaged in homosexuality himself, he expanded his doctrine to state that *anything* done in love is not sin, which left the door open for homosexuals in our group to come out of the closet. Many of them were already married with children, as was the case with Sheba, who was surprised to discover that her husband loved men more than just spiritually.

Sheba was breathtakingly beautiful, but she was aloof and uncommunicative. She soon was transferred to another home, as the leaders decided we had a good team as it was—small, together, potent, and led by our faith that what we were doing was for love. In biblical terms, Breeze represented a Delilah-type seductress, hunting rich and powerful men to use for her own amusement and personal aggrandizement. Sharon exemplified the ever-suffering Mother Mary, ready to sacrifice when chosen. I was the Mary Magdalene, symbolizing the tortured integration of rational thinking and irrational actions. I dissociated my mind and soul from my body as I performed earthly missions of providing sexual pleasures.

In our new home, I requested that the small study be turned into a room for Thor. In anticipation of entering school in the fall, Thor had come to live with me while Cal and Mara hunted for houses. I taught Thor schoolwork almost daily. He was well advanced in math and reading, but I wanted him to learn French. In all the Family homes at that time only English was spoken, and although Thor had lived in France since he was less than a year old, he still spoke almost no French. I had Thor tested at a local Catholic school, and he placed in the second grade, at only five years of age. When Cal had still not found a home by the time school started, I enrolled Thor in the Catholic school. This was not the norm in the Family, but there were no COG schools nearby.

Unfortunately, no one took into account that Thor could not speak French when they put him in second grade. Although he excelled in math class, he didn't tell anyone that he couldn't understand much else. There were no French nationals in our home either, so when Cal and Mara found a home in Antibes, and they wanted Thor back, I complied. I reasoned that most of the children in wealthy families were sent away to boarding schools by their parents, and Thor would not be far away. I could visit him during the week and take him with me on weekends again. If he was going to go to school in France, he needed someone like Mara who could help him with his homework in the national language.

Surprisingly, for having lived in the Family for so long, I was very concerned that Thor excel in scholastic pursuits. I think in the back of my mind, I felt that if the Family did not work out for him, he would have a good education to fall back on, unlike many of the children being raised in the Children of God at that time. Even Mo's prophecy that Jesus would come back in 1993, making Thor only twenty years old when Jesus returned, did not deter me. Mo's prophecies had been wrong before, like the one about the Kohoutek comet destroying America. Every time one of his prophecies did not come true, we were told by Mo that we had misinterpreted what he said, or that the Lord had mercy and gave us more time. He referred us to the story of Jonah, in which God had told Jonah to prophesy that the evil town of Nineveh would be destroyed. Poor Jonah, who didn't want to say the prophecy, just in case it didn't come true, had to spend three days in the whale's belly before he agreed to prophesy. Then the Lord forgave Nineveh and didn't destroy the town after all. I was not taking chances with my son. He might live to be an adult, and there might not be the Children of God around anymore. Although I did not think about it at that time, obviously, at some fundamental level, I was preparing my son for life inside or outside the Family.

Thor moved back with Cal and Mara, who had found a very nice home in the cozy town of Antibes, about forty-five minutes away by bus. They now lived with another couple from the old Show Group, and Cal had a steady engagement performing at a local music club. They were settled in nicely, and their home seemed like a picture of family security. I felt that Thor would have the support he needed in education and fatherly discipline, so I let him go without any trouble, after securing a promise from Cal that I could take Thor to Monaco every weekend and on vacation. Meanwhile, during the week, I often made the one-and-a-half-hour round trip to be with him. Thanks to being free from a normal job or witnessing quotas, this was possible. As I went on long, playful walks with Thor in Old Antibes, surrounded by medieval architecture and the famous castle wall by the sea, I imagined that my life was magical.

Back in Monaco, we began an earnest study of the letters describing the "flirty fishing" ministry, upon Timothy's insistence. An early letter, "Law of Love," written in 1974, told us: "Are you so ruled by His Love that He can liberate you from the rules? Are you willing to lay down your life—or even your wife—for a starving brother or sister? Can a couch be your cross? Jesus said, 'If any man lose his life, for My sake, the same shall save it. Love God . . . and love they neighbor as thyself' (Matthew 22:37–40)" (quoted in "Law of Love" 302c). These Mo letters were illustrated with drawings of naked women with their bodies pierced by a hook, and sexily clad women offering a hook and a look of love to admiring men, with a caption that read, "Hooker for Jesus." The lengthy letters, describing every detail of the fishing experiences, were spiked with quotes asking if we were "willing to do anything for Jesus to help your Fisherman catch men, even to suffer the crucifixion of the hook . . . eaten alive" ("Flirty Little Fishy" 293). Later, when women started to get sexually transmitted diseases, our sacrifice was compared with that of Jesus: "We are suffering for their sins as Jesus did for ours in order that we and they might be saved" ("Affliction" 569:108). However, Mo did suggest we see a doctor.

Now that we were told to accept money from our fish, the financial difficulties that had plagued the Family around the world were considerably lessened. The COG headquarters expected a lot of money from our tiny Monte Carlo home, presumably for distribution to poorer missions in third world countries. Wasn't this the case in most nonprofit organizations? At least the poor, where my compassion always was, were receiving some of the money I made. Along with our required monthly tithe, we sometimes sent extra money to headquarters in Switzerland by American Express checks, made out to a name that we were given in our monthly correspondence.

We met our most generous givers at parties where Sharon and Breeze were commissioned to sing. At one of these parties I met Adnan Kashoggi again. We had been invited by Salim to sing for a small affair to be held in a private room in the Hôtel de Paris. By the way he described the event, I understood that we could flirt. I brought both Sharon and Breeze, and from the amount of money Salim gave me for the party, I knew this was important. It turned out to be a special dinner party for a rich Arab business associate of Salim, and his girlfriend. My experience had taught me that the presence of girlfriends had no bearing on anything. As soon as I entered the dark, paneled room, I recognized our honored guest as the famed Kashoggi from the Cannes party I had attended more than a year ago. His new girlfriend was a stunningly beautiful Italian. Kashoggi did not indicate that he had seen me before, but he was visibly impressed with our music and especially our message. He wanted to know what the lyrics meant, so I translated songs that were not in English for him.

Discussing the event afterward, we thought that Kashoggi had been making eyes at Sharon. However, when Salim met with me later that evening, he gave me surprising insight into the thoughts of the Arab billionaire.

"Adnan would like to know if Sharon is married," he said, when I arrived in his suite after midnight, as planned.

"Yes, she is," I answered. "However, she will be glad to spend time with him if he likes her."

"No. Adnan would not allow that to be," responded Salim gravely. "He will not willingly be with another man's wife."

"Is that because of his religion?"

"I cannot answer you truthfully. I have many friends who are Muslim, and this does not bother them. But Adnan will not do that."

"You know that I am still married," I said quietly, with my eyes averted. I was not sure if Salim had ever considered that fact.

"Of course I know. However, you have been separated from your husband for years, and he is living with another woman, who has his child."

"You know that?" I asked, surprised that Salim could remember details of my personal life with all the international business affairs he was involved in.

"Yes, I know more, too," he responded, looking deeply into my eyes. He broke into a warm smile. "And besides, I am not Muslim. I am Christian Lebanese, remember?"

"So, what did Adnan say? Was he interested in us?"

"Yes, he is very interested. He noticed that you and I pass forbidden glances to each other. He noticed that Sharon is a mother and a mother-to-be. He also notices that Breeze could be exciting in the bedroom."

"He can read people well," I said, amazed at the accuracy of judgment that Adnan achieved through such a brief contact.

"Of course, that is why he does so well in business. Do you think spirituality stops at the doors of religion?"

"Well, would he like Breeze to see him?"

"Yes. A chauffeur will come for her tomorrow night. Will she be at home?"

"I will make sure she is," I responded with my impresario authority. Of course, this transaction made me more of a madam than a manager, but it was for a good cause. Do the ends justify the means?

That is always the big question, and I had decided that sometimes it does not have a yes or no answer. It depends on *what* ends and *what* means. Witnessing to Adnan Kashoggi, who clearly had great influence over a large number of people, seemed comparable to the role of Queen Esther, in the Bible, given in marriage to a heathen king in order to eventually save her people. And as with Queen Esther, who was only one of many wives available to the king, Breeze was pursuing a good end. If she hadn't been sleeping with strangers while here in the Family, she would be doing it out in the world and might end up with a terrible disease. Or a broken heart. At least here, she was protected by God's Spirit.

Breeze began a long and prosperous relationship with Adnan that lasted for years. Every time she met with him for a few hours, she returned with wonderful testimonies of his spiritual growth, and an envelope stuffed with thousands of dollars. With both Adnan and Salim as regular fish, we would never have had financial worries again, had it not been for Timothy's economic plan.

Timothy suggested that we give everything left over at the end of the month, after paying bills, to World Services, whether it be a hundred dollars or a couple of thousand. I agreed. My motives were several. I thought that if I proved to be indispensable in providing large amounts of money to headquarters from my privileged position in Monte Carlo, I would not be asked to go to another mission. I liked being away from top leaders, isolated from homes where numerous brothers passed through wanting sex constantly. I had more liberty of movement and time than anyone else in the Family, and I was close to my son. I was in a perfect situation, and anything I could do to keep that situation just like it was would be fine with me.

Sharon, as usual, was in agreement with her husband. Breeze also consented, provided her own physical needs would be met first. Breeze looked after herself. Within a short period of time, Breeze had acquired an extravagant wardrobe, as well as the most expensive acoustic guitar that could be found. She convinced Timothy to give us each a "flee fund" of a couple of thousand dollars in case we had to escape from France quickly. Considering the illegality and volatility of our situation, this was a wise idea, and one condoned even by our leaders. So for the first time in my life, I had a personal stash of money kept hidden in my "flee bag" in case I needed to split abruptly. I asked for, and received, an extra allotment of flee funds for Thor.

Even with Breeze's constant requests for extras, and the high cost of living in Monte Carlo, we supplied World Services monthly with thousands of dollars. I never kept the books; therefore I cannot state with accuracy how much money flowed through our home to head-quarters. I do know that Breeze became known among the Arab bil-lionaires as a sexual stimulant, and she was constantly booked, hooking new fish along the way. Since we were not required to go by two on dates anymore, I never knew how much she actually wit-nessed about the Lord.

I knew, from testimonies I had heard in Paris, that Breeze was extremely sexually stimulated. But now that I was living with her, I became acutely aware of her unusual passions. Sharing a bedroom with an adjoining bath, I could hear Breeze unabashedly masturbating in the shower, and although at first I was embarrassed when I heard her moaning, I eventually rationalized that this was normal. It must be I who was abnormal. After all, Mo had written volumes on the virtues of masturbation, and how he had started it at an early age, despite his mother's fanatic disapproval. In his letter "My Childhood Sex," he wrote: "[My mother] brought in a washbasin, a little bowl and a knife and she told me she was going to cut it off! I was terrified. . . . I almost never forgave my mother for that, threatening to cut it off and embarrassing me in front of the family. But that didn't stop me. It felt too good to quit!" He encouraged all of us to share sexually when we needed to, and to masturbate when it was not possible to have sex. Since I considered my sexual relations as work for the Lord rather than as filling a personal need, I could not fully understand his perspective.

Listening to Breeze enjoying herself in the shower and bed, on the few nights we were home, I thought that perhaps she had a secret insight on sexuality. Obviously, the Arabs liked her. Although I was open to sexual experimentation, the stimulation came from my head, instead of my heart or body. I relied on fantasy and theory while in bed with the fish, and the enormous literature on sex and orgasms that I read in the letters was processed through my reasoning. I rarely felt what I would call pleasure, and I always avoided kissing the men. Sometimes one man would cause me to become more excited than usual, but when I tried to understand why, I could find no answer. There was not a special way or a look I liked, and I finally decided it was just extra love from God.

However, I felt that Breeze was privy to something I wanted to know. It was a curiosity aroused by intellectual rather than passionate desire. I approached Breeze on the subject one night under the influence of a considerable amount of alcohol. We had been talking with two American tourists who wanted to take us to bed, but whom we had decided were not the type of men we needed to give our bodies to. Instead, we spent the evening dancing, drinking, and dining with them, while they enjoyed our company, and we witnessed sparingly about the Lord.

Our friends finally left us in a popular all-night restaurant around three o'clock in the morning. They had an early plane to catch and had realized we were not going to accompany them to the hotel. Both Breeze and I were wide awake with coffee, but the alcohol and witnessing had left me psychologically vulnerable. I looked at Breeze's big brown eyes that seemed to hold a merry-go-round of joy and happiness. They sparkled brighter than the diamond studs she wore on her ears. In contrast, I thought, my pensive blue eyes portrayed a look that many of my more discerning fish called melancholy.

"What's your secret to enjoying sex?" I blurted out.

"You are a constant amazement to me, Jeshanah," said Breeze, her eyes jumping with gladness at my new interest in her. "I think that's why I love you so much."

"Of course, you love me," I responded, "whether I amaze you or not." I was always ready to take a statement to its most honest point, even if it meant I would lose it over the side of a cliff.

"I mean I love you more than a sister," murmured Breeze, her eyes still sparkling but her smile now gone.

I felt uncomfortable when Breeze stopped smiling abruptly. It usually meant she wanted something.

"Well, are you going to talk to me about sex or not?" I asked casually, taking a sip of my vodka and orange juice to support my pretense of aloofness.

"What do you want to know?" asked Breeze, sensing that I was becoming uncomfortable.

"You obviously do something to the fish that excites them more than most of the beautiful girls at their disposal. But, what I am really curious about, is why, with all the sex you get from men, why do you still masturbate?"

"Do you want the truth? Or maybe you want to keep us in this safe and careful arrangement you have created."

I felt nervous, as if a strong tentacle had wrapped itself around my heart, ready to squeeze the life out of me if I tried to unravel it.

"Tell me the truth, Breeze," I said boldly. "You know I always want truth."

"Except when it touches you personally," responded Breeze in what I knew was an insight of love.

"You want to love me as a sexual partner?" I asked, pretending to be objective.

"That and more," she said, for the first time showing a vulnerability I did not know she possessed.

"I just want to know how you get so turned on all the time," I said, changing the subject, since I did not want to go any further down that road. Breeze respected my decision.

"It's easier to show you than tell you," she said, the twinkle again returning to her eye.

"I don't know, Breeze. I've never been interested in lesbianism."

"Why not? Mo says it's wonderful for two women to satisfy each other sexually. Tell me the truth. Have you ever been satisfied by a man?"

"I don't know. I like being with certain men. What do you call satisfied?"

"I mean an orgasm. How many orgasms do you have when you make love?"

"You mean in all my life?" I answered with my voice cracking. Not only was this conversation becoming embarrassingly honest, but I felt the tentacle squeezing my heart.

"Oh, no!" cried Breeze, throwing her head back in a deep laugh. "I really meant every time you make love. But you answered that now. So, you hardly ever have an orgasm, do you?"

"I think I do," I said, feeling that the only way to find out was to discover what an orgasm meant to Breeze.

"I think you need a woman to touch you," she responded affectionately. "I want to touch you, Jeshanah, but you never let me."

Breeze had touched me very deeply without realizing. She had penetrated into a place I never even allowed myself—my deepest human emotions. Why was I so outwardly hot and inwardly cold? Why could I love my son with the depth of the universe, while I despised the one who made him possible? Why could I write poems of deep-felt love to my special fish, while knowing that every moan and move I made in the intimacy of the bedroom was an act, carefully rehearsed and so fully integrated that I forgot I was playing? Maybe Breeze held some kind of key.

"Are you asking me to make love with you?" I demanded.

"I am asking if I can make love to you, Jeshanah. I don't think you can make love to me, but maybe, I am hoping, you can learn."

What she said made me feel dirty. I had also felt dirty when I had lost my virginity to a boy who didn't even care about me. I felt dirty when I first made love to my husband. The only way I didn't feel dirty was if I detached my emotions from the act of lovemaking. I didn't know why. At first I thought that all women did it this way, and later I convinced myself that I was like this so I could be used by the Lord to love many men and not just one. Now Breeze was asking me to become emotionally engaged in each and every act, whereas disengagement was my most reliable survival mechanism. Those tentacles were so tight now I could feel my blood pumping uncontrollably.

"Okay, I'll sleep with you," I said, downing the rest of my drink.

A conflicting array of emotions seemed to cross Breeze's face. She seemed pleased at the prospect, but sad at my response.

"You don't have to," she said defensively.

I felt guilty for my lack of compassion and respect for her honesty. Mo had written that sex between women was God ordained, and although I no longer took Mo's opinions as the Divine Insight, I would consider the possibility that I was made to like women instead of men. But no, I didn't feel any emotion for Breeze, or any other woman, but sisterly love.

"Let's go home and see what happens," I suggested, hoping to gain wisdom with time and experience.

We arrived back at the home with everyone asleep. The last half glass of vodka that I had gulped down was now taking effect, and I let Breeze lead me to her bed like I let most of my fish take me without protest. But it wasn't the same. I didn't feel a reason to make love to her. I made love to men because I was either told to or believed I was "helping" them. No one told me to do this. There was also a social stigma attached to lesbianism, just as there was shame to prostitution. Lesbianism seemed to be propelled by human sexual desire on the part of both lovers, whereas prostitution usually involved one-sided desire. I fit much better into the prostitution model, where sexual desire on my part was not a necessary requirement. Sexual craving, even emotional desire for a partner in life, had been lost or forgotten by now, and my only desire was an abstract wish to serve others in love.

My fish were in need of God's Love. Our reasoning, which is not unlike some contemporary radical theory, is that women in the world give sex to men in exchange for something else, such as prestige, security, and support in a marriage situation, or money in prostitution. We supposedly gave sex to prove to these men that we loved them with God's Love, and although I eventually took money, the diversity of my experiences shows that money was not the primary motivation. Neither was desire! I could not find a reason to love Breeze sexually; after all, she had a huge reservoir of God's Love at her disposal. In addition, I felt no overwhelming emotional need, no sexual longing, and certainly no desire that could launch me into this new behavior.

"It's not going to work," I finally said. "I don't feel it, and this might ruin our relationship. I'm sorry, Breeze." I went back to my bed and fell into a deep sleep.

Had I the energy and mental development to analyze this incident at that time, I would have eventually wondered why I could have participated in sacred prostitution and not in lesbianism. Clearly, I did have some concept of my sexuality, however weak, even though I consider my years in Monte Carlo as the most spiritually lost time of my life. Years later, a young female member was rebuked publicly in a Mo letter for not providing sex to a sister who "needed" it, but by then I was beginning to consider my own wants and desires and less influenced by Mo. In Monte Carlo, I don't remember ever desiring anybody, and perhaps that is why I did so much for the Family at that time; however, had I been influenced by the previously mentioned Mo letter, "The Girl Who Wouldn't," when Breeze expressed desire for me, the story might have been different.

Breeze never mentioned the incident or tried to entice me in any way afterward. She continued to care for me like a concerned older sister. And even when the opportunity arose for us to be in bed together, it was Breeze who declined.

Salim invited me to dinner on my birthday—June 27, 1979. I was twenty-six years old. I met him at the suite, where he gave me a lovely Cartier necklace of flat gold links. Then we went to a Monagasque restaurant, the Bec Rouge, where Breeze, Sharon, Timothy, and Adnan had been invited to celebrate my birthday at a surprise party given by Salim.

Adnan gave me his present, a gold-chain Cartier necklace, bigger and much more expensive than Salim's. I put it on with Salim's already around my neck, but Salim told me they looked bad together, so I took Adnan's off. We had a lovely evening, my first and only birthday party in the Family. Salim asked Sharon to sing "Forbidden Games" for me, and then he had to leave to attend a social engagement with his wife. Adnan and Breeze sat next to each other, and he whispered something in her ear before he too had to go.

"Adnan wants both you and me to meet him in his hotel suite later," said Breeze when we were alone. We discussed it with Timothy, who thought that was okay, since Adnan was our biggest fish, but Sharon asked me what I thought. I was in seventh heaven because of the love and care I had received from both Adnan and Salim. I knew Salim was with his wife this evening, and I thought maybe he had set this up. It was okay with me.

Sharon and Timothy went home, and Breeze and I went to Adnan's suite. He was not there when we arrived, but she had a key. We sat in the luxurious living room, looking at each other in silence. I knew she was concerned about something.

"Do you really want to do this?" she asked.

"You don't want me to, do you?" I responded, wondering why not.

"No, I don't think it will be good for Adnan to start this kind of thing."

She said this with an expression that I intuitively read as "Please don't do it, I don't want you to." I never understood why, but I respected her choice.

"Okay. I'll write him a note saying that I am not staying because of my attachment to Salim. Does that sound legitimate?"

"Yes," said Breeze with a thankful smile. "I love you."

Adnan found my little note amusing, and he never asked me to be with him again. He sometimes poked fun at my romantic relationship with Salim. I thought that perhaps Salim had told him something

about us, but in retrospect, I think I always acted like I was romantically involved. Salim was my surrogate father, boyfriend, and lover.
For a short time, he fulfilled every male role that was lacking in my
life. All this from a man I never even kissed.

Now that we had the wealthiest fish in Monte Carlo, we could be
choosier as to whom we went to bed with. After Timothy and
Sharon's second baby was born, Breeze and I pretty much became our
own fishermen. We had been in Monte Carlo over two years now,
and we knew who were the locals and the passing tourists. The easy
criterion we had for all new fish was—if they don't stay in the Hôtel
de Paris they probably won't "need" sex. This line of reasoning was
consistent with Mo's emphasis on the rich being the most neglected
group of people spiritually. Of course, exceptions were made for those
who owned mansions on the Côte d'Azur, or had a yacht in the port,
but the tourists or passing casino players were usually only given a
verbal witness. For those who came back to Monte Carlo to see us
again, we sometimes gave a sample of God's Love with a date or one
night of sex. These were the ones who sometimes fell in love, until
they finally realized what we were doing.

Someone who held a possessive love for me was Leopoldo, a short,
stocky, balding, and very jovial Italian man who had inherited a title
and money from his family. Living in his own villa when he was in
Monte Carlo, he drove around in his flashy Rolls-Royce, which I
suspect bolstered a weak self-confidence. I engaged in a relationship
with him that lasted nearly two years. Although he was quite religious, very loving, and usually possessive, I never understood if he
really loved me or my spirit of recklessness.

Leo often took me to Rome with him on business trips. Sometimes
I took my son, Thor, and we would spend the days visiting the famous
Roman sights, such as the Piazza Espagna, the Coliseum, the Vatican,
and the Catacombs. These outings were an invaluable cultural experience for both of us, and I only worried that Thor, at six years old,
was too young to remember them.

During my solo trips to visit Leo in his Rome apartment, I spent
a lot of time witnessing to him. After making love, we read the Bible
together, and I explained our interpretation of various verses. Leo
seemed to really love the Lord, and he willingly asked Jesus into his
heart when I told him what this meant.

That night we were watching television in his bedroom in Rome.

Leo was a dedicated Catholic, but he had never read the Bible very much, so I had been sharing Bible passages with him for months. It was rather late and I had my Bible in my hands, reading verses out loud to him while he surfed the available TV stations. Finally, he switched off the TV and asked me what it meant to be saved.

There were many analogies I could have used, but I chose the one that I knew Leo could relate to best.

"It's like connecting to electricity," I answered. "Think of your life without electricity—no lights, no TV, no hot water. Having Jesus in your heart is like having electricity in your spiritual life."

"I'll do it," he said, seeming to be genuinely interested.

We held hands and he repeated after me a prayer that I had been taught since I was a little girl, and I had now repeated with hundreds of people.

"Jesus, I know I am a sinner and cannot have eternal salvation without you. Please forgive my sins. Come into my heart and set me free from sin."

This was my reward for giving up my life and body. The Bible said, and I believed, that this simple prayer and belief in Jesus was the way to salvation. If this was true, how could such a puny thing as giving sex limit me from leading a person to salvation? These busy, important men obviously needed the intimacy that a sexual relationship provides in order to open up to the message of Jesus' Love. And when someone like Leo sincerely asked Jesus into his heart, it provided me with the inspiration and motivation to keep giving.

Leo also asked me to accompany him on a vacation he was planning with some friends. I only found out at the airport that we were going to Bangkok, Thailand.

Until we arrived in Bangkok, I never really knew the level of wealth that Leo was accustomed to, and I thought a little less of him because of his seeming insensitivity to the extreme poverty at the doorstep of his lavish holiday home. Leaving the air-conditioned, plush-carpeted, and richly decorated hallways of the hotel, I stepped out into a typical Bangkok street, sweltering and humid and filled with noise, with entire families living on the sidewalks. Thailand is the country of silk and precious jewels, say the travel brochures, but I did not know, having lived so long in a bubble, that it also attracted tourists looking for sex and cheap prostitutes.

My bubble burst as I walked the streets of Bangkok. In some areas, little girls would run up to us and pull at my skirt or Leo's pants, asking us to take them to bed for "ten dollar only," showing us ten fingers. Sometimes it was young boys who asked. One night Leo and his friends took me to a show far out in the country. The parking lot around an old warehouse was crowded with rental cars and taxis. Inside, there was a center stage that looked like a boxing ring, and around it were hundreds of seats filled with Westerners of both sexes. Young Eastern-looking girls were performing sexual antics. I was so disgusted I put my head in my hands and started to cry. Leo took me back to the hotel.

I was happy and relieved to get back to my home and family in our humble little Beausoleil house. My relationship with Leo was never the same after this trip, and I was beginning to doubt our spiritual influence on these men.

We had become so well-known among the night crowd in Monte Carlo that regular clients at Jimmy'z sometimes called and asked if any of the "sisters of Jesus" were there. Whoever answered the phone knew exactly who they meant and would come to our table with a message. Despite what this situation might look like, everyone deeply involved with us overcame their initial suspicions of our motives and began to accept that we were doing this for God.

I also began to believe that too much money was going to pay for our leaders' private apartments, and not enough was going to the poor mission fields. After my horrific insight into the life of poor people in Thailand, I contacted a home we had there and discovered that they worked with Cambodian refugees. Without telling Timothy, I started a fund-raising campaign to collect money specifically for the Cambodian refugee mission. I sent personal letters to my fish and informed them that I was raising money for this work, promising that 100 percent of the money would go to the mission in Thailand. I collected several thousand dollars and sent it to the Thailand home, and then immediately started another fund-raiser for one of our homes in India. Of course, I was soon found out by Timothy, who had been contacted by the leaders, and although they openly complimented me for my initiative, I was told that all collections and funds are proc-essed through World Services and I should follow that God-approved procedure. That ended my short career as a legitimate fund-raiser, but it was another step toward establishing my independence. I had done something in direct contradiction to the rules, and I wasn't

My father, John Fred Williams, in one of the few
photographs that I have of him, taken around 1949.
My father had not yet met my mother.

My mother, Elfriede Seeger
Williams, in a photo taken in
the late forties while she was
working at a German news-
paper in Philadelphia.
Shortly afterward, she would
meet my father.

Before my family moved out west from Philadelphia, my grandparents snapped this photo of me. I was two years old.

In 1956, my family was living in Venice Beach, California. My mother is holding my sister Marlene. I'm in the center, alongside my brother, Steve.

My high school senior picture. I graduated from McCaskey High School in Lancaster, Pennsylvania, in 1971. At this point, I was seeing my sister's teacher and had stopped hanging out with the "hippie" crowd at school.

Wedding day for Cal and me in the summer of 1972 at the Ellenville camp in upstate New York. Cal, the drummer in Jeremy Spencer's band, is twenty, and I am nineteen. The long skirt I am wearing was standard for a woman in the Children of God—the bare feet must be attributed to my rebellious streak. The entire camp was present for the "ceremony." Cal and I wouldn't get married officially until I was nine months pregnant with Thor, about one year later.

The nursery of the Essen, Germany, colony. Thor, less than a year old, is in the arms of a nursery worker. The conditions of this particular nursery were quite good by Children of God standards—some colonies did not even have money for cribs at that time. There are Scriptures written on the chalkboards in the background. We were required to memorize two a day.

Cal, Thor, and I appeared on the cover of *New Nation News!*, the Children of God newsletter. While we lived in Paris, photos were always being taken of us. On the outside, we must have looked like well-adjusted models of happiness. Sharing, threesomes, and flirty fishing were to come.

One of the first publicity shots of Les Enfants de Dieu, taken in the
Massif Centrale in France. I'm standing sixth from the right and Cal is
standing third from the left. Also shown are Jeremy Spencer of Fleetwood
Mac; my dance partner, Jon; my busking partner, Nahum; Hopie; Esther;
Micah; James; and Ruth. Timothy, Sharon, and Breeze would come into
the Show Group later, although Breeze's husband, Abraham, was present
here.

I'm posing with Mara (*left*) at
the port of Monte Carlo in
1978. Mara had officially,
according to COG standards,
become another wife to Cal at
this point. Ironically, people
were always telling us that we
looked alike.

Here I'm standing between Sharon (*left*) and Breeze in our Beausoleil home. The three of us were quite a force as flirty fishers. Our home contributed thousands of dollars to the Children of God World Services.

Moses David (*with beard*), also known as David Berg, and his mistress, Maria (*to his right*), surrounded by the Tenerife flirty fishing colony in 1977. Popular magazines like Germany's *Stern* besieged the small island with photographers and reporters. Moses David was forced to flee after the scandal hit the press.

GOD'S WHORES?

BY MOSES DAVID

COVER BY EMAN ARTIST
EDITED AND COMPILED BY JUSTUS ASHTREE

D.O.M.L
No.560

Illustration from the Mo letters, dated April 26, 1976. Many controversial teachings were in this pamphlet, among them the idea that husbands should show their love for God by willingly sending their wives to bed "fish," and the idea that female members of the Family were whores of God. Moses David wrote, "He's [God's] going to *put* so much love in your heart for them [fish] that you're going to *want* to *take* them to bed . . ." (#560:24). Later he said, "God is a pimp!" (#560:27).

Here I am at the Beausoleil home. Although I was part of an FFing house, I always felt that I was doing these acts for God, or a higher cause.

In Perpignan, near the Spanish Basque border, in the summer of 1983. I'm breast-feeding Genvieve, and Thor is ten years old. After the kidnapping and recovery of Thor, I tried to visit him as often as possible.

Charles took this picture of my family, in Liguria, Italy. I'm standing behind Genvieve (*left*) and Athena, holding Jordan. This was one of the busiest times of my life, and I often felt I was living on faith alone. I had no car and had to go out singing every night from 7 P.M. to midnight to earn money. And there were two nursing babies to attend to.

I'm with Thor at a 1995 blues festival in the South. At the time, Thor was living with me. He's now a graduate student in mathematics in Germany.

kicked out or struck by lightning, and my son wasn't taken away from me! Without the fear of immediate punishment, I had gained ground over my own soul.

Although I could fall in and out of "love" with the ease and detachment with which I changed my clothes, sometimes I had a brief belief in the old myth that "this might be the one." Spyros, a plump, darkly handsome, young Greek man, gave me the faint feeling that romance still clung to me like old cobwebs in the attic.

Spyros associated with the cool crowd whom we avoided, which included Prince Napoleon (the pet name we had now given André) and the ex-Beatle Ringo Starr. Breeze and I were at an empty Jimmy'z one evening when their crowd walked in, and we wound up sitting together. I did not feel that anyone in the group was ready for a message, but when I danced with Spyros, I sensed a deep melancholy. No one told me who this quiet young man was. I imagined that he was the friend of one of the men in the crowd. He seemed so shy and self-deprecating, I could not picture him raised as a rich kid.

When we were invited to join them at a private party over at the Hôtel de Paris, we agreed. Unfortunately, it turned out to be a pot party, and since we never took drugs, although we were accused of doing so, Breeze and I became nervous. Spyros noticed that I didn't smoke any pot, and asked if I took other drugs. Of course, this gave me the perfect opportunity to tell him about the Most High—Jesus. His friends laughed, but Spyros listened intently, asking questions and showing interest in my answers about the spiritual world. We talked till the morning, and after his friends left, one of them with Breeze, I joined Spyros in the adjoining bedroom. I was surprised to find that this suite in the Hôtel de Paris belonged to him.

Maybe it was the hazy smoke rings that had engulfed the room during the night, and which I could not help but breathe in, but I had visions of Spyros being reeled into the Family. He was so interested in what I had said about God and the Kingdom. He seemed to be quite sad and discontented with the life he was living, and I thought that perhaps he was not really part of the superrich, but had only stumbled into their path to be used for a while, like they sometimes did with their lowly entourage. I could be his savior from a life of purposelessness.

However, my spiritual reverie was shattered when we made love. For reasons I could never understand rationally, I enjoyed it immensely. This disproved my theory that because I took my sexual role more spiritually than did the other girls, I did not experience orgasm.

But with Spyros that night, it was different. He struck a chord that had not been touched for a long time. I often thought about why this happened on that particular night, because it never happened again with the same intensity. Maybe it was the pot in the air, or maybe someone had slipped me something, although I doubt both of those reasons. There was nothing particularly special about Spyros or what he did either. Also, Spyros was the first male of my age whom I had been with in a long time; he was outside the Family, and I did not think of him as a "rich fish." These factors combined might have allowed me a brief repose from my inhibiting, missionarylike hold on my emotions.

I awoke before he did, and with the light peeking in through the thick, tightly closed curtains, I looked for a piece of paper on which to write him the note that might start him on the path toward God's Kingdom. There on the desk, among other paraphernalia from the evening, was the necklace he had taken off before getting in bed. Holding it toward a small stream of light, I read the inscription. My dream shattered and joined the invisible particles that glittered in the light like diamonds of dust, for the name on the medallion told me that Spyros was no ordinary rich boy; he was the son of one of the wealthiest and most famous Greek families in the world, the Niarchoses. I suddenly realized that for Spyros to forsake all and follow God would *not* be like a camel going through the eye of the needle; it would be more like trying to split an atom with a butter knife. The soul of such a one, raised in the oppressor's world without an inkling of the People's reality, would take a lifetime, perhaps a few lifetimes, to come to a desire for the Truth. This is what I thought— not what Mo taught. Our intentions for Kashoggi, a much older man, had always been that he would be a "king," one who helped our group financially while we ministered to him spiritually. I had been hoping that Spyros would become a disciple, but now, knowing of his extreme wealth, I had no hope for that. Some of my early, radical training suddenly resurfaced. I didn't put this thought into words; that would be sacrilegious in our religion, because God's Spirit could perform miracles on anyone. But I dropped the idea of fishing Spyros into the Family and accepted that if nothing else, at least he got witnessed to.

Spyros remained a friend, and although he proved to be the epitome of the spoiled rich kid, he still had a humble attitude to anyone who seemed to have more inner strength than he. If I ever saw him in a club or restaurant, I walked over, said hello, and usually sat down to meet the people at his table. Poor Spyros was so well educated in etiquette, yet he never knew what to do when he saw me. One evening I asked Breeze to sing him a song that she had written, which I thought appropriate for Spyros. He was sitting with Ringo that night. Breeze started her song, and Ringo made unflattering remarks. Finally, without listening to the words that Breeze was singing, Ringo started mimicking Breeze, but interspersing words like "We love you Spyros, because you are so rich."

"You are such a fool!" I screamed at him, terribly hurt that he would make fun of Breeze. "Why don't you just shut up and listen to the words? You might learn something, having never written a good song yourself."

Ringo laughed ridiculously, but Spyros was offended by my outburst. He took me aside and said that I could not talk like that to Ringo.

"Why not?" I asked, still angry that Ringo had questioned our motives and laid them on the same low level as his own might have been.

"Well, because of who he is. Who do you think you are to talk that way to him?"

"Who does he think he is to talk that way to God's servants?" I retorted.

I was always sorry for Spyros after that evening. I realized now beyond a shadow of a doubt the inverse relationship between material and spiritual riches. I was getting a little sick of all this decadence myself.

Life was not always heavenly living in God's Kingdom within the world's kingdom. I usually drank more than I ate, and when I was completely sober, I sometimes cried myself to sleep. Even though both Sharon and Breeze loved me more than anyone had ever loved me in my life, I knew that if I was not loyal to the Family, I would lose that love immediately. Once I locked myself in the bathroom, sobbing because I felt no one understood me, and I only came out, in shame, after everyone assured me that they also felt that way sometimes. Even so, I knew I was different. When top leaders came by our home,

I shunned them, fearing to be in their revealing light, which exposed my every evil doubt.

Just as the process of internalizing Mo's doctrine of sexual sharing and sacred prostitution had been gradual, so my reawakening was an extremely slow process. Accepting the Family's values was made much easier because everyone around me, even my husband, accepted them, but discovering my own concept of morality was so much more difficult since I was basically on my own. I had rejected the world's conventional moral standards, which seemed hypocritical to me, but if I did not embrace the Family's, what did I have? I was just beginning to think that I might find, on my own, a universal morality, but the thought was frightening, and terribly lonely. Of course, there were probably many others in the Family who at times had similar thoughts, including my own husband though he didn't tell me. No one shared such thoughts. We were conditioned to believe that they were of the devil. They would lead you out of the Family! And we were right—if you kept thinking that way, you left!

By the winter of 1979–80, we could feel that things were winding down. No one could express what was happening, but there was a general feeling of change around the corner.

One morning I came home to hear that Sharon, now pregnant with her third baby, had been kept all night in the Monte Carlo police station. She had been picked up while she was waiting for Breeze in the Loews Hotel lobby. Searching her guitar case, the police found copies of Mo letters, among them the controversial anti-Israeli literature.

These were the letters predicting the invasion of Israel by a united Arab front and condemning the Western world for supporting Israeli expansion. There were many people of Jewish origin in our group, and we understood these letters as ire against the "state" of Israel, not Jews themselves; however, they were considered by those outside the group as evidence of an anti-Semitic stance. We understood Mo's allegiance with Qaddafi as a means to provide us with inside connections to an eventual "Antichrist government." Whether we did not want to jeopardize our good standing with the Arabs, or whether Mo actually changed his views on the Jews, is still a debate. In any case, the accusation of being anti-Semitic was never addressed by our leaders, many of whom were Jewish themselves.

The police questioned Sharon, fingerprinted her, and sent her home in the morning with instructions that she should not return to Monaco. She was told to send the rest of us down to the station for questioning.

We decided to obey police orders; it sounds odd that we had to consider this, but we had lived outside the world's rules and regulations for so long that only Family orders mattered. Timothy went first, so that Sharon would not be left alone with the children. After he returned, Breeze and I went. The officers seemed amused when we walked in. After waiting the obligatory time so that we understood who was in control and how much respect they had for us, we were given mug shots, fingerprinted, and then questioned separately. I was questioned by an older, more mature officer who looked like he never told jokes.

"We know of your every move here in Monaco, ever since you came three years ago," he said, glaring at me as if I had tried to hide my whereabouts from him.

"I'm sure you do," I replied. "I always knew that Monaco had excellent undercover police."

"I have documents of every hotel you have been in, madam," he said, ignoring my compliment.

"Well, then. I am sure you also have the names of other girls besides us. Are they being kicked out too?"

"You better not be smart with me," he responded angrily.

"You told me we are put on the Interpol files and we should leave Monte Carlo and never come back, yet you are not asking us anything about the men we have been with. What's the real reason?"

"This," he said, holding up the Mo letters. "We don't want trash like this in Monaco."

I understood. They could avert their attention from drugs, and stolen money, and high-class prostitution, but political consciousness was too dangerous to bring into Monte Carlo. They probably knew that we had both Jewish and Arab friends, and if we promoted literature like this, we could start a war here.

However, they did not realize they had nothing to fear. First of all, Sharon, Breeze, and I were much too politically naive to subvert anyone. Furthermore, the superrich were much too concerned about wealth and power to become involved in international affairs on the basis of idealism. There was no money in it. But I believe the Monte Carlo Police thought they were ridding Monaco of subversive influences.

Back at home, after praying and discussing the matter, we came to the conclusion that all good COG members come to when change happens—it must be the Lord's Will! We had been ordered to never set foot in Monaco again, and advised to leave France also, since our visas were long expired. We had kept a three-month visitor's visa for years by crossing the Italian border every few months to receive a stamp. It didn't fool anyone. But I was worried about what it meant for Thor and me.

Within a few days, our whole team had been invited to join the home in Athens, Greece, where the Family was starting a new music ministry. I wasn't personally interested in moving there, and I also feared that Cal would never let me take Thor so far away.

I went to visit Cal's home and explained our situation. He was at a loss as to what to do. Mara and he were very happy in Antibes with the other singing couple. Thor was doing well in school and was already speaking French fluently. What was I going to do?

That night, as I tucked Thor into bed, my heart began breaking a little more. There was no way in the world I could ever leave him again. It seemed like there were only two options open to me: go to Athens, which meant leaving Thor, and was therefore out of the question; or reconcile with my legal husband, Thor's father. I knocked on Cal and Mara's door.

"Can I come in and talk to you?" I asked quietly.

Cal opened the door and came out alone.

"Mara's sleeping already," he whispered. "What did you want? Can't it wait till the morning?"

"No," I said, feeling the tears coming. "I'll do whatever you want, Cal. But please, let me stay with Thor." I burst into uncontrollable sobs, instinctively knowing that all was too late.

"What do you mean by staying with Thor? When you left me, you left Thor too. You understand that, don't you?"

"Yes. I know that now," I said in between sobs. "But I'm sorry. I'm sorry for leaving you. It was wrong of me. I admit it. I should have stayed. I am so evil and selfish."

The thought of not being near Thor was so dreadful that I was ready to live as a second-class wife, not even have a relationship at all with Cal, as long as I could stay here. I was in a bad situation, and all I had ever learned was that it must be my fault. It was a black-and-white explanation, but it was all I could think at that time.

"I wish you would have realized that earlier," mumbled Cal under his breath.

"I do, too. I am so—so—sorry," I cried, with huge heaving sounds now. "What can I do? I will make it up to you. I will do whatever you say from now on. Please let me stay here. I don't want to go to Greece."

Cal put his hand on my back as I buried my face in my hands, trying to muffle the sounds of my heart being pummeled into a bleeding pulp.

"I will have to talk to Mara about that. I would agree to you living here, but I have to respect her wishes also."

Cal left me on the couch alone, and I cried a flood of tears, nearly drowning in the depth of despair. Finally, I raised myself from the couch and floated to Thor's room as if an angel were carrying me. I lay down beside him, holding his six-year-old body close to mine, and hoping I would die before I woke up.

The next morning, I knocked on Cal's door while Thor ate his cereal.

"Come in," he called.

He was sitting at the desk already with a cup of coffee, obviously with something heavy on his mind.

"Mara doesn't think that would be a good idea," he said sadly.

"What can I do then?" I asked, dumbfounded but having expected this in the back of my mind.

"You can stay here temporarily, if you need to. But eventually you will have to find another home." Cal seemed truly empathetic. He assured me that I still had visitation rights. Now all I needed was to find another home nearby.

I walked back into the kitchen as if nothing had happened, took my coffee, and asked Thor if he wanted to go to the park. Obviously, reconciliation with my legal husband was not a viable option. Overpowered by my desire to be near my son, I had to come up with another plan.

Later that day, I returned to our Beausoleil home and had an unexpected visit from my friend Paolo, a handsome Italian who had picked us up hitchhiking one night. He lived right across the Italian border, and I had been to his house a few times. Paolo, who was far from being rich, lived by himself, and he seemed terribly lonely. Since I first met him, I thought he might become friends of the Family, or even join one day, although neither Timothy nor Breeze thought he was "sheepy."

I had felt that there was something special about Paolo when I first witnessed to him, despite the dreariness that he carried around and threw into the atmosphere like the Sandman sprinkled sleep. Breeze told me he satisfied the aspects that she thought were necessary for my ideal type of man: shoulder-length brown curly hair, expressive eyes, and a huge chip on the shoulder. I laughed off this assessment, but the fact that he was here at my house waiting, just when I was desperately trying to decide what I would do in the immediate future, seemed more than a coincidence to me. I thought that perhaps he was sent to help me during this difficult time. He was thirty-three years old, just the age of Jesus when he was crucified. Perhaps Paolo was ready to die to himself and start a new spiritual life. In my confused state of mind, I confided my situation to Paolo that night.

"I don't want to go. I want to stay here to be near my son," I told him at last.

"Oh!" he said, a man of few words. I thought he might appreciate it if I got right to the point.

"Can I live with you?"

He looked at me with what I thought was fear in his eyes.

"That might be difficult!" he said.

"Why? Do you have a girlfriend in Italy?" Whenever I was at his small apartment, I saw no signs of another woman's presence.

"No!"

"Well, what's the matter? I won't stay long, if you don't want me to."

"I'll think about it," he said and left.

Paolo said he would come by the next evening, but he never showed up. Nervous and frustrated, and not knowing where to turn except for the Family, I was at the end of my rope. I had to call him.

"Why didn't you come?" I demanded, secretly fearing that he was my last hope to stay near my son.

"I don't feel good," he replied.

"Do you have a fever?" I asked.

"No," he said and was silent.

"What's wrong?" I asked again, pressing for a response.

"I can't drive."

"What do you mean you can't drive? You drive here all the time. Is your car broken?

"No!"

"What is it, Paolo? You can trust me." I sensed fear in his voice—great fear.

"I am here to help you," I continued. "God loves you, Paolo, and He sent me to help you."

"I can't drive when I feel like this."

"Feel like what?"

"Feel like I am going to die."

His voice sounded distant—worlds away. I knew he was in deep trouble. I had heard about depression before, but we had never acknowledged any medical basis for this disease. I was sure he needed the Lord.

"I'll be right over," I said. "I'll take the next train."

Realizing that I could actually be helping Paolo by him helping me better supported my crazy idea to live at his house. With absolutely no doubt that I was needed, I had no fear for personal safety, even though I had known Paolo for only a month.

I packed my bags and made the half-hour train trip and ten-minute bus ride to his home. It was late at night, but I felt safe in the small, sleepy Italian village nestled at the foot of the Piedmont mountains.

Paolo, I found out, had been taking tranquilizers for years. He was now up to five or six a day, but even so, he sometimes was afraid to get out of bed. I couldn't understand this fear, but I knew that God could help him. I stayed with Paolo that night and the next day, witnessing to him about God's love and power, and reading the Bible with him. He agreed to try to stop using tranquilizers. He also agreed to my coming to live with him.

When I told Timothy my plans, he was not happy.

"What are you going to do in some godforsaken Italian village? You will be so bored there, not to mention the waste of God's time and talent."

"What talent do I have? I can't sing or play an instrument very well. All they want me for in Athens is to have an extra available girl."

Timothy looked hurt. Perhaps he wasn't sure what he would be doing in Athens either.

"I think she would like to stay near her son," interrupted Sharon. "I believe that is a good reason. If she can win Paolo, well, praise the Lord!"

"You can't spend the rest of your life following Cal and Thor around," said Timothy. "Besides, I'm sure God will give Thor back once you forsake him in your heart."

I flinched at his words, and Sharon nudged Tim with her elbow.

"I think you're making a good decision," she said. "And we will always have a place for you in our home."

Breeze couldn't imagine my staying with a nobody like Paolo, who owned a pet store. Breeze might have understood me emotionally, but she didn't know the diehard idealism that flourished where love should have been. Besides my desire to be near Thor, I thought that Paolo needed the Family at this time of his life, and I would rather take care of a sheep than be around bossy shepherds.

I told Cal the news about moving in with Paolo. Since I would not have much to do all day, or so I thought, I could come and stay with Thor as much as I wanted. Cal expressed concern about my future, but I assured him that I really "loved" Paolo, and I thought I could bring him into the Family. The more I told people about Paolo becoming a Child of God, the more I convinced myself. Before I moved in with him, I had told myself that bringing in a disciple would be the masterwork of the Monte Carlo days. After all the money we had made, the parties we had attended, the men who had asked Jesus into their hearts while lying naked in bed with us, this was the coveted crown—winning an eternal soul and body into God's Kingdom. It was a dreadful reasoning!

9

○ ○ ○

Crossroads

It was a cold January evening in 1980, my first night as a resident in Paulo's small apartment, located on a cobblestone road in a tiny Italian village. I was completely isolated from anything or anyone familiar. The apartment had a small living room, a bedroom, a kitchen, and a bath, and was more than five hundred years old. Paolo had remodeled every room and installed central heating, a luxury in this small town. I had been in so many homes that were not mine, I did not find my new predicament unusual. Cognizant of the reality in my life that nothing lasts very long, I was enjoying my new independence. Except for being physically dependent on Paolo, emotionally dependent on access to Thor, and spiritually guided by the Mo letters, I could pretty much do as I pleased.

The first thing I took advantage of was listening to Paolo's music collection of early rock and roll, hard rock, and many of the bands I had missed during the 1970s and 1980s. When Paolo came home that first day, I turned the music off, conditioned to feel guilty about doing what I liked to do. However, since Bob Dylan had recently been saved, the whole Family was listening to his Christian songs now, and Paolo bought Dylan's Bible-based records for me. They were the first worldly recordings I had owned in ten years.

I had just turned off the stereo, and Paolo was now pacing back and forth between the bedroom and the bathroom, where his tranquilizers were sitting abandoned in the medicine cabinet. He had agreed not to take any more tranquilizers once I moved in, and I had spent most of the evening praying for him every time he wanted to go to the medicine cabinet. It was late at night, the neighbors had all already turned off their lights, but Paolo could not get to sleep. Trying to substitute Jesus for tranquilizers, I spent hours reading the Bible aloud to him and praying. But he still could not sleep. I followed him out to the living room and sat down on the couch in the dark. The only light came from a lamp in the bedroom that shone through the open door.

"Paolo, come here and sit beside me," I called to him as he paced past the bathroom door.

"I don't want to," he snapped.

"I think you should pray this time, Paolo. I always pray for you, but if you pray for yourself, it will have more power."

Paolo looked at me with what seemed like hatred. Normally, he appeared slightly disturbed in a gentle way, but he now wore an aggressive glare. I was apprehensive, but I returned his glare without breaking contact. I saw more fear in his eyes than I felt in my own heart. I told myself that I was safe.

"I want you to pray, Paolo," I repeated with a firm voice.

He turned around and stalked into the kitchen at the end of the hall. As he lingered there in the dark, for about twenty minutes, I quickly went over in my mind the various scenarios that could take place here in this isolated apartment in this deserted town where no one knew me and I couldn't even speak Italian. I said my own prayers silently, knowing that faith could overcome any obstacle.

When Paolo finally returned, his distraught face looked as if he had been through hell. He fell to his knees and bent his head down, as Catholics are taught to do when they pray.

"I don't know how to pray," he said after a few minutes had passed in silence.

"Say what is on your heart," I suggested.

"Help me, God. *Aiutami, aiutami,*" he kept repeating in Italian.

After what seemed like a very long time, he got to his feet. His face looked better, and he seemed tired but content. Evidently the prayer had dispelled the hold of the tranquilizers, and I breathed a sigh of relief.

Looking into his eyes again, I saw he had something to tell me. "What is it?" I asked.

"Do you want to know?"

"Yes, I need to know."

"Will you leave me if I tell you?"

"No. I won't leave."

"When you told me to pray," he began apprehensively, "I heard a voice in my head. It said to kill you. While I was in the kitchen the voice told me to take a butcher knife and come in here and kill you."

"Is that why you went into the kitchen?" I said, goosebumps rising on my arms at the thought of what he could have done.

"I wasn't going to do it," he responded defensively. "I think I went into the kitchen so the voice would stop. I went in there to get away from you because the voice did not like you."

"My spirit is much more powerful than that puny voice," I said, remembering Mo letters that told us how the devil tries to scare us when he knows he has already been beaten. I pictured an enormous, powerful angel on my side and a shriveled, bent-over little demon whispering into Paolo's ear. Now I was sure that Paolo would come into the Family. Even the devil knew it, and he was making his last stand.

I succeeded in helping Paolo substitute faith for his addiction to drugs and therapy. I did not feel a sense of power over Paolo after this; instead, I felt an enormous burden of responsibility. I was now his spiritual mother. I had to nurture him, feed him, protect him, and educate him until he was mature enough to be on his own. It was as if I had been through a difficult birthing experience, and the baby had been born alive, but traumatized. Tired as I was after giving birth, I knew that the hard work had just begun.

Convincing Paolo to forsake all, a Family requirement in order to join, took time. Paolo was by nature selfish, stingy, and possessive. Not only did he not want to share me, he didn't like the idea of giving up his coveted worldly possessions. Paolo pampered himself with fashionable clothes, comfortable furniture, and good food. He had a huge double closet full of the latest Italian fashions and dozens of shoes. I used to laugh to myself that my clothes took up only about one-tenth the space that his clothes did.

Paolo was also not willing to share his money. I brought my flee fund money with me, and to provide an example of true communal actions, I deposited the whole amount, about two thousand dollars, into his savings account. However, Paolo insisted I come to work with him at the pet shop every day, and although he gave me money to shop for food, I never had any spending money of my own. One evening, as we passed the only jewelry shop in the town, Paolo pointed out a gaudy gold cross with Jesus on it and indicated that he would like to wear a cross now that he was a Christian. I offered him one of my Cartier necklaces, suggesting that he ask the jewelry shop owner to make a trade. Even though I was unaware of the value of the Cartier at that time, I knew it was worth much more that the cross. In the back of my mind, I thought that maybe Paolo would surprise me by exchanging my Cartier for a cross for him and a ring, or necklace, for me. When he showed up with only the cross, and said that the shop owner had given him nothing else, I was disappointed, but I dashed these thoughts from my mind. Anything I could do to show Paolo God's true love was worth it.

Paolo's mother lived nearby. His father, a Calabrese, had deserted her with two small sons when Paolo was very young. She supported them by working as a nurse, but as a typical Italian mother, she spoiled her boys, giving them everything they wanted. She came over every morning, after Paolo had gone to work, to make his bed, clean his house, and take his laundry. In the evening, she brought a warm dinner over for him, or he ate at her house.

As I began my household duties, I thought of what Timothy had told me about wasting God's talent. He was against my living with Paolo, and he still wanted me to come and live in Athens with them. But living with Paolo served many grand purposes: It was helping Paolo break his dependence on legal drugs, giving him a goal in life; it gave me a place to live so I would not have to go to Athens, which would break my connection with Thor and perhaps with my own soul; and it took me from the detached experience of loving many men to learning to love one man.

Meanwhile, I took the three-hour round trip on the train and bus every weekend to pick up Thor. My son integrated well into the

Italian country life, camping out with us and going fishing; however, Paolo, who was the poorest conversationalist I have ever met, was even less talkative with children. There is a Bible verse that says "a man who keeps quiet is esteemed wise," and I thought that perhaps Paolo had deep thoughts. As time went on, I discovered that he just had nothing to say.

A few times I floated the idea of bringing Thor to live with us, but Paolo was averse to the idea. He said it was better for Thor to be with his father. Meanwhile, I had completely changed my own lifestyle for Paolo. I was now a dutiful housewife with a good sleeping schedule, regular meals, and lots of rest. Within a few months, I became pregnant. Even though I had not practiced birth control throughout the years of offering myself, I had never become pregnant. Therefore, to be having Paolo's baby was further proof to me that he was a disciple. In retrospect, I was just taking better care of my body.

All full-time disciples sent 10 percent of their monthly income into the COG headquarters in Switzerland, but since Paolo did not want to do this, we were put on the lowest status. That meant simply that we did not receive the "Disciples Only" (DO) letters, and we needed permission to visit Family homes. Of course, Cal never tried to enforce this rule, and I could go and come freely at his house, but otherwise, I was estranged from the COG. Sharon, Tim, and Breeze wrote to me from Greece, inviting me to come if I found out Paolo was not a sheep, and to bring him if he was. I could do neither. Now that I was pregnant, I would have to do my best to keep him connected to the Family, even if it meant living with him apart from a Family home.

The new Family rule, according to the latest letters, was that if a baby resulted from relationships with a fish, it was God's way of showing that the fish was worthy. Therefore, the bait (me) must stay with that fish and keep him close to God's Family. Nothing was mentioned about love except that God can give you the love you need. For many years I waited and believed that love was coming. Sometimes I even fooled myself that love was there, that I just had to acknowledge it. Years later, I heard the cynical words of a Dylan song, "Love is just a four letter word," and I thought how true that was in my life. But for now, my time was absorbed with teaching Paolo how to be a Child of God, and I had no time for inner-self thoughts.

Unfortunately, my student was not a willing learner. He, at the same time, was trying to teach me how to be a typical, subservient Italian wife. The first day I went to work in his shop, he yelled at me for arriving late. He let me do all the dirty work, such as picking huge ticks out of the infested country farm dogs and sweeping the dirty dog hair away from his grooming area. After working in the luxury of Monte Carlo for three years, it was quite a change for me, but I had learned to be content in whatever situation I found myself in my service to the Lord.

Paolo was nicer to me after I became pregnant, and his mother, who had long ago resigned herself to her station in life as a single abandoned mother, was the epitome of self-sacrifice. She took it upon herself to train me in her image and likeness: how to shop daily from store to store, picking up the freshest pieces of meat and vegetables, making pasta from scratch, sewing curtains, crocheting baby clothes (she tried to teach me to knit but I have always been afraid to have knitting needles around children), hanging up pretty curtains. I followed her respectfully, but without enthusiasm. What I really planned was to get Paolo and me into a Family home somewhere as soon as possible.

In the spring of 1980, Cal informed me that he and Mara were going to go back to America. Almost everyone who had been in Europe for a while was encouraged to go on to other mission fields like the Far East or South America. First they would have to go to America and raise funds. Mara was pregnant with her second child, and since I was also, Cal thought it might be a good idea for us to get divorced so that we could marry our new mates. I discussed this with him at length, and we planned on meeting in America, and then going together to a mission field and starting a home consisting of Cal, Mara, their little girl, Thor, Paolo, me, and our new babies. That would keep Thor with both of us, and I liked the idea of having help in training Paolo to be a disciple. All I had to do was convince Paolo to move to America.

Paolo had already been to America when he had worked on cruise ships. He was not interested in returning. He was more interested in going to Canada or South America, since he had never been to those places. I explained that first we needed to get married, which meant I had to get divorced, which was easiest accomplished in America.

He seemed to agree. Assured that I would be following soon, I agreed to Thor going with his dad to the States ahead of me.

Cal left with Thor before the summer, and I promised to help pay for the divorce. He handled the whole procedure in New York, where his parents lived. Meanwhile, Paolo and I were to start gathering funds to leave and meet them when summer ended.

As the summer months passed, Paolo seemed less interested in leaving. I pleaded with him to put the shop up for sale as he had promised, and although he kept saying he would, he did nothing. Finally, in November, seven months pregnant, I gave him an ultimatum.

"Paolo, we agreed on a plan before Thor left," I reminded him. "I trusted you. I never would have let Thor leave if you had told me you were not sure."

"You can't do anything about Thor anyway," he replied. "You gave Cal custody of Thor."

His words jolted me out of my delusional fantasy. Pathetically, I had not counted on Cal asking for full legal custody, which he had done once in America, but I had continued to have faith in the plan. Now, it became clear to me that even Paolo was ready to betray my trust in him. I had given Cal custody in order to obtain an uncontested divorce. That was the only way that he would do it, and with him in America, with Thor in his possession, there was little I could do. The divorce papers also said that I had deserted them. I complained about this statement, but Cal said he had to give some excuse for getting divorced. Paolo, the only other person I ever talked to at that time, had encouraged me to sign the papers also, and now he was using this against me.

"Yes, I did give up custody!" I hissed at him, angry that he could be so insensitive to my feelings. He was there when I received the papers from Cal, when I cried over the desertion claim and the custody. Paolo knew how much those statements hurt me.

"But I trust Cal, and I still do," I cried. "And I thought I could trust you."

"Do you expect me to leave a good business, and go to America where I don't know what I can do?"

"You are going to America to be part of God's Family. If you don't want to do that, then I don't want to stay with you."

"What about the baby? God gave us that baby for a reason. We are supposed to be together."

"God gave me Thor for a reason too, Paolo, and I am going to stay beside my firstborn."

Paolo laughed condescendingly, an irritating habit he resorted to when he didn't know what to say.

"I am leaving here with or without you, Paolo. You can't keep me here. We aren't married yet, and you can't prove fatherhood either," I added, not knowing if that were true or not.

We were on chilly terms for the next couple of weeks. Since I had put the money Timothy had given me into Paolo's bank account, I had virtually no money. I contacted my mother and sisters, who were willing to help me. My mother had been reading all the anti-COG literature she received from church groups that explained our unusual marriage relationships; however, she was still horrified to learn that Cal lived with a pregnant woman in New York, while I lived with a stranger in Italy, and was also pregnant. I had been in touch with her through letters, but I never had given her the details of my life. Other than news about Thor's growth, my letters were filled with Bible verses supporting our ministry. Now that my mother heard about my divorce, she preferred I arrive with a husband-to-be, but said she would send me the money if I needed it to leave Italy. Paolo, sensing that I would do this on my own, gave in. He put the shop up for sale, and we left before Christmas. We arrived in New York in December 1980, with the news that John Lennon had just been shot and killed.

"Great entrance into America," said Paolo sarcastically.

Paolo and I began to live in my mother's house in Lancaster, Pennsylvania, and we were married a few weeks before I had my first daughter. Only my mother was present at the ceremony held at the justice of the peace's office, and she took us out for pizza afterward. Paolo had not bought a wedding ring for me, despite having over ten thousand dollars in the bank, so my mother gave me an heirloom ring she had been saving. It was too big, and I eventually lost it while doing dishes. My second baby was born in the local hospital, and we named her Athena.

Back in Lancaster, I caught up with all my family's history. I knew that my sister Marlene, who had visited me in New York before I'd left for Europe, had died in a car accident, but back in my home,

I finally had the time and space to allow myself to mourn. Many times I looked at the old pictures of her and remembered how I had hauled her to the antiwar march on Washington when she was only fifteen. Ruby had married a drug user whom she felt sorry for, and was now divorced and trying to start a new life with a baby. Karen and Ingie were living in Florida and doing well. My brother, Steve, was in prison again.

Cal and Mara joined us in Lancaster, and we rented a house and lived together for a few months while trying to raise money and decide which mission field to go to. My mother was terribly upset that we were living together, imagining the most horrible sexual transactions taking place, but actually, we never shared at all. Everyone had their individual problems to keep them preoccupied. Paolo had plenty of money from the sale of the shop, but Cal was dead broke. In COG philosophy, we should have shared our money with Cal, but Paolo was not ready for that. He still had a hard time sharing his money with me.

None of us were particularly good friends, but friendship was not valued in the Family. I don't think that any of us would have even kept company had we known each other outside of the Family. Our interests, likes, and dislikes were so different. But in the COG, all that mattered was God's work, according to Family doctrine. As for me, I would do anything to stay near my son.

It soon became evident that Cal, now almost thirty years old, was not happy with Family policy. He had stopped sending in his 10 percent, and had started drinking and smoking. One day I found out that he was also smoking marijuana. Like many people who control their own negative urges by condemning them in others, I confronted him about his vices during morning devotions. I wanted everything to be laid out in the open so I knew where we were going. Cal stormed out of the room, and Mara looked at me sheepishly.

"You guys aren't in the Family anymore, are you?" I asked, dumbfounded by my lack of discernment.

"Cal's just having a difficult time," she replied. I thought as she said this that she must really love him. How strange to love someone in the Family enough to support their shortcomings.

"Mara, you need to let me know. I have a new disciple I am trying to train. He can't be seeing Cal smoke dope. What is happening with you two?"

"Okay," she confided. "We both have trouble believing Mo now."

"We always had trouble believing Mo," I answered. "But what about serving God? Do you think the Family is still a legitimate alternative to the system or not?"

Having had a recent taste of the system life, both with Paolo in Italy and now back in America, I concluded that the Family was still a better way of living. I didn't like the loneliness of living in the so-called world. Of course, I hardly had time to make friends, but with work and children to take care of, I didn't see how any mother could have time for a social life. However, most of all, I didn't think I could live a life without a goal, and I saw my goal as living for the Lord one hundred percent. No Christian church would take me in now. There was basically nowhere for me to serve the Lord but in the Family.

"You know that Cal has not been happy in the Family for quite some time," continued Mara.

"Is he in or out?" I demanded to know.

"He wants some time to think about his life, about what he's going to do, now that we will have two children."

"Cal has three children. What does he plan on doing with Thor?" My heart was racing frantically. Cal had legal custody of Thor, and now he was planning to leave the Family. What would he do with Thor? It was my worst nightmare come true. I had not counted on Cal becoming a heretic—and having custody of my son.

"I'm going back to France to have my baby," she said, ignoring my question. "Cal is going to stay with friends in California and raise some money."

"I want to know what he is going to do with Thor!" I said more emphatically.

"You'll have to talk to Cal about that," she said, even though I was sure she already had discussed the matter with him.

Cal informed me later, after he had calmed down, that he would let me take Thor until he situated himself and his family. I knew that could take months or years. As long as I had Thor, life made sense.

Thor was now eight years old and had been to four different schools in his life, not counting the Family schools he had attended as a toddler. He had lived in four countries and in over a dozen different homes. It was a lot of moving; I had moved often as a child also, but I had thus far never analyzed the psychological implications of that factor on my life. Thor made friends wherever we went; however, he was not doing well in conduct at school, which I attributed to the system's poor way of teaching and disciplining. I started to teach Thor again at home, and when we moved, I did not put him back in public school.

Paolo and I bought a small travel trailer and, together with Thor and Athena, we started down the East Coast on our way to South America. On the way, we were joined by a COG family from Italy with four little kids who lived in a tent.

By the time we arrived in Florida, it was hot, humid, and buggy. We found a home in Miami that processed COG missionaries on their way to South America. The Italian family separated from us there, and started working on raising more funds, while we ended up in a trailer park in Jacksonville. Paolo went to work as a waiter, not wanting to sell literature on the streets. I stayed home with Athena and taught Thor. When Paolo complained about my not making any money, I sold the gifts I had collected in Monte Carlo. I eventually sold all the jewelry, including the Cartier gold chain, and Salim's painting. They brought in a lot of money, but much less than they were worth.

Our trailer had no air-conditioning, and poor little Athena was covered with heat rash. In addition, since she had suffered a high fever after her first vaccination, Paolo insisted that she have no more shots, and I was always afraid she would come down with some childhood disease she had not been vaccinated against. Paolo had become very strict about our diets and medical needs, fanatically embracing the Family's policies of avoiding doctors. Although all my children have been relatively healthy, they also all went through the childhood diseases that most children were vaccinated against, such as measles, chicken pox, and whooping cough. While in Florida, Athena acquired a red rash all over her body, accompanied by a fever for three days, but I never knew what it was. By the time I took her to a doctor, she was already better.

Also, during our stay at the trailer park in Jacksonville, Thor came running home one day from the pool with his hand covering a profusely bleeding forehead. It was the first time I had left him at the pool under the care of a neighbor, since I'd had to run home and change Athena's diaper. Paolo was away, and I didn't drive, so a lady from the nearby trailer park store came to my rescue and drove us to a clinic, where I was relieved to hear that Thor's cut could be sewn up with a few stitches.

Finally, I received a letter from Sharon, who told me that a new music ministry was being started in Puerto Rico. It was easy to obtain clearance to go to Puerto Rico; also, Family members could still collect food stamps there from the government. We put in our application for Puerto Rico and received the okay immediately. After selling the car, and leaving the trailer with a dealer to sell for us, we arrived in Puerto Rico in time for the ovenlike August weather.

Our first week in San Juan was spent in a tiny rented room with no air-conditioning. I lay on the bed in the shaded room with the fan blowing on me during the heat of the day, while Thor and Athena played in the wading pool we bought and put right outside the open door so I could watch them. I had to bring them in every twenty minutes so they would not get heat stroke. In the evening, I took the children for a walk on the beautiful beaches. Meanwhile, Paolo scouted San Juan for housing and work. Unless we lived in a home, Paolo would never understand how to live by faith. COG members did not work for money at that time; they sold literature on the streets or sang in restaurants and cafés. Since I could not speak Spanish, and I had to watch the children, I did not see how I could do either in this heat. Finally, I hit on an idea.

Paolo had always wanted to learn to play the guitar, and the Italian brothers we visited had started to show him a few chords. He had bought a guitar in Italy and brought it with him through all our travels. I convinced him to play a few chords while I sang—on the buses. The buses were air-conditioned, or had a good ventilation system, so it was better than keeping the children in the hot motel room. I took Athena in a stroller, and Thor collected up and down the bus aisle while Paolo played the guitar and I sang. After a few weeks, Thor started to sing with Paolo and they went out alone, since Athena often slowed us down.

I was worried about Paolo taking Thor out alone. There had been a few incidents when Paolo had hit Thor harder than I thought was necessary. Thor had been his usual rambunctious self while we were on a long driving trip, and Paolo had reached the end of his patience and slapped Thor hard across the face. His mouth was bleeding, and I yelled at Paolo for hitting him so forcefully. Even though corporal punishment was condoned in the Family, we were supposed to talk to the children first, and let them know how they would be punished. In addition, I wasn't sure if Paolo would watch my eight-year-old son well enough in the crowded San Juan streets. I never had the feeling that Paolo was as concerned about Thor as a father should be. He was not mean to him, but he was not sensitive to a young boy's needs, such as when to take a break and when to buy him an ice cream.

During our first month in San Juan, we visited other colonies searching for a place to live. One evening we visited a large home outside San Juan where they were having a get-together for the members in the area. I had not been in a regular Family home for years, and I was shocked at the filth and disarray of the house. The brothers and sisters were sweet, but somehow different from the Family I knew in Europe. I felt extremely uncomfortable, and I later learned that these were all people who had not received clearance to undertake a mission, so they congregated in Puerto Rico. Most of the members who could not obtain clearance were actually incompetent. Our socialist philosophy was to take anyone into the Family who believed in Jesus, wanted to forsake all and live communally, and would obey the Mo letters and leadership, but I now began to realize what difficulties that entailed. Some of our members had come from very poor, undereducated backgrounds, and we were not properly trained in social reeducation. Although some of these people eventually learned to clean up their houses, teach their children to read and write, and earn enough money to support the colony, many of them stayed in pretty much the same condition as when they joined—abject poverty. It was the first time I was aware of a huge class difference existing within the Family, and I was not sure of the causes or implications. After dinner, the leader of the home, a huge brother from Chicago, suggested we all put our names in a hat and pick a partner for the night. I declined, saying that we were not spending the night here, but he insisted that I at least share before going home. Paolo also was not interested in having sex with a name he picked out of a hat. We left before the names were chosen.

Within a few weeks, we found a couple to live with. They were clean, well-mannered people who had already received clearance to Argentina and were just staying to raise more funds. We moved to a small village called Humacao, rented a large, airy villa, and went singing in San Juan. This couple stayed pretty much to themselves in the second-floor apartment of the villa, and we never shared sexually. Sexual policies, I learned, varied greatly from one Family home to the next, as well as at different time periods in the COG.

One day I got a call from the leader of a house that was underground.

"Hopie heard that you are in Puerto Rico," the brother said. "She wants you to come up and visit us."

Once again, Hopie, Mo's daughter, was my savior. A car was sent down for Paolo and me, and brought us to a campground situated on a beautiful mountain about an hour's drive from San Juan. There were roughly twenty trailers and large living tents pitched under the trees, with a kitchen and a huge covered patio by a pool. It was a picture of heaven-on-earth, and seeing old friends just made it more celestial. There were a number of musicians from our Paris days, all of whom I knew well. Most were married now and had children. There were also singers and musicians from Italy whom I had met in my travels. Then there were the big leaders, whom everyone knew. It was definitely the place to be in the Family at this time.

The latest push in the Family was to recruit members back into the group. Flirting had been toned down now; we were giving sex only to men who were very influential or wealthy. The new, elite ministry in the Family was making videotapes of Family songs. This camp in the mountains of Puerto Rico was a gathering of our best talent, and more was on the way.

One of the significant "backsliders," as we called them, who had been brought back to the Family by Hopie's personal initiative was an extremely talented young man named Gabriel. He, along with all the other "prodigal sons," were treated royally. They were given the best houses, the nicest clothes, use of the cars, and were instantly made leaders. Mo said we were to reach the world through music, radio, and television, and we needed good musicians, technicians, and others with entertainment-industry skills to do it. Gabriel was multitalented, and besides writing scripts, performing, and directing the shows, he was one of our most successful public relations men, opening doors in the South American music world that would have taken us years to even find. For a short while in Puerto Rico, he was treated like a king. Many years later, he was to become one of the first victims of the "victor camps," where rebels or leaders who had disobeyed Mo in some way were humiliated by verbal lashings and public spankings, forced to confess before the colony every "sin" they had ever committed, subjected to sleep deprivation and exorcism, and separated from any source of help. However, that would come years later. In the camp near San Juan, our little paradise, it seemed like no harm could touch us! With intelligent and capable people like Gabriel around, I began to have more faith in the Family again, and the depression and horrific conditions of the San Juan homes that I had recently witnessed were soon forgotten.

Hopie, who seemed to have a special liking for me, was her usual, happy self.

"Praise the Lord, honey. It's great to see you again," she told me cheerfully. "When I heard you were in Puerto Rico, I thought, well, Jeshanah has to come up here. She's an old Paris Show Group performer. So what have you been doing? I heard you lured a fish into the Family."

"Yes, I did. When Monte Carlo closed down, I went to live with a fish in Italy."

"Well, praise the Lord. Good for you. That was Dad's main objective, to get souls into the Kingdom.

"I want you to stay up here in the music camp," continued Hopie. "Is your fish with you still?"

"Yes, we had a baby and got married."

"Praise God! Two souls for his Kingdom. Well, can he sing or play music?"

"No, not really. He started to learn in Italy."

"I never knew an Italian who didn't love music. I know what he can do. I bet he's a great cook. Italians love good food. Why don't you and, what's his name, honey?"

"Paolo."

"Why don't you and Paolo stay here and take over the kitchen? We could use some better cooks here. And I'm sure they could use you in some of the dance numbers, if they start doing shows like we did in Paris. That was great, wasn't it. The Lord's Spirit sure moved in Paris."

Paolo and I moved up to the camp within days. He recognized a good situation when he saw it, and the camp was a true haven. He was also given a little special attention, being the youngest disciple there, by years. We bought a little pop-up trailer to place alongside the RVs. Although Hopie said we were to be in charge of the kitchen, the practical leaders felt that Paolo was too young in the Family to be in charge of anything. He was relieved just to be there in the camp, where our daily needs were met by the community and we did not have to go singing to raise funds.

Soon after arriving, I found out that Sharon and Timothy had come over from Greece and were living on the island. When I finally talked to Sharon on the phone, I realized she had changed drastically; however, it wasn't until I would meet her, weeks later, that I understood what a complete transformation she had made. But for the time being, both Paolo and I focused on adjusting to our new communal life.

Like in all Family homes, sharing was taken for granted in the camp. The concept of "one wife" was now widespread in the Family. Mo's words "God's in the business of breaking up little selfish private worldly families to make of their yielded broken pieces a larger unit— one family—one wife" ("One Wife" 249:9) were taken literally now. Some homes even set up regular, weekly "sharing schedules" to ensure that everyone got equal opportunity. The ideal was to become one with every member in the home, not just with your own mate. Paolo, like most men, had *not* joined the Family to share sexually with many women, but he participated in the schedule until he was asked to go with a sister he found unattractive. After a brother explained to him that God's Love does not discriminate by outside beauty, Paolo reluctantly agreed to go with a sister he had refused repeatedly. However, he talked badly of the girl afterward, so the leaders wisely considered Paolo a special case, and he was no longer encouraged to share. Since I had become saturated with sex, I was more than willing to pass up any opportunities to share, using the excuse that Paolo was alone. Sex was a chore for me by now, and since we did not use birth control, I was always afraid of becoming pregnant.

My old rebellious and dear dance instructor, Salome, was also at the camp. She now had three small children, and from what I understood, one was from a fish. Salome, as a nursery worker, had always expressed to me her feeling that there were enough children in the Family, and she did not want to add to the number. She kept to herself in her own trailer, rarely coming out for fellowship. Rumor had it that she not only refused to share with brothers; she would not have sex would her own husband unless she could use birth control. Since birth control was absolutely not allowed in the

Family, as far as I knew, I imagined that they had a sexless marriage. I envied her.

During our stay in the camp, Mo asked the Family to video women dancing in various forms of the striptease, which he called the "heavenly houris" dances. In new letters written at this time, such as "Glorify God in the Dance," Mo described how we should dance in these videos as if we were making love to him or the Lord. Like most of his new ideas, they had been tested previously at selected homes. Since ours was a special, underground home, we were allowed to see some of the original tapes that had been sent to Mo from the Greece home. I was interested in seeing Sharon's dance. Hopie gave us a little prep speech before showing the video.

"Now this is the second video we sent to Dad. He was not pleased with the first one, and especially with a few of the girls whom he felt were not dancing in God's Spirit of freedom. Thank the Lord for Dad's insight, and that he is never too proud to let us know when we are doing wrong. Amen?"

It seems that Sharon, among others, had danced with such sexual inhibition that Mo had rebuked her and said that it was time for that girl to receive the Holy Spirit, since evidently she had not yet. He also suggested that she drink a little more wine before performing her dance for him, and he gave specific instructions on what he wanted to see—more sex!

I was shocked when I saw Sharon's second dance. She was a different person from the kind, sweetly shy girl I had known and loved. Her eyes seemed spooky as she penetrated the camera with a flirtatious, come-hither look that was not the Sharon I knew. Other girls on the video had danced and undressed in a sexy, but awkward, manner; however, Sharon, whom I remembered as one of the most modest women I have ever known, masturbated openly before the camera as if she were a professional porno star. She was brazen, brassy, saucy, and bold—the ultimate sexual plaything for a man with unbridled sexual fantasies. I thought that she must have become one of Mo's own women, and it took my breath away as I realized how close I had come to being one too. Perhaps it was my mother's prayers, or my own innate defiant nature, but somehow I had missed being chosen by him. In a rather warped way, I entertained the thought that perhaps he *did* have spiritual insight, and he knew I could never give up my soul to the point that Sharon had. I didn't want to believe it was the same woman I knew, and as I went to bed that night, with a heavy heart, I pondered why Mo had picked poor Sharon. Sweet, sweet Sharon—the lily of the field, I used to call her! She was no longer lily-white; she was now the red, red rose of Sharon, covered, smothered with the blood pouring from her wounded soul. These were my thoughts after seeing the person whom I had loved most in the Family dancing before her king!

I was asked to perform a houri dance the next day before a video camera, and I wondered what I could do that would not be criticized by Mo. Intuitively, I now knew that I was safe, since Mo went after the women who had a malleable inner core. Knowing that I would never be among Mo's inner circle strangely gave me more faith to stay in the Family. I had been a socialist before I joined, and I never liked this hierarchical system that had developed in the Family anyway. As long as I was not part of the leadership, I should not take blame for any of their mistakes. The bottom line was that we were still preaching God's love and salvation. These naked dances were only for the elite, and the upper echelon historically degenerate and are replaced. I decided to do my dance like the person I was—a woman who loved to dance for the dance's sake, not for Mo, or sex, or pornography. My warped mind was bent on excusing Family perversions, and I had become quite good at it. Declaring that leadership would evolve to eventual perfection was one of my best ploys of self-deception.

Choreographing my own dance and designing the stage scene between two trees, I began by dancing in the nude behind a sheer muslin curtain with a stage light shining from the back. Nothing could be seen but my silhouette as I danced. I let my body flow, spin, and spiral to the music. Of course, there was always the possibility that Mo would send a message saying that I was not in the Spirit, but I had already survived that experience years before. After a few weeks, Mo did have a message for me: "Tell the Uneager Beaver that I liked her dance."

I heard this compliment from Hopie while I was at a dinner party at the residence of one of the leaders, where Sharon lived, and my anxiety of finally meeting with Sharon and Timothy overshadowed any reaction I might have had to it. Sharon had lost about twenty pounds and was thinner than I. As she looked at me, she said, "I love you," but her eyes looked past my heart or soul to some faraway place only she could see. I thought that she must have achieved either sainthood or zombiehood, and I wasn't curious enough to want to find out which, which was very unlike me. I was a little scared. Sharon reminded me of a happy victim—the ultimate evil paradox. Instead, I talked at length with Timothy, who was watching the children so that Sharon could entertain at the dinner table. His boyish face still looked naively hopeful as he explained to me that Sharon had a "special calling."

"I heard Hopie say that Mo liked your dance," Tim told me gleefully. "He doesn't say that to everyone, you know, especially not on their first dance."

"Yeah, he also called me the Uneager Beaver again," I replied, but I could see that the meaning of this comment went over his head.

"Oh, don't worry about that, I'm sure he loves you."

Actually, I wanted to say that I was thankful that Mo still called me the Uneager Beaver, which suggested he would always hold the story I had written against me. Now that I had witnessed the change in his wife after becoming an "insider," I liked the freedom and safety of being an outsider more than ever before. I had never been very close to Timothy, so I did not say anything, and Sharon was now much too far away to ever talk to again. She was like one of those monks who achieve enlightenment after years of social isolation. If that was enlightenment—I didn't want it.

The camp was full of outsiders like myself. We seemed to be a bunch of freethinkers who had been temporarily handicapped by ideals, opportunity, love, or other psychological/emotional anesthetics. Almost everyone living in the camp eventually left the Family, and at least one of them committed suicide after leaving. But I never heard of a suicide while in the Family, and certainly those days on the mountaintop kept all of us preoccupied. We were too busy to think about what we were really doing then, and it was only after we left, if we were able to spend time alone with ourselves, that the wastefulness of our lives could be understood. During those mock "days of heaven on earth" in Puerto Rico, I was oblivious to the approaching storm.

Most of my concern was over my son, Thor, who was now eight years old. He was at an awkward stage of childhood development, made more confusing by recent Mo letters on how to raise children.

Because of our free-sex lifestyle, sooner or later the subject would have to be discussed with our children. Eight-year-olds want to know why Mommy and Daddy are sleeping in someone else's trailer.

More distressing than the sexual aspects of raising my son was the discipline that was being taught to all parents. Paolo took the disciplinary rules very seriously, and on a few occasions, he took Thor into the woods and whipped him with a stick. Each time Thor received a spanking, I wondered if his own father would have done the same. Thor asked about his father sometimes, and I said we would probably see him soon. But after these spankings, Thor especially wanted to see his daddy, and my heart would break. If God truly does punish us for our sins, I know that the worst way He can punish me is through my children; for this reason, I have often lived in fear. Nothing ever made me as anxious as the thought of what effect my actions would have on my children. On the other hand, there are never easy problems or easy solutions, as I was soon to learn.

Near the end of the year 1981, I received a letter from Cal telling me that he was out of the Family for good and that he wanted Thor back. With the letter was a one-way ticket to France, where Cal now lived with Mara. I was sent into a complete panic. My plan was utterly destroyed. I had not counted on Cal becoming a heretic when I had signed those divorce papers. The only reason I had given him custody of Thor was that I believed we could all be together eventually, or at least live close to each other. To complicate matters, I now had two children, with two different fathers. The ideal was to all live together. That was not going to happen now, and I could not figure out what to do. I wrote Cal that I would not send Thor until some agreement could be reached on visitation. I was willing to return to Europe, if necessary, but for now, I was relieved that Thor was in my possession.

One day Cal called the San Juan home, and asked if I would come to the phone that evening with Thor so that he could talk to him, which I felt was certainly good for both of them. I was hoping that we could come to some sort of agreement during the call. When Cal phoned as planned, I explained to him that I did not use the ticket he sent because I wanted to be sure that he would send Thor back to me sometime. He said he was upset at first, but now understood and that maybe we could work something out for the future.

It was already dark outside, but we had to return to the camp, so we said good-bye to our hosts. Paolo was driving and I was in the front seat, holding Athena, who was almost a year old and still nursing, while Thor sat in the back. As we turned a corner and headed down a deserted street towards the highway leading out of town and to the camp, a car suddenly headed toward us. Before Paolo could swerve out of its way, it backed into us and rammed our car.

"The doors," I screamed. "Lock all the doors." A dark-haired man came running out of the car toward us. I thought we were being robbed and I frantically locked my door and the door behind me. Thor was on the seat behind Paolo and I could not reach him.

Everything happened so quickly, and I was in such an emotional panic afterward, that I can't recall the exact details of this incident, and those involved have contradictory reports. I know that Thor was taken away from me at that time; I remember I was relieved to see my ex-husband, Cal, come toward me in the dark of the night, so I knew Thor had not been kidnapped by a stranger; I came to the dreadful realization that Cal was taking Thor away and I might not see him again.

In a state of near hysteria, I was taken by Paolo back to the Family in San Juan.

Paolo took me inside the home and I sat down while he talked to the leaders, handing them an envelope Cal had given him. They called the camp and then explained to me what had happened.

"Jeshanah, listen! He took Thor for good. He's not bringing him back."

"He can't do that! I have Thor's passport; he can't get out of here without it."

The home leaders came back into the room and opened the envelope. It was a letter from Cal.

"He has been to the police already," they explained, "and he is threatening to give away our locations and everything he knows about the Family if you don't give him Thor's passport."

"But he doesn't know where the camp is," I protested. Athena was crying now, and I tried to nurse her but no milk came. The leader's wife took her.

"He knows enough," he said. "You guys should stay here tonight. They will call in the morning."

I looked around in bewilderment. Were they going to let Thor be taken from me? Forever, like Cal said? Wasn't Thor worth saving?

What's wrong with these people? This is my son! I looked to Paolo for help, but he didn't respond. I didn't know what he was thinking—I never did! Was he going to help me or not? Could I count on him when my emotional energy was depleted?

"No! No! You can't make me do it," I screamed hysterically.

"You need to get a good night's sleep," said the leader's wife, who had already laid Athena down in a baby cot. We were given a space in a spare room.

I couldn't close my eyes. Athena and Paolo slept all night, but I stayed awake, rocking myself as tears flowed down my cheeks. Maybe in the morning, I would hear that Cal had changed his mind. Maybe Thor would refuse to go with him. Maybe the leaders would force Cal to make concessions to me. All I wanted was a promise that Thor could see me. I would go back to Italy. I would not go to South America, not if Thor was on another continent. There would be a change in the morning, I was sure of that. "Sorrow lasts for a night, but joy cometh in the morning." That's what the Bible said. Still, I stayed awake all night praying and weeping.

We heard the next day that all the top leaders had fled the island during the night. There was too much bad publicity about the Children of God and many angry people in America were looking for the leaders, many of whom were right here in our camp. Groups like the one called Free COG, standing for "Free our children from the Children of God," and deprogrammers, who kidnapped adult COG members and tried to un-brainwash them, were becoming more powerful. In addition, individual Family members were now embattled by lawsuits from mothers or fathers who had left the COG but whose spouse and children were still in. Cal had a lot of information about us—leaders' legal names and addresses and what they looked like—and they were afraid. They suggested that I give Cal whatever he wanted. Hopie, who had also left the island, sent a special message saying that it was all in God's hands, and if I trusted Him, He would give me the desires of my heart.

At that time, I did not mind that they left. I knew that the top leaders always protected their identity and location, but I couldn't believe what they were asking me to do. Paolo drove up to the camp to get the passport and some of Thor's clothes. Meanwhile, Cal called and talked to the leader at the home. Cal had been in San Juan about a week, studying the movement in and out of the San Juan house, which he found by following a brother home from the post office. He had called to make sure we would be there with Thor that night; then he and his brother had planned the kidnapping. He wasn't about to make any deals, and all the chips were stacked on his side of the table. I was in a state of shock when Paolo took me to the airport to meet with Cal. I still hoped that I could persuade him to change his mind.

Cal met me alone at the planned location, without Thor. He said he thought it would not be good for Thor to see me in this state. I was a wreck from being up all night and day crying.

"Cal, you can't do this to me," I pleaded.

"You were going to do it to me," he responded spitefully. He was a different person from the one I had left a year ago. He was tough and much more sure of himself.

"No, I wasn't going to keep Thor away. I wanted to work something out with you."

"What could we work out? You are in the Family, and I am not. You want to live in South America, and I live in France."

"I would not have gone to South America."

"That's what you say now. But you would have taken him and disappeared. Why didn't you send him back with the ticket I sent you?"

"I know it looks bad, but I was afraid to send him. I didn't have any proof that you would let me see him again."

"You're probably right. I don't want Thor having any contact whatsoever with this perverted cult you're in. You guys are nuts. Your leaders are all f——ing perverts. Where are your leaders now, huh? They've all left you by yourself, haven't they?"

I couldn't listen anymore. I knew he was right, but what could I do? Agree with him? It wouldn't get me Thor back. And what about Paolo and Athena? I held my head together as if to stop it from exploding. Like Tolstoy's Anna Karenina, I seemed to have been left without a choice. There was no road open to take. I would have to forge one for myself, but not now. I was too weak, too confused, too close to the edge! Knowing he was taking Thor for good, right now, this very instant was all that mattered. I turned to Paolo for help.

"Paolo, do something!" I cried. "Find out where he's going. Please don't let him take Thor without knowing where he's going?'

I sat on the nearest bench and buried my face into my hands while

Paolo gave Cal the passport and suitcase. Paolo had let me down. He did nothing at all. Maybe he liked his position in the Family now, near top leadership. Maybe he just never liked having Thor around, a bothersome, constant reminder that I had been married to someone else. But I had helped Paolo in his darkest hour. Now, I wanted and needed his help in my darkest minute, and he did nothing! I would have to take care of myself! They were gone! My beloved had been yanked out of my heart and it was bleeding profusely. Would I become a zombie like Sharon? Was that how God did it? After all, the Family did not plan this one. Lifeless, I let Paolo take me back to the San Juan home.

I didn't want to see anyone. I stayed in the little room they had given us for two days and two nights. Not even Athena could make me come out. I nursed her and handed her back to Paolo to take away.

After crying all the tears I had left, I lay folded up in the fetal position, praying to die. Then I stopped praying, and anger took the place of any false hope I had stored for God to do something. I was given messages from the leaders that God wanted me to sacrifice Thor as a test, and He would give him back. However, not one of my friends from the camp came to comfort me. During those tortured, guilt-ridden days of passing judgment on myself, the Family, and the world, I finally came to a verdict.

This was not between me and the Family, I told myself. It was between me and God. What kind of God would ask Abraham to sacrifice his only son? Why put a man to a test like that? I had tried to understand the reasoning, and as long as I had not been so intimately touched, I could. But no longer. I had found at least one truth in my heart. I could not trust a God who would ask this of me!

I went to my knees and raised my clenched fists upward.

"I am not a man!" I cried. "*I am a mother!* And I won't pass that test. I won't even take it! *I will not sacrifice my son!*"

I dropped to the floor, and while a coat of scales fell from my soul like a snake's skin being discarded, I closed my eyes and slept for the first time in three days.

10

Living in the Looking-Glass Mirror

After Thor had been kidnapped in Puerto Rico, I told Paolo that with or without him, I was going back to France to look for my son. At first he tried to convince me to stay, but when he saw that I actually meant it—that I would leave without him—he said he wanted us to stay together. We sold our trailer to some Family members, who I think gave us money for it because they were glad to see me leave, and together with Paolo's leftover funds we had enough to buy stand-by tickets back to Italy.

It was February 1982, and I was almost thirty. In a French village above Monte Carlo, we stayed in the converted garage of a lady friend I had known before we left. While Paolo scouted around for business opportunities, I rested at home and watched Athena. In the evening he drove me to the Loew's Hotel, where I landed a job as a cocktail waitress.

Our plan was to save some money, borrow some more, and open a health food store in Italy. Paolo had become interested in health food nutrition while in the Family, and there was a trend toward healthy living under way in Italy. Meanwhile, I wrote a letter to Salim, explaining that my son had been kidnapped by my ex-husband, and asking for his help.

His lawyer called me within a few days and told me they had hired a private detective to locate Thor. I knew only that he probably lived in France. They had moved from the place where I had sent mail and left no forwarding address. I did not know Mara's legal name, or the name of her parents, but I did know Cal's legal name. While I waited to hear again from Salim's lawyer, I lived an anxious, limbolike existence between the piano bar in Loew's and the garage-home outside of Monte Carlo. One night a man, who had appeared two evenings in a row, stayed late, following me with his eyes.

It was almost closing time, and I brought him his check. Without taking his eyes off my face, he reached into his suit jacket and pulled out a badge. I looked at it briefly and then looked at the silly, I'm-in-control expression he wore.

"What does that mean?" I asked. "That you don't have to pay?"

The grin fell quickly from his face.

"I think you know what this means," he replied in a thick French accent. "We don't want you in Monaco. I think I've made my point."

I left my station and clocked out, deciding to leave by the underground employees' entrance and call Paolo from another location. As I walked through the well-lit streets of Monte Carlo, I recalled the many nights I had walked those same streets with Sharon and Breeze. It seemed like another world ago. It was.

Paolo had found a suitable location for a store near the popular seaside town of San Remo. He borrowed money from relatives to open the store on a shoestring budget, and we lived in a small room in the back. I spent the next few months helping Paolo set up an herb and natural food store. While waiting for customers, I wrote, scribbling in pen and ink on looseleaf paper reams of fictional stories. They were all eventually put in the trash, having been written more as a kind of personal therapy than for anyone to read.

Finally, I heard from the lawyer. They had located Cal, who now went by his legal name, Jerry. He lived and worked in Canet Plage, near Perpignan, which was on the other side of France, by the Spanish border.

"He says you can never see your son again," the lawyer told me matter-of-factly. "He tells me that you are in a strange cult that abuses children, and that your son was abused by you and others in this cult. Is that true?"

"He was in the same cult as I was," I replied. "But I am not in it anymore."

"Does he know this?"

"No. I can't write to him to let him know. I don't have any way to communicate with him."

"I will let him know. I will see what we can work out. But you must be telling me the truth. Are you out of this cult?"

"Yes," I replied truthfully. We had not written to the Family or heard from them since we had left Puerto Rico almost a year ago.

I waited anxiously for weeks. Finally, I received a call from the lawyer. She said that Jerry had agreed to talk with me, and if it was all right, she would give him my phone number.

Jerry called about a week later. After discussions back and forth, which lasted for over a month, he said I could come and visit Thor. But he included a long list of do's and don'ts. I agreed to anything he said.

We planned for me to take the trip during the Christmas season. Paolo's shop would be less busy during the quiet time after the holidays when everyone had already spent their money. Since I was now eight months pregnant, Paolo thought Athena should stay with him. I took the long train trip by myself, hardly seeing the beautiful French scenery as I envisioned my first encounter with Thor in over a year.

Jerry met me at the train by himself. He wanted to talk with me awhile to be sure how I was doing and that I would not cause any emotional scenes. I assured him that I would do exactly as he told me, and I would not weep in front of Thor. When I entered the small town house they had rented, I saw Thor playing with his half sister in the yard. He had grown tall and thin, but he still had his distinctive red hair. All his babyness was completely gone, and he portrayed a maturity that I had never recognized before. I felt as if I had lost my little boy forever. But when he turned around and looked at me, all his childlike innocence came rushing back into him, as if a floodgate had been opened. With love in his eyes that only I could recognize, as his natural mother, he came running to me and jumped into my arms. My big stomach was in the way, but that didn't stop him.

"Whoa. Your mother's pregnant, son." said Jerry firmly. "Calm down and act like a man."

Thor disregarded what his dad said, as he told me excitedly of things he had done since moving to France. He took me to his room, where he had a set of mechanical toys, which he had made into some sort of flying vehicle. He pulled out a game board that could be converted into about twelve different games, and after explaining how each one was played, he asked me which I wanted to start with. I played with him for hours, as I observed his happy face and remembered that he had never been allowed to play with toys in the Family. Toys were something systemites gave their children to hook them on material things. It was a ploy of the devil. If so, the devil knew how to make children happy. Thor's face was radiant, and I hoped that some of it was because he was glad to see me. His dad must have also talked to him about not displaying too much emotion, because it wasn't until I put him to bed that night that I saw tears in his eyes. He quickly brushed them away and turned over saying, "I'm happy you're here, *Mommy.*" He had called me Mommy, and he would continue to call me Mommy until he was well over twenty years old.

Late that night, after the children had gone to bed, I talked with Jerry and Mara, who was now called Mona, her real name.

"Thor seems genuinely happy and content here, " I said wistfully.

"Yes. In the beginning he was telling us all these things we should not be doing—like eating white sugar, or watching TV, or me smoking cigarettes," said Jerry with a laugh. "But he soon started to like the system way of life much better, and now he doesn't even want to talk about the time he had in the Family."

"Has he mentioned me often?" I asked, getting to my main concern quickly.

"No. Only the first few weeks," replied Mona in her usual truth-be-told manner. I usually admired her Libraish balance on life's most emotional issues, but this time it hurt too deeply. However, I knew better than to cry in front of them. I had promised no emotional displays.

"Well, I suppose that is better for Thor. How is he in school?"

"He had to be put back because he forgot most of his French. But he does very well now, especially in math," said Jerry. "Of course, he's had a few run-ins with other kids. One in particular was a bit messy when he broke the nose of a policeman's son."

"Oh, no!" I cried. "We have always taught Thor antiviolence!"

"Oh, don't give me that peace bullshit. You know Mo talked about killing every Antichrist Israeli, and every non-Christian goes to the fires of hell. Real peaceful stuff!"

"That was just a madman's ravings. I never believed that either, and I certainly never told Thor that."

"Well, don't worry. Thor is a good boy. And his fight was really to protect his sister. Seems this boy pushed his sister off a swing, so he punched his nose."

I knew that Jerry had been quite a fighter, growing up on Long Island, but I made no mention of this. He seemed almost proud of his son.

I went to bed late, and the next morning, I took Thor to the beach, despite freezing weather. We played among the sand dunes all day, and that evening I felt a chill. I ignored it. For three days, I spent all day with him, exploring the surroundings of Perpignan with my son. I wanted to be able to imagine every minute of his day. How could I leave him? Of course, I would have liked to stay there and never leave. But life was not so easy. I had another child in Italy, and I had promised Paolo I would be back by a certain date. He had work to do and could not watch Athena indefinitely. Also, I promised Jerry I would not make a scene and beg for Thor to come back with me. This was a beginning in reestablishing my connection with Thor. I told myself that I would work things out. However, leaving Thor was an emotional wrench on my spirit that I was not acknowledging, though my body did. When I left on the train to return home, I had a high fever. Eight hours later, when Paolo picked me up at the station in Italy, I was almost delirious.

My fever raged for three days, and then a doctor was called. He diagnosed me as having pneumonia, and given my pregnant condition, he suggested I be kept in bed and taken care of. I was moved to Paolo's aunt's house, and for days I was oblivious to this world.

"You must think of Athena, and the new baby," I remember Paolo's aunt telling me every time she tried to spoon some homemade broth into my mouth and I refused. I think I again wanted to die. It seemed such a good idea.

After seeing Thor so happy and content in his new surroundings, I thought to myself that I had been a very bad mother. I was now a very unhappy wife, and although I loved my daughter, Athena, I would probably not be a good mother to her either. Why should I go on having children? Why not just die now? I had no will to be healed. I seemed to have made a mess of what was most precious in life to me—motherhood. Thor now had a new mother, and for Athena—better no mother than a bad mother, I thought. I wanted to die, and I was not afraid of death.

Then I remembered that I had rebelled against God. "Curse God and die," Job's wife had told him in his darkest hour. Good old patient Job had not cursed God, however. He said, "Though He slay me, yet will I trust Him."

Job was another story I did not like. It was a man's story. Who would want to live after all his children had been killed, just to learn a lesson? So what that Job got more children back? They weren't the same ones. How could God imagine that one set of children could replace another?

It seemed to me that God was still on my case. He wasn't going to let me live happily and He wasn't going to let me die. One thing was sure though. When I finally did die, I would have a whole lot of questions to ask.

Paolo kept bringing Athena in, saying she needed me and was crying for me. Athena was like a doll. She had the beautiful Italian features of her father, and the defiant fire of her mother. She had always been a handful. When she was a newborn, screaming her lungs out with colic, even the nurses in the hospital said they never saw a baby cry so long and so hard. She wasn't going to sit back and take anything she didn't want to. I thought Athena would do all right in this hard, tough world, but she probably needed a mother's love as much as Thor did. I decided to get well for her.

We wanted to have our next baby at home. When the midwife arrived at our old stone house in the tiny village, I was already quite far along in my labor.

"This bed is too low! Put her on the kitchen table!" she commanded. She was a big, heavy Italian momma, and she was uncomfortable stooping to our low bed as she prepared me for delivery. My baby was born on the kitchen table on a tiny lane called Canevai, meaning the dog's way, in an old, picturesque Italian village by the sea. The small stone house she was born in has since become a national monument because it was built in the year A.D. 500. It had probably been the birthplace of many babies, and she was the last!

When they brought her to me, wrapped in a rough blanket, she was sucking on two fingers. We had chosen the name Genvieve, after the patron saint of Paris. As much as Athena was noisy and lively as a baby, Genvieve was quiet and calm. I often checked her crib to make sure she was still alive.

I spent most of my time writing, crocheting, and raising the children. I started to teach Athena to read when she was three years old. She was bright and eager to learn. I taught her in English, and spoke English to the children all the time since their relatives spoke only Italian.

One day, Paolo came in with a man who looked vaguely familiar.

"Hi, Jeshanah," he said with a huge smile that I had almost forgotten. "You remember me, don't you?"

He had an Asian face, but an American accent. Holding a guitar in his hands, and carrying the trademark lit-bag that all good Family members have, I knew he was a COG.

"Well, I see you don't remember my name. I'm Sojourn. And this is my daughter, Crystal," said the stranger as he held out his hand.

I looked down and saw the little girl for the first time. She also looked Asian, and had a warm, friendly smile. I offered her some candy, which she refused sweetly. Then I remembered that Family children don't eat candy.

I had met Sojourn in Paris, but having met hundreds of people briefly at that time, I hardly remembered him. He remembered me of course, since I was in the Show Group. He could not believe Paolo when he told him I had left the Family. Sojourn and his wife, Maggie, along with their two little children, spent the next few months parked outside our house, eating in our home and staying inside with us most of the time. They both tried to persuade us that the Family had changed.

"You are so talented, Jeshanah. You must come back and use your talents for the Lord," Sojourn told me one evening. "We need more leaders who are concerned about children."

"I don't want to be a leader. I never did. Listen, I love the way you guys are, and how you live so freely. But the leaders are not like that. People change when they get power, in the Family as much as in the world."

"That's why we need people like you, Jeshanah. You have the power and the heart to be a good leader."

"But she doesn't want to, Sojourn. She just told you," interrupted Maggie. "She has three children now, and I am sure that keeps her busy enough."

I was thankful that Maggie included Thor as one of my children. Even though I saw him only twice a year, at Christmas and in the summer, he was always on my mind, and I guess Maggie realized that, being such a loving mother and a caring person.

Separation from Thor was still a source of grief for me. Although Jerry said I was allowed to visit him whenever I wanted, Paolo did not give me much free time. Now that we had two children, Paolo did not want to take care of the little girls while I was gone, and the train trip was too long to take two small children alone. I had visited Thor only one more time in the next year, when we all took a vacation there in the summer.

"If nothing else, you should stay with the Family to be an example to Thor," said Sojourn, seeming to read my thoughts. "He has no spiritual training with Cal."

"I don't think you should be prying into Jeshanah's life," said Maggie.

They had a strange relationship. I knew that Sojourn, who was a mixture of Hawaiian and black American, used to be homosexual. Although homosexuality was subtly allowed in the Family at one time, the goal for men was to be able to have sex with women also in order to produce babies. All former homosexuals were encouraged to find mates of the opposite sex, and Maggie seemed to be one of the few women willing to accept a man who liked men. In return, Maggie, a quiet, usually unobtrusive person, had an adoring husband who was gentle and mutually submissive in his marriage relationship, a real rarity among Family men. They talked to each other with equal respect, and I never saw Sojourn openly disagree with his wife, or use his God-given power as "head of the household" over her. On the contrary, he usually asked her what to do, and obeyed her slightest hints of disapproval, as he did now.

"I'm sorry. You're right, Maggie. Jeshanah is really probably in the Lord's Will. I should not meddle."

I could not help but notice his humble reaction to Maggie's suggestion, and how different it was from how Paolo and I related to each other. Unfortunately, Maggie was not around to stop Sojourn from talking to Paolo about joining.

Paolo was not doing well with our health food business. We had borrowed heavily to open the shop, and there was no more money to borrow. He eventually sold the shop to a rich banker's daughter from Torino. After paying off our debts, we had enough money to buy a mobile home and set it up on a piece of land owned by Paolo's aunt. Paolo began selling health food in the Italian markets, and encouraged by Sojourn, I began going out singing. Together with Sojourn and his daughter, I took Athena and a guitar, and we hit the open cafés up and down the Italian Riviera. Maggie stayed home to watch her little boy and Genvieve. We were living a communal life again. It had all the benefits and none of the disadvantages caused by leadership. Finally, Paolo told me he wanted to rejoin the Family.

I had mixed feelings. Ever since Thor had been taken from me, I had lived life with half a heart and half a will. I was not at all happy with my marriage or my situation, but as a mother, there was no alternative for the time being. Joining the Family at that time gave me hope that Paolo would have other sources to fulfill his emotional needs. I didn't think I could ever fulfill them. I had married him to bring him into the Family, and I had expected help with his spiritual growth. If he wanted to join again, perhaps that would be the best course of action for him and for our marriage. When Paolo had "joined" the Family the first time, he did it only to stay with me. This time it was a decision he was making, and I probably went back into the Family because of him. It seemed to be the lesser of two evils, as the saying goes. Without Thor, I wasn't completely happy anywhere, so if Paolo felt better living in a community, I did not have any strong opposition to it.

Of course, I did feel that the leaders in Puerto Rico had let me down, but maybe that was my own fault in a spiritual way. I felt that I had been wrong to associate myself with the elite of the Family. Maybe they were the only ones who were corrupt. Perhaps these kind, humble members were different. Also, the Family had recently experienced another "revolution" within their group, and all leaders were demoted. From what Sojourn told me, most members were living quite independently of leadership and rules.

I told Paolo that I didn't care one way or the other, that it was his decision. I didn't want to get the blame for this one, as I had gotten for everything else we'd done up to then. And I didn't want it to interfere with my visits to Thor.

It was the year 1985. The Family had changed in many ways. Joining simply meant that we sent in 10 percent of our income, and they sent us the Mo letters and supported some of the poorer missionary fields. "Missionary work" was now the volunteer work we did in retirement and nursing homes, hospitals, and orphanages.

This was the part of the work that I enjoyed. With Sojourn's talent as a musician, I taught the children a small dance routine, and we put on performances at social institutions across northern Italy. The children liked performing, and after every show we talked with the old people, the sick, or the poor, holding their hand and telling them about Jesus. We often received a free dinner from the Catholic sisters or social workers who ran the place, and we took pictures to use in the brochures we carried around. Eventually, we traveled for days in our trailers like Gypsies, from one town to the next, performing with the kids. I was pleased to be bringing light and happiness into the lives of those who were institutionalized, but I had a few worries. What if Jerry found out? And what if I got pregnant again?

I talked to Paolo about using birth control, but he would not hear of it. He warned me that God was against birth control, and dire things could happen to me if I went against God's Word. He had internalized Family and fundamentalist Christian doctrine much better than I ever did. In addition, since he was the head of the family, and he did not want me using birth control, it was forbidden. I wanted to obey my husband this time, but I secretly tried the rhythm method, counting my days carefully, and avoided having sex on the days that I would be most fertile.

As for Jerry finding out, he was too far away from us to know what we were doing. He had agreed that Thor could come visit us in the summer, so I planned on spending that summer at our trailer in Paolo's hometown. This time while we were in the Family, we were on the bottom rung, but we had no leaders over us. We could pretty much do as we pleased as long as we witnessed and sent in our tithe. Living on the Italian Costa Azzurra, we were close enough to the tourist beach towns to sing at cafés and restaurants, which provided us with funds.

When Thor came to visit us on vacations, we discovered that he was a talented musician, having studied music and theory in the French Conservatoire. He became the star of our show. Whenever I took him to sing in restaurants along the beach, we made twice the money. I played guitar and sang, while Thor played the accordion or tambourine, and then collected the money. He was a natural-born showman, having been raised in the Show Group, and no one could resist him. He was eleven years old when he started singing with us and virtually never stopped until he struck out on his own. Sometimes he wore odd-looking hats for emphasis and used them to collect the money. We gave him a small percentage of the money to take home, but I was worried about his father finding out. I preempted this by calling Jerry. My ex-husband was a typical musician who would be thrilled to hear that his son had inherited his performing genes. I didn't think this would risk my seeing Thor, and I was right.

"I wanted to know if you mind if Thor goes out with us?" I asked him on the phone.

"What does he think of it?"

"Well, I took him out a few times, and he likes it."

"Does he collect?"

"Yes."

"Well, what do you know. I guess if he doesn't mind, it's okay with me. How much do you give him?"

"Ten percent."

"Ha! I doubt if that will keep him content for long. But if he's happy with that, it's okay with me."

Thor played and sang with us for the next couple of years, and each year as he progressed, he was given a bigger cut. He went from playing tambourine to playing guitar. By the time he was fourteen, he was singing and playing guitar, and I was collecting, giving him 50 percent. But it was worth it. By then we were making two hundred dollars a night. Jerry moved his family back to Nice when Thor was fourteen, less than an hour from us by car, so my son came to our house almost every weekend as well as all summer. I thought that I must be doing something right now—and oddly enough, I was in the Family. Singing with my teenage son gave me some of the happiest moments of my life. The fabulous weather allowed tourists to sit in the open cafés by the beach and enjoy the lovely Italian seaside. Thor and I had our regular restaurants and cafés in every town along the coast. We planned our work systematically, making sure we kept good relationships with the restaurant owners by not coming too often, and we hit a different town every night. The more popular resorts, such as San Remo and Diano Marina, were saved for the big nights of Friday and Saturday.

Living a gypsy lifestyle brought us into contact with other Family gypsies. What I liked best about that time during the early 1980s was that all the ambitious leaders had gone to the "mission fields" such as India, South America, and the Far East. Remaining in Europe was the equivalent of staying in the United States, which meant you couldn't make it as a missionary. No one in Europe bothered us about our spiritual state, and as long as we sent in a decent 10 percent, we were left alone. However, many of the struggling Family homes wanted us to join up with them. As I traveled from home to home, I realized that not only had I previously lived a privileged life in the Family, but I also had a strength that made others want me near them.

Without birth control, I conceived again while Genvieve was still a baby. I felt sorry she would have to grow up so quickly now. When my third daughter, Jordan, was born, eighteen-month-old Genvieve stood next to the two-day-old baby lying on my bed with her eyes wide open, with her two front fingers stuck in her mouth as usual.

After receiving invitations to live in various homes, we chose to stay in a new home opening in Nice because it was closer to Thor. Around this time, the publications from the Family, which I usually never had time to read, talked about the life and teaching of Davidito, the little boy Mo's lover had with a fish. The Davidito Series, as these letters were called, explained how the parents themselves, or the nursery workers, should teach the children about sex. One Family publication included a picture of the nursery worker putting Davidito to sleep by fondling him. Later, Mo issued a statement that he did not approve of sex with minors and renounced any writings saying that he did, claiming that someone else had written that. It was difficult to know what Mo actually did write since he renounced anything that caused trouble.

By this time the Family homes were spread all around the world, and the Mo letters, especially in the area of sex, were followed in varying degrees. Some women in the Family never shared sexually with anyone but their husbands, while some husbands forced their women to do so. I heard stories of wives being physically punished for disobedience, but I never saw this with my own eyes.

It sickened me to read anything that seemed to condone any type of sex with children. In all my travels, I never met a family that actually did this, and I inquired everywhere I went to see what the others thought about the Family's child-sex education. No one ever admitted to pedophilia. Nevertheless, years later, I heard tearful confessions from ex-Family members who said they or someone they knew molested children under pressure from their leaders. I am thankful that I was not in a home with leaders—not until the very end of my time in the Family.

The brothers and sisters at the Nice home felt the same way I did about teaching children how to engage in sex—that is it was a sick thing to do. When he was younger, Thor had been with children who had been encouraged to explore each other's bodies, and he did not retain happy memories of this. The idea of showing young children adult sexual organs, and actually teaching them how to use their immature sexual parts in an adult way, was even more perverted. But I could not face this issue at that time. Unfortunately, Paolo and I didn't talk about it; we avoided the subject altogether. When letters arrived that discussed childhood sex, no one in the home mentioned them. I hardly read any letters now anyway, but lived only to raise my children. We were not even sharing among the adults here in Nice, and I believed that no one made sexual advances toward the children.

Around this time I called Salim to thank him for helping me find my son. I had sent him a thank-you card years earlier, but I had never thanked him in person for his help. I told him I was living in Nice and he immediately made an appointment with me to meet in the Hôtel de Paris.

I was extremely nervous. Not only was I five years older, but I had borne three more children since I had last seen Salim, and there was nothing new I had to offer but the same old message. I was surprised when he wanted to make love to this thirty-one-year-old mother of four, who had done little to keep her youth or beauty intact.

"Why do you like being with me?" I asked after a most mundane exchange. Despite my numerous sexual experiences I had not learned any of the special tricks or unusually stimulating procedures that are rumored to keep men interested. Why did Salim want to see me when he could pay for the best and most beautiful of the elite's high-class call girls?

"You have a strength that no other woman I know has," he responded, as if the answer had always been on his tongue ready to fall out.

"What do you mean? You know so many women; some are much stronger and much more sophisticated and experienced than me."

"That is all outward strength. It is not the same. You can uncover secrets of life. And although it seems like you are weak and submissive, it is only because you choose to be at this time. When I make love to you, I feel strength within me. You are strong!"

This was the longest and most revealing piece of personal information that Salim ever gave me. Salim had always kept a very powerful image before me, and anyone else I saw him with. I was surprised that he had let his guard down, even for a few minutes. I looked at him carefully. He still had the same iron-clad expression, but his eyes had become softer. He withdrew back into his powerful-man mode, and I did not see him again for years. But the insight that he had shared with me, whether it was true or not, stayed with me forever.

The Nice home, like all pleasant situations in the Family, did not last long. We found ourselves on the road again, this time traveling with our family in an old RV to one of my favorite cities, Venice. There we found a deserted farmhouse in the milk-producing region of Pordenone. I was sent to the owner of the house, a wealthy industrialist who had bought the property on a whim and later decided that raising cows was not his cup of tea. He flatly refused to even rent the house to us, although we had suggested he give it to us free in order to keep it from being vandalized and lie in disrepair. We had been taught never to take no for an answer, and I went back to him about half a dozen times. Each time he became more friendly, and as I showed him our photo album full of pictures of the children and me singing in nursing homes and hospitals, he softened a bit. After more than a month of persuading and bargaining, he agreed to let us live in the house rent-free, and we agreed to refurbish the old place and bring it back to life.

"I don't really care if the house tumbles to the ground," he said. "I don't need the income from it, and I don't ever plan to sell it either. But I don't want you guys causing any trouble out there."

Paolo and I invited another couple and their children to help us fix up the grand old stone farmhouse. We quickly learned that this area of Italy was a provisioner's paradise. There were factories of every kind all over the place, and we established regular contacts with Benetton clothes; Parmalat milk, cheese, and yogurt; and many others. We literally remodeled the house with supplies we got for free, but it was labor-intensive work. I spent most of my waking hours, when not physically involved with the children, scraping, cleaning, and painting the old walls and beamed ceilings.

There was no central heat or indoor toilets. The large kitchen had a huge wooden stove, and the enormous living room, covering half the downstairs, had a fireplace with seats on the side, so you felt as if you were sitting inside the fire. However, it did little to heat up the rest of the house. There was one other room downstairs, which had a private entrance and no heat at all. Upstairs were four large bedrooms and a center hallway large enough to serve as a den. There we placed an oil heater that we had procured from a factory in the area. Walking out on the back patio from any of the downstairs rooms, one was greeted with the beautiful Friulian pastureland. A cement sink with a water pump constantly gave us fresh springwater that had a sulfurous taste, but was sanitary and healthy. My daughter Jordan spent hours at this pump, drinking and playing in the water. The barn, which was in terrible disrepair, housed old machinery, and eventually we filled it with chickens. It was a pastoral dream come true for an old nature lover like myself, but unfortunately, I could never be completely happy. Thor was farther away from me now, which meant he could only come for the summer, and I was still not happily married. Knowing that bad marriages happen to the best of people, I consoled myself by raising my children with all the energy and love I found available.

All my children started learning to recognize letters from the time they could talk. Athena was already a proficient reader at the age of four, and she often helped me to teach phonics to her sisters. I also taught them to dance and sing, and we performed at hospitals, schools, and nursing homes regularly. Different Family members visited us periodically, and some stayed on indefinitely. The house was big, and extra Family members usually meant more hands to do the work, and more income. That was until we were graced by the presence of "leaders."

One day they finally arrived—my old nemesis from Germany, Naomi, and her husband, Samson.

As I suspected, Naomi and Samson stayed only a few months before moving on to their mission field, but not before they almost ruined the open access I had with my son. As usual, Thor came to visit me in the summer. Although Naomi had suggested that the presence of a "systemite" kid might be a bad influence on their sheltered children, I insisted on this one, and they eventually acted as if they had heard from the Lord to allow him to come. When they saw how much income he generated through singing with me in Venice, they quickly changed their minds about him being a systemite and tried to recruit him back into the Family. Of course, Thor, at thirteen, was much too smart, and had been too indoctrinated by his father on the evils of cults, to even consider this invitation. But the strange behavior of his mother, who lived with people in her own house who told her literally what to do every minute, was confusing to him. I tried to explain that I believed in communal living, and one took the evil with the good, until the evil became too much. At his young and tender age, he was forced to struggle with the dissonance of the moral dilemma between idealism and the corruption of absolute power. Even though Jerry eventually realized that I was back in the Family, he believed that Thor was mature enough for exposure to a radical ideology he once believed in himself. I had talked with Jerry back in Nice, before I left for Venice and Pordenone, and wanted to bring Thor with me. He agreed, but told me that he knew we were back in the Family.

"I'm only in it because of Paolo," I said. "I don't have many choices in my life."

"I feel sorry for you sometimes,"said Jerry, as he shook his head. "But don't worry, Thor knows enough about the Family to never want to join it. Just keep him away from the leaders—okay?"

Naomi had put Jerry's faith in his son to the test by enticing him to join us, and Thor had passed with flying colors. I remember controlling my urge to tell Naomi to back off, and I watched to see what would happen. Looking into my son's bright eyes, I saw him weigh the lifestyles in his quick, observant young mind, and he decided the system had more to offer him. I was truly happy about his decision. Maybe he could make it out in the world. Obviously I could not!

During the time that Naomi and Samson were in Pordenone with us, another couple, on their way to serve God in Eastern Europe, had stopped by our home for an extended stay. Paolo and I were away taking Thor back to his hometown. We stayed longer than planned, with the excuse that we were making money singing with my son along the coast. When we returned, I discovered that the other couple's four-month-old baby was terribly sick. The poor Italian mother was holding the baby, who looked like a limp rag doll, draped over her outstretched arms. In her pain and despair, the mother recognized that I could help her.

"Don't let the children come in here," I said to Paolo as he opened the kitchen door, having parked our RV in the field by the fountain. "There's a sick baby, and I want to find out what's wrong." Fortunately, I had just been in Genoa, where the story of a small child in the Family who had died from meningitis a few months earlier was still the major topic of discussion and prayer. I had researched the symptoms, and this baby, lying almost dead with an extreme fever, seemed to have the same condition.

"We're taking care of this," barked Naomi, who came in from the living room and ordered the mother to take the baby back upstairs to the cold and drafty second floor. "It's none of your business, of course, but we have been praying about this situation with the baby's father. The Lord has shown us that the mother has a spiritual sin which needs to be confessed, and then the baby will be healed."

"Oh? What sin does she have?" I asked, curious as to what reasons they thought God would have to let a baby and mother suffer so.

"She is rebellious to her husband."

"Well, I don't believe it. I don't think God is keeping that baby in pain because the mother has problems with her husband. I want that baby to see a doctor. Right now! Do you know what meningitis is? Do you have any idea how quickly a baby can die from it? And did you know that your own children, Naomi, might be exposed to this terrible disease right now?"

"My children are protected," Naomi said rather weakly.

Just then her husband, Samson, came in. He spoke directly to Paolo. "I think you need to take Jeshanah out of here. She is standing in the way of God's work."

"Oh, how ridiculous! How can anyone stand in the way of God's work?" I was furious, and I was going to get that baby to a hospital if I had to drive it myself. But I had not driven a car for over twenty years, and I had no license. I would have to go for the jugular vein—the dreaded authorities.

"Paolo," I cried, turning to my confused husband. "Do you realize that this house is legally in your name as the only Italian resident? These foreigners are your guests, and you are liable if this baby dies in this house and you did nothing about it." I didn't know if that was true or not, but it could have been.

Both Paolo and Samson had a shocked look on their faces.

"We're going to pray with the father about this again," said Samson, taking Naomi with him upstairs.

Paolo asked that I go out into the RV and stay with the children. In a few minutes I saw the baby, the mother, father, and Paolo get into the car and drive off. I went into the house.

"The Lord showed us it was time to take the baby to the hospital," said Naomi without looking up at me.

Thankful, I went back to the RV and put my children to sleep without dinner, reading them a story and holding them close. Paolo returned hours later with the news that the baby did indeed have meningitis, but it was hopeful that the baby's life could be saved.

Later, after the baby and his mother had spent two weeks in the hospital, a visiting sister told me that the doctor had looked at a picture of Jesus hanging up on the wall and pointed to it.

"You can thank Him that this baby lived," he said dramatically, "because this was a miracle."

The baby's parents never came back to our home. The father implied at other homes that I had interrupted God's work of making his wife submissive, and that it might take years before she learned that lesson again. Clearly, here was a father willing to sacrifice his son. I wondered if he too had been quoted the story of Abraham? Did he imagine that God was going to stop this baby from dying at the last minute because he would obey God's voice and give him up willingly? What would that prove? But the mother of the baby sent me a message, through a sister, saying that she was grateful that I'd saved her baby's life.

This experience not only had given me further insight about my own strength—which Salim had seen but I never did—it also prepared me to stand up to any leader who came our way. This fearlessness in the face of leaders was not enough, however. There were more lessons for me to learn. There was still the struggle between God's Will and free will to be resolved. Before Thor had been kidnapped, I had not believed I possessed any free will once I submitted my own will to God's. Now I fluctuated between what I was told was God's Will and what I felt was my own free will; however, as long as I continued to think in terms of this dichotomy, of only two polar opposites from which to choose, that fence-sitting vision that disturbed my thoughts at inopportune times would always bother me.

After Naomi and Samson left for Yugoslavia, we were graced with the presence of Emma, the former wife of Jeremy Spencer, who had now become an artist in the Family and was living underground somewhere in the world. Emma was the mother of five or six children with Jeremy and another three with her new mate, Giacomo. I was curious to find out about her oldest children and how they had fared being raised in the Family.

"Where is Teddy now?" I asked when she first arrived, wondering about her oldest son, whom I had watched as a child and who was now about eighteen years old. I had read nothing about him for a long time in *Family News* letters.

"Oh, Teddy has forsaken God and the Family," she replied coldly. "He backslid in the Philippines, and I don't know where he is now." Emma, who had once been a top adviser on motherhood in the Family, with responsibilities for organizing our best schools and nurseries, now seemed tragically unconcerned about her own offspring.

"Don't you have any contact with him at all?" I asked, projecting the pain I felt about my own son onto the concern I felt for poor little Teddy.

"No. He has chosen his path. No child has had as much opportunity for spiritual growth in the Family as Teddy has had, besides Davidito of course. And if he has rejected the Lord's work to follow in the steps of Satan, he'll have to make it on his own. Of course, I pray for him, but really, it's in the Lord's hands now."

The fact that Emma could talk so objectively about the loss of her firstborn gave me chills that penetrated deeply into my heart. I remembered how devoted she was to Teddy and her little girl when I lived with her years ago in Ellenville. I never trusted her again, and I tried to keep my own children as close to me as possible. Such a cold, hard attitude was certainly not conducive to raising healthy kids. Her "good" children received special attention and had become quite snobby. The little girl who was about Athena's age bragged about her singing exploits in India, and showed off her beautiful Indian sari. When we visited the nursing homes, however, the little girl was either too shy, or too aloof, to hold the feeble, wrinkled hands of the old people, as Athena did naturally.

Later, I discovered that Emma's oldest daughter, now in her late teens, already had two children, no husband, and was living somewhere in the Far East. Her fourteen-year-old, Andrew, whom they had brought with them to our home, was under constant condemnation because he had not been accepted into the coveted Family teen camp in Hong Kong, where his younger brother now lived. Emma let us all know that Andrew had some serious spiritual problems, but that with God's help, he might work on them and be accepted next year.

The teen camps were just starting up, and so far were only in the countries in the Far East, where we had many disciples and where most of our leaders were. Mo's own son, Joshua, who had a few teens himself, headed the huge teen home in Hong Kong, which we read about in our *Family News*. There the teens, most of whom had been raised in the Family and never attended system schools, were taught skills like carpentry, had computer training, and learned to play musical instruments. There was little emphasis on academic education. Evidently, there was some kind of admission procedure to go to teen camps, which I was not interested in since I never planned to send my kids to any of them.

I took Andrew out witnessing and provisioning with me whenever I could. He seemed to enjoy my freedom and spoke openly with me.

"I want to be a truck driver when I grow up," he told me one day.

"But we don't have truck drivers in the Family," I replied.

"I know," he answered, looking at me with hurt, inquisitive eyes. He was a tall, handsome boy who probably had superior intellectual abilities that had never been stimulated. "It's the only thing I've been taught to do, though, since I am not a musician. I drove a truck when we lived in the Philippines."

I realized that he meant he would leave the Family, just like his older brother, Teddy. We were told not to talk about Teddy around the children, and since I didn't want to bring up painful memories I changed the subject.

We talked at length about the possibilities "out in the world," and I was pleased that my own son had all those opportunities to choose from as well. Sooner or later, I would have to come to terms with choices in my other children's lives, but for now, they were safely innocent and ignorant of adult decisions and mistakes. Much later, I found out that Andrew had indeed left the Family and enrolled in college to study theater. Truck driving is a legitimate career path, of course, but I felt that the quiet, sensitive Andrew had other talents to offer the world.

With so many children already in our home, I was anxious about not becoming pregnant again. The Family policy was still "no birth control" of any kind, and my husband Paolo was strictly adhering to that rule. Since we rarely went to doctors, I did not know what was available in the social health system in Italy, so I tried the rhythm method again, and again, I became pregnant.

It was September 1986. I was thirty-three years old, giving birth to my fifth child in a hospital in Pordenone. The nurses were excited, since I had agreed to use a new birthing chair they had bought and none of the local Italian women would try it out. I told them I would much rather sit during birth than lie down. When the contractions came hard and strong, they put me in the chair, only no one had taken the time to figure out the complicated stirrup and strap system. The cold metal felt icy next to my hot, sweaty skin, and while they tried adjusting the stirrups up and down and over again, I held my legs open, pressed tightly to the sides of my bloated stomach, and pushed and pushed. Out came my second son.

Paolo wanted to give him an Italian name, so we called him Michelangelo, after the great Florentine painter.

After Emma's departure, we enjoyed a few months of raising our children with a few lowly but sweet family members. Our peace was short-lived, with the unfortunate arrival of two new leaders. Judah was an American who claimed to have a degree in journalism. He was a cynical man and his large, bearded face showed little sign of empathy or compassion. His wife, Anna, a thick-skinned Italian beauty, had not borne children gracefully. Thankfully, we never shared with any of these Family members since we were supposedly not engaging in any sexual sharing between couples due to the venereal diseases that were spreading around the Family. Adults entering Europe from Eastern countries were particularly told not to share at all. On the other hand, the letters about having sex with underage teens were explicit. A series of letters supposedly written by Mo about a fictional future end-time supergirl named Heaven's Girl was circulating among our teens. In these illustrated letters the young teen has multiple sexual relationships with men of all ages. With each new letter that arrived, I became more worried. Heaven's Girl became a sex fanatic. Then a new series titled Heaven's Girl was sent out with an artist's depiction of Mo in bed with a teenager. I confronted our new leaders immediately on their opinions of these letters. They were conveniently vague.

"What do you think?" asked Judah, without batting an eyelid.

It was a moment of truth and I failed miserably. If I confessed that I didn't approve of Mo or any adult man sleeping with teenagers, I might as well leave the Family, which was an option I had not yet discussed with my husband. Paolo and I never talked about the implications of these letters. Parents in the Family had become like the people we had despised when we were young revolutionaries—those who "turn their head, pretending they just don't hear," as Bob Dylan says in "Blowing in the Wind." I wanted to make sure my own children were safe now, and later I would address the issue of what was going on in other homes. At the same time, by accepting a deviant collective conscience, I was beginning to doubt my own virtue.

"I think it's Dad and Mamma's business what they do in their household. He is supposed to be the Prophet. But I don't want my girls exposed to adult sex. Is that clear?" I answered.

"Don't you think that Mo is God's Prophet for the End-time?" asked Anna, completely avoiding the question.

"Actually, I have serious doubts about that, yes. But whether Mo is a Prophet or not doesn't bother me at all. What bothers me is people taking Mo's letters as if they were God's Word. And if you really want to know, I don't even believe everything in the Bible is God's Word either. A lot has been tampered with through the ages."

"Why are you in the Family then?" asked Judah suspiciously.

"I'm in the Family for the community. I'm in here because I still think it's better than the system. And right this minute, I'm in here because this is where the father of my children is. I lost one child, and I don't want to lose any more."

"No wonder you guys are doing so badly. And we were told it was Paolo," replied Judah, rubbing his chin as if that discovery took a lot of mental effort.

"Well, it's me. But I'm also the one who got us this house you are living in. And if you want to stay here, I want to know what you think about sex with children."

"You have no right to come in here and demand us to answer your questions," shouted Judah. "You made your point. Don't worry. I won't touch your precious little girls."

The Family was not free of the bureaucratic problems found in the system. I wasn't in this hierarchy, but I still had minimal power in my own house. I spoke to Paolo about my conversation with Judah, but he thought I was imagining things. Since our children slept with us, in our own bedroom, he said we had nothing to worry about. The letters about sex and children did not seem to bother him so much. He said that it wasn't really having sex. Mo never said to have actual intercourse with children! Like most of us, he probably did not read these perverse letters, but they were there, like a cancer eating any ideals we had left.

Everyone I talked to convinced me that I was taking these letters too seriously. I began to think that I really had a problem after all. But what problem was it? I thought about it for hours as I lay awake in bed at night. I recalled an incident that had happened about a year before, when my mother and sister Karen were visiting me in Italy while we were alone at Paolo's hometown. Karen mentioned that it was terrible how we let the children run around naked on the beach. Actually, most of the Europeans do that also. We got into a heated discussion about nudity, and finally she said what was on her mind.

"I read that the adults in your group show their naked body parts to their children, as a way of sex education. Is that true?"

Suddenly, as if a window of my past life had been opened, I saw my father showing me his penis.

"Well, what's so bad about that? Dad used to do it," I answered.

"Oh, you're disgusting! Dad never did that! You're just making that up because you're in this group! You're sick!"

She talked to my mother about this, since my mom and dad had already been separated when she was still a little girl. My mother assured her that it was not true. Coincidentally, my mother also had a severe epileptic attack while she was visiting at this time. I don't remember if it was before or after this conversation. It bothered me so much that I closed that window to the deep past.

As I lay in bed and recalled this event, I thought perhaps I was afraid of something in my past. Not one of the other adults living with us seemed as concerned about sex and children as I was. I did seem to have a problem with sex. Maybe it was I who was perverted by an evil and sick mind. On the other hand, those who did not like the Mo letters left the Family. What was I doing here anyway?

I had a lot of time to think about it. Soon after my outburst with our new leaders, I was restricted to my room for two hours of extra word time and prayer a day. I welcomed this restriction since I used it to get much needed sleep. But I also did a lot more thinking than praying, and I didn't read the Bible or Mo letters. Why did I still let leaders tell me what to do? Because I had grown accustomed to it maybe? It was a habit—part of living communally. But why did I live this way? My ideals were gone. My curiosity about a different lifestyle had long been satiated. Like Alice in Wonderland, I had seen enough. My dream was over. I came to the conclusion that I was only in the Family now because Paolo wanted to stay. I had to convince Paolo to leave.

However, Paolo seemed to find life in the Family easier than life in the Italian system. Although he worked hard, he had no rigid work hours, and all responsibilities were shared by a group of adults. If money ran low, we had a choice of going out as witnessing teams to sell tapes or singing in restaurants. Paolo was also convinced that the system was a bad place to raise children. Because of his own traumatic experiences as a child, which had left him and his brother with forms of depression, he did not want his children to have the same condition. Two of his cousins had died drug-induced deaths. He saw the Family as a haven from a cruel world. He appeared to like having rules and regulations to guide his every act so that he didn't have to think, make decisions, or take the blame for anything. Even though I know he did not agree with the letters either, he truly believed that his children were safe here.

Unlike Alice, I could not seize the tablecloth in my hands and shake everybody off. This was real life—not a dream! I spent a few months vacillating in my ruminations about who was crazy, I or they. In my weakened state, I was reproached by Judah and his wife for making Paolo use condoms, which I had recently insisted upon, so he stopped using them and I became pregnant immediately.

When I was about three months pregnant, Judah and his family moved to another home. We were expecting a new family soon, and I started cleaning out the bedrooms upstairs in preparation. As I went through the drawers in the children's rooms, where Judah's girls had slept, I came across a spiral notebook. I thought I could reuse it for school if there were enough empty pages, so I leafed through it. The name of his oldest girl, who was about eight, was written on the first page. I turned another page, and the drawing leaped up at me as if I had been grabbed around the throat and choked.

There, drawn in pencil, was the replication of a fully erect penis.

I gasped. I shut the book and breathed deeply, trying not to scream. What had gotten into me? I had seen drawings of penises in Mo letters before. But this was a child's book. And it appeared to be drawn from looking at a live model. The detail was too precise. I opened the book and frantically searched through the other pages. It was full of penis drawings, at different stages of erection.

"Oh my God!" I thought to myself. "Did this happen in my house? Was a little innocent girl taught to draw her daddy's penis while I was sleeping in the next room? What a horrible person I am. And how much have my own daughters been exposed to?" Athena was seven years old. Was she included in these lessons?

I took the book as evidence and went to the window to check on the kids. Athena was playing on the swing we had hung under a spreading oak tree. Genvieve was dressed up in her long princess dress, playing at some fantasy about being married to a prince. She had long, curly blond hair, and whenever a small boy visited our home, my four-year-old would make him be a prince. She lived in a fantasy world. Jordan was by the fountain, throwing flowers, leaves, and bugs she found into the pool that had formed from the running fountain water. I couldn't believe that my precious little ones had been touched by this evil. From a deep recess in my soul, the part that I had shut off because of a long-ago pain, I had a premonition of repeated history. I did not know what it meant, but I knew I had to protect my children. Michelangelo was asleep in his cot. At barely a year old, he had been touched by none of this. And I was never going to let that chance come. I gathered up the children's passports and hid them in the pages of one of my books. I took the book outside and hid it again in the barn. That evening I confronted Paolo, showing him the horrible notebook drawings.

"We don't know that these were drawn by her, or that they were even drawn here," he said, pushing the notebook aside as if to take it out of his sight and so out of his mind.

"Of course, they were drawn by her," I protested. "And so what if they were not drawn here in this house. This is pornography. What if Athena saw this?"

"You don't think Athena has seen the Mo letters?"

I realized with a gasp how foolish and blinded I had been. What was to stop the children from looking at the Mo books with fully detailed sex organs drawn for the adult readers, or so I wanted to believe. And even the children's newest comic books from the Family, the much-read Heaven's Girl series, included the naked man's body. He was right. Athena had seen pictures like this.

"But this has been drawn by a little girl! Don't you see the difference?"

"What are you worried about? They're gone now!"

"But they'll send more leaders to us. Paolo, I don't want my children exposed to this. I'm leaving."

"Where are you going? And how are you getting there?" Paolo laughed, knowing I could not drive.

"I'm writing my mother. She will send me money to leave Italy. I have the children's passports, Paolo. I'm leaving."

Paolo's face dropped. He looked in the drawer and saw that our passports were gone.

"I'll find them," he said weakly.

"No, you won't. And what can you do? I have proof, just like Jerry did. I can get the kids if we go to court. But I know what it's like to have a child taken from me, and I won't put you through that pain, Paolo. I'm leaving, but you can come if you want to."

Paolo softened drastically before my eyes. I knew I would make it out.

"What will I do for work?" asked Paolo. "We've been in the Family for years now. I can't borrow money again from my family. How will we live?"

I felt truly sorry for Paolo, especially since I had introduced him to the Family to begin with. But I knew it was Paolo who had decided to go back, so now I would make this decision without my ever-imposing guilt feelings.

"Are you saying you will leave the Family for good?" I asked.

"I'll follow you and the kids, not because I want to but because you are making me."

It took a few more weeks to encourage Paolo to do this. A new family had come to the farmhouse, and it seemed like everything would be fine again. Paolo tried to convince me that Judah was a special case, but now that my eyes were opened to the reality of the Mo letters, I saw sexual innuendos everywhere. I was insistent. Many years later, when we had been out of the Family for years, I asked Paolo why he had wanted to stay in a group where there might have been child abuse.

"I did like everyone else," he answered without hesitation. "I put it out of my mind. I thought this would never happen to us. We all thought, well, it didn't happen to us. And living in a community gave me security. I didn't know how I would get a job if I left or how to support my family. The community gives you security."

Finally, we left in our RV. Paolo was still complaining about how he was going to support us all. He told the new people that we were only going on a faith trip and we would be back. Everyone knew I was having problems. I was also pregnant, and pregnant women, everyone knew, sometimes act funny.

I didn't care what they thought of me. I had enough thoughts of my own. Should I stay with Paolo? He was the father of the kids, after all. And he was so weak. Maybe I would stay with him until the kids were a little older. At least I would stay until the baby was born. I couldn't make any decisions now. All I wanted to do was get away.

There were about eighteen thousand members in the Family at that time. There were now six fewer.

11

○ ◐ ●

Like a Rolling Stone

Globs of blood were coming out of me as I sat in pain on the toilet seat. There was a blood trail from the bedroom to the bathroom. I felt sick as I looked at my pieces of fetus floating in the pink toilet bowl water. The girls were in the yard playing. Michelangelo was crying in his highchair, waiting for more food. I leaned over, squatted, and pushed hard. There was no use trying to save this now. Maybe God was punishing me for leaving the Family.

"No," I thought, as I grew dizzy from losing so much blood, "this will be a blessing, not a punishment."

When Paolo arrived back at the trailer, after going out to look for work, I asked him to take me to the hospital. One of the advantages of living in Italy, married to an Italian, was their socialized health care system. I knew I should see a doctor after what had just happened.

"Why?" he asked. "The blood probably washed it all away. These things are natural, you know."

"I just feel I should go to the doctor, that's all."

Paolo went down the street and asked his mother to watch the kids while he took me to the hospital.

I was advised to stay overnight and get a D and C, which is a uterus cleansing, the next day. The doctor suggested that I have my tubes tied after he heard I'd had five children and this miscarriage, but Paolo was insistent that I should not do it. He promised to let me use birth control, and I inserted an IUD, which made my menstruation longer and, for the first time in my life, painful. But it was worth it.

With our trailer parked in the garden plot of land that belonged to Paolo's uncle, we were mainly concerned about bringing in daily income. Paolo spent a few months selling our leftover Family tapes, while I took the girls out singing. Although Paolo was not happy to be working in the system again, I was thrilled at the limitless possibilities open before me. However, after a few years, I realized that in Italy married women with children already had their place established for them. It was in the home, serving her husband and children.

Since we now were living in Taggia again, and Jerry was living with his family in Nice, Thor was less than an hour from me. A tall, lanky boy at the difficult age of fifteen, Thor often had serious arguments with his father, and he was now free to come to my house whenever he wanted to. Although the Family always preached that God would punish those who left, I instead felt blessed. With Thor close by, I could see him every weekend, and he soon became an integral part of our little family show group. An agent signed us on to perform at small theaters, but because of the travel involved, and the little financial recompense, I created my own music business. Under the name of "Happy Songs," I developed a program introducing English to children in elementary school through singing and games. We performed at most of the local schools, and the local paper ran an article on the girls singing in a school, comparing us with the *Sound of Music* family.

When Athena, our star, enrolled in school, I began taking her on a public bus in the morning to another town, and picking her up in the afternoon. I still could not drive, and Paolo now had a job as a salesman, which kept him out most of the day. We had to stop performing, and our singing was limited to hospitals and nursing homes. In the summer, I made use of the tourist beach towns, taking all the children to sing on the large pedestrian streets. The money that the sweet Italians, who absolutely love other people's children, threw in our guitar cases helped to pay for children's clothes and other necessities.

My good friend Charles, who had always helped us financially, giving at least one thousand dollars as a gift every time I had a baby, invited us to spend vacations in his St.-Tropez home. I went out singing in the St.-Tropez restaurants, and brought back quite a bundle. It's not that I was a good singer or musician; I was neither. But, by now, I had a tough skin. Once, when singing in Villefranche, an American man at the first café/restaurant gave me the equivalent of one dollar and said, "Here, go get some singing lessons." Since we needed lunch money, I had to keep singing. At the next café, a young Arab gentleman sitting with a beautiful woman asked me to sing a special love song for her, and he slipped me a hundred dollars under the table.

Whenever Thor came with me, we made twice as much. He now kept half the collections, but he was worth more musically. Having studied for seven years at the Conservatoire in Nice, he was a virtuoso on many instruments. At fifteen, he was tall, sported bright red hair, and was shy about his hormonal changes. Sometimes it was painful for me to watch as he struggled through the complexities of being a teenager. Like most fifteen-year-old boys, he was less mature than girls his age, and as far as I knew, not very interested in them. Perhaps I was in denial that my darling little boy had grown up. I was only now addressing the reality of adulthood myself, having lived in never-never land for fifteen years. I never talked to Thor about sex, or the sexual experiences of the Family, but I gathered that his father had told him a lot. One evening, after we had just finished singing at our best restaurants in Diano Marina, a hip beach resort, we bought some delicious Italian ice cream and sat on a bench to wait for our train home.

"Why did you leave Dad?" Thor asked me out of the blue, licking at his cone hungrily and pretending not to be very interested.

"There were many reasons, honey, but you were not one of them. You were the reason I stayed with your dad, and why I am still friends with him. I will always love him as your father."

I could see tears welling up in Thor's green-blue eyes. His face was becoming bright red.

"Why did you do that to him?" He started crying. "How could you do it?"

"What? What did I do?" I asked frantically. I knew he wasn't talking about divorce.

"You know. Dad told me everything. How you went with other men—lots of them."

Thor was slobbering now. His ice cream had dripped down around his hands, and as he tried to lick it, the sticky melted stuff was spreading down his chin and neck. I tried to wipe his face with my napkin, but he pushed me away.

"You must be a bad person," he continued. "I know how it must feel to have the girl you love go with someone else. You cheated on him! Poor Daddy! Why did you do that, Mommy?"

I was beginning to understand that Thor must have had his first pangs of puppy love. He also had been told too much by his father, at too tender an age, and without a balanced view. But how was I to explain all this to a sexually budding fifteen-year-old boy? Despite his protests, I drew him to me and held him tightly. He melted into my arms, as the cone he held in his hand fell to the stony ground under our bench. His favorite flavors of ice cream spread across the sharp rocks, covering them with sweetness. I wished my love could do as much to the rocks that had been thrown in my little boy's heart.

I listened to him sob uncontrollably, as the last big cry of his childhood opened a door into maturity. I prayed he would not be afraid. I prayed he would eventually hear my side of the story, because I knew it was too early to tell him right now. All I could do was hold him and hope that he felt my tremendous love.

"There is more to the story than what your father told you, sweetheart," I whispered when he finally calmed down. I wanted to tell him everything from my point of view, but I believed that it would confuse and upset him even more.

"Whatever you think about me, I hope you know I love you very much. I always have and always will."

"As big as to the sky and back," said Thor with a smile, using an expression we shared when he was a child.

"As big as to the end of the universe and back," I answered, wiping away my own tears. "Come on, we have to make the last train."

We were all living in a small one-bedroom trailer. Our garden was beautiful, but in the winter, with four small children running around, the cramped space seemed unbearable. Then one day I noticed an article in the paper that gave me an idea.

There were dozens of tiny villages in the mountains around our area. With populations under three hundred in the winter, swelling in the summer with tourists and foreigners, the villages' schools were constantly under threat of closing down. I read of one town near us that was lamenting the fact that their one-room elementary school house would no longer have enough children to be eligible for public support. I called the mayor of the town and told her I had three school-age children, and one more on the way. If she could find us a decent house at an affordable price, we would move to her town. Within days, not only had she found us a house, but she also offered me a job running the after-school program. I talked to Paolo, and we accepted. We lived in this village, located over six hundred meters above sea level and still with a view of the ocean, for a few months. Then the mayor of Apricale, a neighboring town, called Paolo and offered him a huge house for a ridiculously low rent. Since Apricale was closer to the main roads and the beach area, we moved our family into an elegant old stone house, with four bedrooms, living room, den, kitchen, and terra-cotta floors. This was the beauty of old Italy.

I spent the first two months cleaning the three-story home, which had belonged to the mayor's family but been unoccupied for over a dozen years. After whitewashing all the walls, scrubbing the broken terra cotta, and covering the cracks with linseed oil polished to a shine, hand-sewing lace curtains for the windows, and designing hand-made high beds for the children to keep them off the cold and drafty floor space, I finally had time on my hands to think about life. Paolo worked in the tourist towns along the coast selling publicity for the newspaper, and without a car or even a driver's license, I was forced to live a village wife's life.

I walked the girls to school every morning through the stony path-ways that turned and twisted around the medieval town set on a hill. The Italian children wore little *grembulas*, which are a type of apron, over their school clothes, and I had made the girls grembulas of faded jeans and lace. Athena was eight years old, with brown inquisitive eyes that questioned everything. Genvieve, at six, had retained a baby-face expression of naïveté and innocence. Her long blond hair was worn in two braids, and her expressive mouth was either smiling or round with wonder. Jordan, my cute little doll daughter, who scowled when everything was not exactly how she wanted, was only five, but she attended the same classes as her older sister in the two-room schoolhouse. Together, they made up a third of the school, and as the only half-Americans, in a town whose inhabitants spoke a dialect not even the Italians understood, they were always the outsiders. Their friends were the children of other marginal dropouts, the recently arrived Italian and German hippies who were buying up small, deserted farms around Apricale in order to "live off the land." The mayor of the town had learned to recognize these new residents as his only hope for the town's survival. Most of the natives' own children had moved to the bigger cities to start their families. Still, there was a deepening gap between "us" (the locals) and "them" (the newcomers). I watched this real-life drama from the sidelines, and ironically, I was included as "us" since my husband had been born and raised in Liguria, and included as "them" because I was a foreigner. Due to this precarious access, I was often asked to serve as a liaison between the two camps when disagreements arose over town politics.

Thor, who was now an independent teenager, came to visit whenever he could. He had not only become an accomplished musician but also excelled in math, and had been selected for the difficult math track in the French schools. That guaranteed him a college education in the prestigious colleges specializing in math and science. I was so proud of him. Through our talks together, I knew he had a deeply inquisitive approach to life, and would find answers to questions that I didn't even know to ask.

I usually brought Michelangelo, my youngest son, to the preschool, which Apricale provided for all the under-school-age children. He attended unwillingly, and often I let him stay with me in the piazza, playing in the morning sun while I took a cappuccino at the only café and read or wrote. However, on those winter days when it was too cold to play outside, and it took the house, with only one wood-burning stove in the kitchen, all day to heat up, I thought Michelangelo would be more comfortable in school, where he could also learn Italian. We still spoke English at home, and I continued to teach my children to read and write in English. During those winter months,

I took a heater into the tiny, windowless room we used as an office, and with an old portable typewriter I had bought secondhand, I wrote stories to keep my troubled thoughts from clogging up my mind.

It was the fall of 1990. I had been out of the COG for almost two years, and I was ready to write another children's story. I had never heard of the symbolism of a labyrinth before, and I started this story without knowing where it would go. It led me through a labyrinth ritual. The story line told of a little girl who discovers that she can jump into a tall calla lily growing in her garden and slide down into the underground world below. The lily's roots open into a labyrinth through which the girl must discover the answers to many of life's basic questions, such as why is there evil, where does it come from, and what can one do about it? I read the story to my children as it unfolded, and they remained enthralled, so I sent it off to one editor in the States. When I received a rejection letter, I switched to writing adult stories.

I wrote intensely, listening to 1960s music as I worked, and with the Bible and Mo letters cluttered around my desk. Writing was the only way I knew to clean out my guilty conscience and express the cry of one truth-seeker who failed to find truth. I was thirty-seven years old, had been in college for only a semester over twenty years ago, and had not been allowed to pursue any type of academic research during the fifteen years I spent in the Family. But due to a natural inclination to include eclectic knowledge, my writing was interspersed with quotes from a range of sources: Bob Dylan, Francis Schaeffer, Leo Tolstoy, B. F. Skinner, Moses David, and the Bible. I sent in a twenty-four-page thesis to *Rolling Stone*, which rejected my article. I decided I must be too religious for the radicals, and I resigned myself to try to learn the system.

This period of writing proved to be therapy for my questioning soul. I felt I had to empty myself of a polluted perspective before I was free to file new material. Writing was an emptying process, but it was only a small beginning. There seemed to be a bottomless pit to empty. After winter passed, and the cherry trees began to blossom on the lovely hillsides, I put the typewriter away, left my windowless room, and joined the children while they played on the sun-warmed stones of the town piazza.

During this time, Paolo was constantly changing jobs. He was unhappy with his working prospects, and when he met a member of a religious commune from America who had started a community in Sus, a small village in western France, he asked for their address. He took us to visit the community, which looked much like the COG, in the early days before sexual liberation. Everyone in the hundred-odd-member commune shared food, housing, clothing, and work responsibilities, as they ran an American-style coffeehouse and built futons, and other hippie furniture, to sell. Marriages were sanctioned by the leaders, and children were taught, disciplined, and cared for by everyone. The most notable difference between this commune and COG was that the women wore head scarves and were even more subservient to their husbands than the Family women had been. Their marriage ritual included the wife kneeling on the floor before her husband, while he placed the scarf on her head. The symbolic scarf, which the wife would forever after wear in public, was a constant reminder that the wife is under the man's rule, as the Bible supposedly commands. I was liberated enough at this time to think to myself that even the system has a better symbolic act, with the man kneeling to the woman as he asks for her hand in love and devotion, but, alas, Paolo thought communal life offered the ultimate set of rules. The leaders of the group convinced Paolo that until I bowed my head to him and wore the head scarf, our marriage would always be bad. Paolo told me on our third evening that he was joining.

"Fine," I said. "I'm taking the kids and leaving." My first reaction, although it did not last long, was relief that Paolo wanted to stay, followed by an urge to take my children and run!

"How are you going to do that?" he asked with assurance. "I have the car, and you don't have any money."

I knew I was stuck without resources. We stayed another few days, and either through subconscious manipulation on my part, or because I was truly desperate, I felt that maybe I should think over the possibility of joining. I somehow convinced Paolo that I would join, but that we should first go back home and get our belongings. Once back home in Apricale, I called the only Christian friends I knew, Baptist missionaries who worked, of all places, in Monte Carlo. I went to visit them and told the story of the commune through tears and weeping.

"I only want my children to be happy and healthy," I cried. "Maybe I should join this commune with Paolo. They aren't doing anything bad. I don't think they abuse the children. But I just can't see myself submitting to Paolo, and I don't want to raise my girls to do that. But maybe that is the answer. Maybe I have never found the answer because I have not submitted to a man."

"You have submitted to many men, from what I understand," said the missionary wife, who was somewhat liberal and very pragmatic.

"Oh, that was only in the flesh. I have never submitted my will, my spirit"—I was searching for the right word—"I have never given up my soul to a man—that's what they are asking me to do."

The husband of this woman was a very open, sensitive man. At one point he put his arm around me while I cried, but he had nothing to say that could comfort me. After all, even in their Protestant religion, the wife was ultimately obedient to the husband. However, they did meet with Paolo and convince him not to join that group, but to attend their church instead. Their support seemed to be enough for Paolo.

After the episode, I took a walk with my children along the beautiful mountainside trails, with all sorts of wildflowers blooming in the spring breeze. Sitting under the cherry blossoms, with a view of the Mediterranean Sea below us, and the blue sky that reached across Europe like a secure blanket covering a divided bed, I felt more lonely and lost than ever before in my life. Here I was living in the most charming place on earth, with the most adorable children I could ever hope for, with a husband who said he loved me and wanted to work on our marriage, and I felt utterly hopeless, as if my soul was desperately struggling to keep from dying. Why did I feel this way? Tears rolled down my cheeks as I clenched my teeth and tried to keep the sobs noiseless.

I walked back to where my children were playing joyfully under the trees. They couldn't wait till the cherries would be ripe and they could pick them, but then I would have to explain to them that these cherries belonged to someone else. We could only pick and eat the cherries that belonged in our family, or to some nice person who would allow us to pick their cherries. This is life. This is not the Garden of Eden that I read about to you at bedtime. From some memory storage in my mind came the words, "There is no truth outside the gates of Eden." Fine, I thought. I'll ponder that. But what if there is no Garden of Eden either?

The next few months passed as if I were stuck in glue. The days went by, the calendar pages were flipped over, but I did not feel that

I was getting anywhere. I thought I had already emptied myself with the writing. What else was there to empty? Where did one find answers? Why did some look, while others did not? Was I doomed to eternal seekership? How could I be a good mother and a truth seeker at the same time? Truth seekers are always rejected and criticized by the contemporary majority who don't want to rock the boat. They have had the truth for two thousand years, and if I couldn't recognize it, then there was something wrong with me. Just be a good mother, I told myself. But how could I be a good mother when I felt like a hypocrite and a fake; when I felt like I was teaching my children to live a life that did not make me happy or fulfilled; when I really thought the purpose of life is to seek truth, love, and happiness, but I had given up? The paradox of my two most urgent, emotional needs—the search for brotherhood and the pull of motherhood—was tearing me apart.

Paolo was unconcerned with my dilemma. Either he could not understand it, or he did not want to be bothered by it. When I annoyed him with existential questions, he suggested I might be crazy. My only intellectual support, Charles, who had remained a friend to us throughout the years, offered me hope that I was not crazy but instead, just beginning to explore another level of understanding. Through conversations with him, I was able to recognize a ray of light inside myself. Perhaps I was not without resources, but during that dark time I felt utterly helpless. Against my will, I cried out for empathy to the person who was supposed to be closest to me. Maybe I was a hopeless romantic after all, but I believed that my husband— the one to whom I gave my body, but who also wanted my soul— would, should, could understand me!

Instead, Paolo avoided my questions about why I was so unhappy. We began to argue over every decision involved in living together, from the big ones to the small ones.

"Help me! Help me! For God's sake, help me!" I screamed one evening, as I lay completely prostrate on the cold floor at Paolo's feet.

As I listened to Dylan's song "Like a Rolling Stone," I realized how I used to make fun of the "systemites" and the people who "hung out" at churches. Now I was scrounging for a spiritual meal, and I was on my own. I didn't even know where home was anymore. How did it feel? Enough to drive one crazy.

A few weeks later, I woke up in the early morning hours hearing a child cry. It was still dark outside, but because we left a light on in the hallway, I could see out through our open door. Our bedroom was situated next to the children's room, which was right at the top of the steep stone steps. There, on the platform at the top of the steps, I saw a little girl, covered from head to foot in dripping blood. She was about the age of my youngest daughter, who was five. I couldn't tell who it was because the blood hid her facial features. It could have been my middle daughter, who was seven. She just stood there in the hallway, crying.

In that split second of realization, I imagined that my daughter had fallen down the stone steps, crawled back up while blood from a head wound splattered her body, and was now at my door crying. I screamed out in terror and pain. I could not move or make an intelligible word.

Paolo rose quickly from a deep sleep.

"What? What is wrong?" he asked, looking at me as if I were a madwoman.

I pointed to the little girl, still standing in the hallway. I could do nothing but scream. He looked to where I pointed and then back at me.

"What is it? What are you pointing at? What do you see?"

With a chill of fear running down my spine, I realized that Paolo did not see what I saw. I looked at him for an instant, my eyes wide with disbelief. When I looked back to the hallway, the little girl was gone.

"Go look at the girls," I cried, as I found my voice again. Maybe Paolo had not seen her since he just woke up and had not focused his eyes yet. Maybe my bloody daughter had gone back into her bedroom, frightened by my screaming. But I could not move to go look for myself.

Paolo went into the next room. All the girls were now sitting up in their beds, awakened by my screams.

"They are fine," said Paolo when he came back. "What is the matter with you?"

I got out of bed now, and ran into the next room, followed by Paolo. There were my three girls, all sitting up in their beds, and all without a drop of blood on them.

"What's happening, Mommy?"

I gave them all a hug, as I touched each one to make sure they were fine.

"What was it?" asked Paolo.

"I must have had a nightmare," I said with fear still in my eyes. "I'm going to stay in here and sleep with the girls. I don't want to let them alone now," I said, lying down and trying to act rational. "Please, tuck the girls in. It's still night. We need to sleep."

As I lay in bed, with my eyes open or closed, I saw demon faces. We had acknowledged the presence of demons in the Family, and although I had never seen one, I prayed and rebuked them while in the COG, like I was told to do. Now, as I lay awake in bed, I had little to go on but what I had learned in the Family.

"I rebuke you in Jesus' name," I said silently.

I had no tools to fight with but religion. I repeated the name of Jesus over and over, and quoted all the Bible verses I could remember. That helped me to make it through the night, but the days were worse.

When Paolo woke me to get the children ready for school in the morning, I knew my experiences of the previous night were not over. My whole consciousness had been altered. I felt as if I were walking in a world that was not real to me. I did all the rituals that were required: washed, dressed, fed the kids, took them to school, came home, cleaned the house, prepared lunch, etc., but all the time, the real me was in another place, looking on at my dissociated self. At night, demons came back and tried to convince me I was crazy. In the day, I walked around as if I were a zombie. Paolo finally grew concerned.

He took me to a doctor who was a homeopath and used natural cures. He diagnosed me as having had a nervous breakdown induced by stress and poor eating habits. Natural doctors seemed to attribute everything to eating meat and processed, chemically enhanced foods. I was put on a strict diet of brown rice and vegetables, and given natural vitamins and other homeopathic remedies.

However, after three nights of demonic visions, as I lay in my children's bed, desiring to be close to them since they were the purest form of love I knew, I looked the demon in the face and laughed.

"You have no power over me, so why don't you just go away. I am protected by angels," I said, using the only references I knew. "I have Jesus in my heart. I have light, and you are darkness. You cannot exist inside me. You can only bother me from the outside. I am not crazy. If I were, you would be inside me, and you're not. You are out there!"

The demon faded away. Others came, but they all faded away. I never saw them again after that night. Sometimes, years later, whenever I started to lose faith in myself, this fear of demons would come again. But it only took remembrance of the light within me to make it vanish.

12

○ ○ ○

Breaking the Shell

Your pain is the breaking of the shell that encloses your understanding.

—Kahlil Gibran

Charles gave me a book when I first left the Family. It was M.
Scott Peck's *The Road Less Traveled.* As I read through it, the desire
to know my purpose grew in intensity. Charles gave me other books
as well, mostly written by recent Nobel Prize winners, and I reread
the classics, which I found in a local English library. I soaked in these
books as if I were dying of thirst, which I was. My husband, who
never understood my interests, had given me only one book in our
fourteen years together. It was written by a beautiful Italian television
actress and was about how to keep your breasts firm. I had nursed
five babies now, and he thought I was worried about what shape my
breasts were in. I wasn't until he gave me the book.

I knew the direction for my new life was to go back to school. I
had worked as an English teacher for the British School in San Remo,

Italy, for a while, and when I asked the director why I received half the pay that other teachers got, he told me, "You don't have a degree." At first I wanted a degree in order to make more money, but the more I read and realized how little I knew, having lived in an intellectual vacuum, the more I wanted to go to school just to learn. Early in 1991, I tried to go back to college, but everyone laughed at me: my friends, Paolo's Italian relatives, the college administration. They all told me, in one way or another, that at thirty-eight years of age, with four children at home, higher education was not an option. At least not in Italy. But if I could not go to school there, I would have to go somewhere else. As if others were conspiring to help me, my sister Karen called from the States, offering me her house if I wanted to come to America. I had been thinking that I could go back to school if I lived in America, but I had not told anyone. I had kept in touch with my family through infrequent letters and small Christmas gifts, but the last time I had talked to Karen was when she came to visit us in Italy three years before. She had no idea that I was thinking of returning to America. But here she was on the phone telling me that her husband had taken a job out of the States, and I could use their house in the southeastern part of the United States. She thought it was time I come home.

The last time I had been in the States was when Athena, who was now ten years old, was born, and even then, I was there for only a few months. All together, I had been away from America for eighteen years. Discussing the possibility of going back with Paolo, I suggested that we try our luck in America for a few years, and if it didn't work out, we could always come back. Paolo finally agreed, after he lost his fifth job. It took us months to sell everything for the money to buy tickets, and by that time Paolo had found another job, which was going well for him. He now wanted to stay in Italy. We were back in the trailer again, and with the tickets already in my hand, I said that I and the children were going. Paolo stayed in Italy another five months before joining us in America.

The hardest part of going back to America was being separated from Thor, who was now eighteen and ready to graduate from high school. Ironically, his father also wanted to return to America, and Thor had already been thinking about it himself. He would attend college in France, since his grades were good enough for him to make use of France's academically vigorous, but free, universities. However, he would visit in the summer, and he was already thinking of going to graduate school in the States. My four younger children were excited about going to the country where almost everything came from—the movies, the music, the latest fads, their mother! I told them I would kiss the ground when I arrived, and I did.

Returning to America, however, was more of a cultural shock than I expected. My sister no longer lived in the city where I landed, but she sent a friend to meet me, for which I was extremely thankful. I had only recently learned to drive, and the seven-lane highways looked terrifying. My mother came down from Lancaster right away to stay with me and help with the children, but I still felt estranged from her, having been emotionally absent for twenty years. I was busy learning how to live in America, in this hot, humid city where no one walked anywhere, grocery stores were open twenty-four hours a day, children did not play outside but in the play areas of fast food restaurants, and people did not visit without calling you to make an appointment. I didn't have anyone to visit me anyway! Often, I went to sleep crying silently, so the children would not hear, wondering how I would make it in this harsh environment. There was nothing to do but persevere.

First I had to find a job. I drove the half hour to the first city rapid transit stop, rode the underground train to a center city connection, and descended into a corridor filled with police. Two men had just been shot at the entrance to the station. It took another two hours for me to find the office for my first job interview. I had dressed in an elegant silk pants suit that I had seen women in France wear in offices; however, the lady behind the desk looked at my pants with my bare ankles and said, "You really should wear a skirt and stockings to an interview." Stockings in 90-degree weather, I thought, remembering that Esther had told me the same thing years ago. As I sat in the cool waiting room, I thought of my four children and elderly mother back at the house with no air-conditioning. They must be so uncomfortable. Tomorrow I'll go out and buy some kind of wading pool for them to sit in. Finally, a man called me into an office for an interview; however, the stress of the day was so great, I started to cry when he asked me why I had come back to America. On the way home, I decided it would be easier to work in one of the cheap family restaurants down the street from our house in order to earn a few extra dollars in tips. I was hired immediately and began working the night shift, returning home at three in the morning.

Meanwhile, I looked for a school for the kids. Apprehensive about sending the children to a large, impersonal public school after the small, one-room schoolhouse they were used to in Italy, I went to every private school in the area, offering to work in exchange for free tuition. I didn't have a degree, but I knew two languages and had taught English to children in Italy. Surprised by *two* job offers, I took the one that gave me a small stipend plus free tuition. It was a Christian school with about one hundred students, in kindergarten through twelfth grade, and my children adjusted well, even excelling in the school's basic academic courses. At first I was a teacher's assistant, but within three months I became the first-grade teacher and taught Spanish to the high school students. When the principal found out about my evening job, he offered me a better stipend so I could quit working at the restaurant. I think he was embarrassed that one of his teachers was a waitress. No one knew that I had been in a cult, and I never talked to anybody about it.

I had called Paolo to let him know how hard it was in America, and that maybe we should just consider this a visit and we'd all come back. But he already had his mind set on coming. It was no easier once he arrived; in fact, for me it was harder. Now I felt responsible for our poverty and guilty for having taken the children away from beautiful Italy. I had almost given up the idea of going back to school when, during a visit to my hometown of Lancaster, my old friend Jan told me I could go back to school on a Pell grant. She had received her degree while she was a divorced mother, and the Pell paid for it all. So I applied and soon I was going to college full-time in the evenings, while I continued to work as a teacher during the day. After my first quarter, during which I received all A's, I knew I would be able to handle it all, but Paolo discouraged me all the way. Later, in Christian counseling, I was told that it is very difficult for a man to accept a wife with a superior education, but that wasn't a good enough reason for me to stop college.

Charles had lent us money to invest in a mobile pizza trailer, and we began working the fairs to supplement our low income. For one year I went to college at night, taught during the day, and helped in the pizza business over the weekends. I studied literally every spare minute: I carried note cards out onto the school playground at recess, had my kids read college texts to me while I drove, and covered my books with flour and tomato sauce as I read while making pizza. I made straight A's my first year, but my marriage with Paolo had reached a crisis point.

It wasn't only because of school! Paolo had become more difficult as he saw me gain more independence. I knew inside myself that it was only a matter of time before we would have to separate, but since I was working in a Christian school and attending church, the counsel I was receiving left me feeling guilty about even thinking of divorce. It was my father's stay with us in 1992 that provided me with the key to moving on.

My father was in a veterans' nursing home in Pennsylvania, and I took my family to visit him. Frail, skinny as an old TV antenna, and hardly able to remember who I was, he asked me to bring him home. The doctors told me he might live a month or a few years. Almost eighty years old, he suffered from emphysema after smoking two packs of cigarettes a day all his life, and he had weakened an otherwise strong body from alcohol abuse. After discussing it with my mother, who had been living apart from him for over twenty years, we decided to bring him home with us. I watched in amazement as my poor mother fell into the same reluctantly obedient role I had observed her enacting when I was a little girl.

"Freda, Freda," my father would call from the other room.

My mom would drop the dishes she was doing and run to him, complaining on the way.

"Get me a cigarette," he said when she arrived. He was too weak to walk very far, and I kept the cigarettes hidden, out of his range.

"You are only allowed one per hour," she replied.

"It's been an hour," he yelled at her. "Get me a cigarette."

"Oh, all right, but you won't get one for another hour, you know."

This same scene was repeated about every hour throughout the day, and my weakened old mother obliged him every time.

She complained about him constantly, however, and I told her not to answer when he called.

"Well, he might need something important," she said.

"Well, don't give in to him," I answered, without thinking of the multiple meanings this statement could have. Suddenly, I understood.

I had always experienced a block to understanding my confusing emotions about men, and I felt like I had now found the key. A child first learns about relationships from her parents. There are few "perfect" marriages, but my parents definitely had a very peculiar one. My mother was the only one who supported our family emotionally, and she received no support for herself. She gave constantly, yet often without joy! She argued with my dad, complained about his drinking, cried when she discovered he had stolen the family savings, yet in the end, she always gave in to him. She disliked my father deeply, yet she gave and gave and gave—it was the Christian thing to do. I remember when I was a young girl my mother and father slept in different bedrooms, and sometimes my father would go into her room. I heard her complain, and then the complaining would stop. He did not come out.

"Why does she keep giving to him?" I thought when I was a little older and knew what he was doing in there.

And here she was, an old but content lady, still giving herself.

My father died in my house less than three months after arriving. I had taken him to the VA hospital for a checkup, and the doctor basically told me that he was on his way out. We discussed putting him back in the hospital, but even the doctor saw no point in it, and my dad expressed an earnest desire to go back home.

A few days later, I was sitting with him on the porch. He was in the rocking chair, struggling to say something to me while I held his hand. Listening earnestly, my heart sounding like the clock of the universe on the quiet porch where we sat, I thought that maybe he would say, "I love you, Miriam." I don't think I ever heard that from him. He raised his arm weakly with the first two fingers of his hand sticking out like a priest about to bless a congregation. I felt he was dying—dying peacefully while I held his hand, after having lived a life of alcohol-induced confusion and turmoil. What was he going to say with his dying breath? He could not get it out as he coughed and sputtered.

"God loves you," I said, hoping that he would go to heaven. I said a prayer for him as he looked into my eyes with what seemed like an understanding of the meaning of life. Finally, his voice came back and he said the words he was trying to say, bringing his two fingers close to his mouth as if to kiss them.

"Gimme a cig!"

I smiled. Was I a spiritual fanatic or what? I got his cigarette and lit it for him, but he just let it burn away, seemingly content to know it was there.

I had to leave him to take my mother to the dentist. She thought he would be all right till we came back, and I left one of my daughters to sit with him on the porch. Charles, who was visiting us at the time, also came out to sit with my father. When I came back from the dentist, Charles told me he had passed away peacefully.

I never saw my mother cry over his death—not when we checked his pulse to see if he was dead, not when the coroner came, not at the funeral. Maybe she cried in the seclusion of her room; she had always been a very private person emotionally. I cried because he was my father, but I thought to myself, "I would not cry if he were my husband either—I would be relieved."

The moral of the story unfolded like a dream to me. I was continuing this subtle, yet life-sucking form of oppression. I had unconsciously learned it from my mother, and I would be passing it on to my daughters. I was always giving in to my husband, Paolo, and hating him a little more each time I did it. I didn't know all the psychological theories of why daughters continue the dysfunctional models set by their parents, but I knew I had to stop it! I was not teaching my children love; I was showing them how to learn hate and pretend that it was love. Forget the "wives obey your husbands" rule! There was no reason in the whole universe good enough for me to give love lovelessly.

I finally took the first step to breaking that long chain of oppression, and struggling against the self-condemnation that I felt rising in my heart from years of church indoctrination; I separated from Paolo. I promised to stay nearby with the children, but I felt it was dishonest and unhealthy to live under the same roof with a man with whom I felt less of a connection than with a stranger. Yes, he was the father of my children—but why? Because I gave him sex to lead him to the Lord, to keep him in the Family, and finally to obey some rules that I was no longer sure who made and why. Trying to keep the family together for the children would ultimately perpetuate the cycle of oppression I wanted to break.

I discussed the separation with my children, and did so periodically, asking them if they had any questions, any problems, any preferences of where and with whom they wanted to stay. I will not say it was easy for them; however, they have always been honor roll students in the public schools they now attend, and they have told me they like it better this way because Daddy and I used to fight all the time. I question my daughters often, wondering what they remember from the Family. One of my daughters told me that her earliest childhood memory is that of her parents arguing.

Paolo and I went for about a year to a marriage counselor, and I took the children to see if they would reveal any hidden anxieties in counseling. We were told that our kids were some of the healthiest children, emotionally and psychologically, that they had ever seen. "Whatever you are doing," the counselor told us, "it's working with these kids." What we were doing was attempting to have an amiable, intelligent separation. Paolo paid a decent child support, saw the children at least twice a week, and they went to his house on weekends.

I started attending day classes at another college, working part-time, and living in a trailer again until I saved enough money to move into a house I bought with my mother. We split the down payment and the mortgage, and she helped me watch the children while I finished school. My mother was still a giver, but now she was giving where she desired to give. I asked her many times if she wanted to go back to her home in Lancaster, which she now rented out, but she always told me she'd rather stay with us. She was an immense help, and just her presence in the house made me feel safe when I was gone. Three years later, I graduated summa cum laude with a bachelor of science degree, and I was accepted into graduate school with a graduate research assistantship.

During my first few years back in America, I looked to the churches to provide me with understanding and spiritual support, but after about three years, I finally realized that I was not going to find a resting place for my soul within traditional organized religion.

Thor visited us every year, and I discussed my search for truth with him. Now twenty, he had grown into a tall, thin young man with a tousled mop of red hair, a sharp mind, and a spiritual orientation. Although he had become a talented musician, played in a band in France, and earned all his money through music, he was intent on getting a good education and continuing his own search for truth. His father was now divorced also, and living in Colorado, so Thor lived alone while finishing college in France. We spent hours together discussing our past lives in the cult and our present lives in the world. At that time, Thor saw the world through the eyes of a mystic.

One day as we drove down the interstate, he explained to me that he saw God in everything.

"Of course," I responded. "I can see God in the trees, in nature, in children. But what about that," I said, pointing to the city sky-scrapers that just came into view. "Do you see God in that?"

Thor had a peaceful expression as he smiled and gazed out the window at the highway. "I see God in the tar on the highway," he said.

I looked at the material on the road, as intensely as I could while driving. I detected little sparkles in between the black.

"Yes, I can see some beauty among that too," I responded rationally. "But what about child molesters. God cannot be in a child molester."

"God is in everything and everybody. At least in the way you understand God."

"Well, okay, let's define God, then."

"You first."

"God is Love. Well, let's not talk about Love. Its meaning is too distorted. God is truth—absolute Truth. But where can one find absolute Truth? In churches? In religion?"

"There might be absolute Truth," he responded, "but it is not in the domain of dogma."

I agreed heartily, since it was about that time that I stopped looking for truth in church and religion.

Yet I felt strangely very "spiritual." I noticed little miracles happening around me constantly, and I felt guided by dreams that I could not remember. I identified with the "paradigm shift" that some avant-garde scholars were predicting. I could not help but notice that the old paradigm characteristics were definitely masculine in nature, such as competitiveness, individualism, power struggles; whereas the new paradigm called for cooperation, community, peace, and nurturance. I was on the verge of embracing feminist thought, but for the time, I was interested in understanding my involvement in the Family.

My 4.0 grade point average in college had proved to myself and others that I was not stupid, a common accusation leveled against those who join cults, and in my case reinforced because I was a blonde. Now I seriously tackled the question of why I had spent most of my life in a cult. I had not been led blindly, since I knew what I was doing and could have left at any time. Yes, I had perhaps been blindly idealistic. My ideals were those taught by the Bible, such as "Greater love hath no man than this, that a man lay down his life for his neighbor." "All that believed were together and had all things in common." "Lovest thou me [Jesus]? Feed my sheep." But I was also an extremist. Someone told me how to live these words to the extreme, and I followed, along with about twenty thousand other people. I was also self-sacrificial. I was willing to be used for a greater cause. But a cause greater than what? Than capitalism? Perhaps idealistic extremists should stay away from religion and politics, but I did not know that at eighteen years old. I also did not know the difference between religion and spirituality.

In every upper-division class I took in college, I made use of my experience while conducting research on cults or the Children of God. Eventually, this line of research led me to the study of women's issues; but in the beginning, I was intent on understanding what had happened to *me*. One of the best explanations of cult experience was written by William Kephart, who created a valid typology of people who join cults. I identified with the "deep feeler," who, according to Kephart, views social problems on a grand scale and identifies emotionally with social issues much more strongly than does the average person. He claims that the "deep feelers" do not usually feel that they are victimized, since their emotional involvement is often for the masses. I did not like to describe myself as a victim, or if I ever used the word, I said I was a willing victim. I think children in general are victims, as well as any person who is physically, emotionally, or psychologically dependent on others. The question became why had I allowed myself to be willingly abused, but the answer to that was still hidden.

Most cult analysts claim that cult members are alienated from society. However, that in itself was not a sufficient reason. Many people I came to know outside the COG were also alienated. In addition, there was a growing number of ex-cult members now living in the world who were still alienated. Perhaps knowing the cause of alienation in each individual would shed light on why one person dealt with alienation by becoming a criminal and another by becoming a prostitute or a monk and so on. I believe that in the COG we received relief from alienation at the price of exploitation. There were no blanket answers.

During my graduate studies I learned some amazing theories of social interaction, which I tested on my experience in the cult. One of the classical theories in sociology talks of a "collective consciousness" that becomes an entity of its own in society. One learns, obeys, and internalizes the morals from the collective consciousness of the group, and in my case, having rejected the consciousness of mainstream society, I adopted first the counterculture's, then those of a new society, the Children of God. I did not realize, of course, that morals eventually become internalized; I would not even have known what the word "internalized" meant at that time. But my experience and subsequent reflection showed me that everything I had been taught as morally wrong in society was questioned and often replaced by the group's new morality of "love."

Emile Durkheim wrote of the impulse we have to seek harmony with the society to which we belong: to adopt the ways, thoughts, and actions of those who surround us, to obey without reason solely because the moral maxims possess social authority.

But why did I not internalize the morality of normal society? Why had I chosen—actively sought out—an alternative? Classical social theory explains that society is like an organic body, and one part of it cannot be infected by a disease without affecting the whole; therefore in times of crisis there will arise currents of disillusionment that create a sort of social malaise. At this time, religious systems might spring up to reduce the feeling of the senselessness of life. Those who experience this alienation often look to these new religions for relief from their pain. In the late 1960s, America was undergoing an internal crisis that resulted in a proliferation of what scholars call "new religious movements," but which are commonly known as cults. Without clear goals or a sense of direction, the (usually young) people who are most sensitive to society's sickness often join what they see as an alternative. That is what I did. But the question still remains, why me?

I hope that this story of one cult will not instill in the reader the simplistic idea that all new religious movements should be stopped. Consider the fact that Christianity started as a cult. What I do wish to impart to every person who considers new fountains of truth is to seriously consider the source! And lines must be drawn. I believe any group that condones child abuse needs to be rooted out. Those are not merely weeds!

Through much research, I had begun to find academically sound reasons for why some highly idealistic people join cults and participate in a destructive moral system, sometimes, as we have seen in Jonestown and Heaven's Gate, to the point of mass suicide. I still did not understand why *I* did it. Nevertheless, I continued to explore cult involvement as I talked with the growing number of adults, teens, and children who left the Children of God over the years. And there were many.

In 1990, the total membership of the COG was reported to be eighteen thousand, and it remained at about this level for years, as the number who left were replaced with newborn babies. Researchers estimate that hundreds of thousands of people from my generation have been involved with cults at some point in their lives. For those who joined as adults, reorientation into the "world" was always difficult, but for children raised in the cults, it was traumatic. I became acquainted with a few organizations that gave support to those who came out of a cult experience, but inquiry showed me that these support groups were usually religious, and often steeped in dogma. In fact, one of the ex-cultists I worked with had been "kidnapped" (forcefully taken against his will) by a hired deprogrammer, along with his brother, while they were both in the Children of God. They were kept in a hotel room for days and supposedly deprogrammed from all the brainwashing they had experienced while in the cult. Upon their release, his brother went home, but he promptly rejoined the COG and stayed a few more years.

I wanted to have some contact with others who had been in cults, if for no other purpose than research, but I didn't want to get involved with a church-influenced organization. Then, in a coincidence which I eventually recognized as the serendipity that occurred frequently in my life, an ex-COG member, my old friend Ruth, moved to the city where I lived and organized a meeting with other ex-Family members. Together with another single mother and a couple, Rose and Bishop, who had been out of the Family for about twenty years, we planned a national reunion of former COG members.

The reunion, held in a park in Atlanta in 1993, drew not only former Family members from across the nation, but also the attention of the national media. The focus on us—amplified because of the recent event in Waco, Texas, involving the Branch Davidians—was short-lived, but through it we established a network of ex-COG members that has grown exponentially. I was interested in helping former members discover themselves, but I was also interested in their stories. It was wonderful to see and hear from my once beloved brothers and sisters. Some of them had turned to drugs; many returned to Christian churches; others had tried to salvage badly made marriages and had failed. However, most tragically, there was a great number of women who now struggled heroically to raise their children and find a stable means of support: often alone, misunderstood, and looked down upon by others, especially if they told their story. Clearly, the women of the cult had suffered greatly, and compared with many of them, I felt fortunate to be so far along the road to recovery.

Sociologist Steve Kent, an expert on the Children of God, reports that "the most manipulative use of feminist rhetoric against women occurred in the Children of God, where its leader . . . subjected women to numerous pregnancies, traditionalistic family roles, subservience to men, prostitution, physical violence, and general sexual exploitation." I was now a witness to the results of such indignity. I had a feeling that I had passed through this abusive cult for a reason. But I was not yet ready to understand its significance. First, I needed more revelations about myself.

Other than higher education, my search for meaning led me to read many of the popular books that were currently reflecting the baby boomer midlife consciousness. With my belief that nothing was too sacred to question, I was on the path to questioning God. I read with an open mind and heart the contemporary works of Clarissa Pinkola Estes, Matthew Fox, Scott Peck, Alan Jones, James Redfield, Rosemary Altea, and others—all writing on modern spirituality. Jones claims that to mend the world, one needs self-knowledge. I was on a search for my original self so that I could know her. I had reached the midlife decision that Estes talked about—whether to be bitter or not—and I chose not to be. Little had I known that I would receive the "gift of tears" along the road to joy!

One of my earliest influences among popular nonfiction writers, after leaving the Family, was Scott Peck. In his book *A Different Drum*, he sets forth in layman's terms the stages of community building, which are very much like the stages of faith development. He explains the four stages—*pseudocommunity, chaos, emptiness, and [true] community*—as a developmental process that those seeking to build community must pass through. When Peck came to speak in the city where I lived, my supervisor at college gave me her ticket since she could not attend.

During the question-and-answer session, I asked Peck what he thought we could do about the poverty in the world, or even in America. His answer made clearer to me than ever before that there are many forms of poverty. I had been working on pulling my family out of economic poverty, but I still had forms of my own emotional and psychological poverty to contend with. However, I didn't have the financial means to seek qualified outside help.

Later, when a Peck-inspired "community-building workshop" came to town, I received a scholarship and attended the workshop for three days.

On the first day the facilitator told us to write down any dreams we might have that night and to talk about them the next day.

I woke up about 5 A.M. sobbing uncontrollably. I had just had a dream, and I could recall it vividly. Not sure if I was awake or asleep, I went through the dream again in my mind, and I felt as if I were there.

I was a little girl about seven years old. My mother was away at the hospital having her fifth baby. My brother, who was two years older than I, was hiding somewhere in the house, and I guess my two younger sisters were being taken care of by someone else. I seemed to be alone with my father. It was dark outside, being January, and I was playing in the alcove at the front of the living room with a doll I had just received for Christmas. I was pouring her tea when I heard my father calling from the middle room, right before the kitchen and at the foot of the stairs. It was dark in there, and he was slouching on the couch. He always slouched that way, and he mumbled as he talked.

"Miramm, Miramm, come here!" he muttered.

[Lying on my bed at forty years of age, I felt the fear, loneliness, and helplessness that I had felt at seven years old, as acutely as if I were there again.]

"Where is Mommy?" I cried to myself. "Why isn't she here to protect me? Where is my brother? He should be here playing with me. I don't want to go in to Daddy. Why isn't someone here to save me?"

"Miramm, come here, I said. Come to Daddy," he called again from that dark place.

I put the tea things away in the case and lay the doll inside the bench box we used for toys. I wished the doll could help me. But she was lifeless. I never played with her or any dolls again.

I walked into the room dragging my feet. The familiar smell of my father, of cheap wine, filled the air. My father was on the couch with his penis out.

"Come here and hold this, Miriam!"

I didn't have to write the dream down. I could remember it vividly now whenever I wanted to.

When I went to the workshop that morning, I waited for others to say something. There was a much smaller crowd since some of the people decided that this wasn't for them. No one had a dream to tell. The facilitator kept looking at me, as if to say, "Tell your dream." Finally, I started, as tears welled up in my eyes. By the time I finished, I was sobbing, and so were a lot of other people in the room. Then, one by one, half the people in the group began recounting sexual or emotional abuse that they had suffered as children. Some seemed much more terrible than what I had experienced; a few, like mine, had never been remembered or talked about before; but all were traumatic. I felt an emptiness inside, and I realized that before this emptiness I had been living in chaos.

I began to understand something about my soul from that point on. The issue in my life was not *only* cult involvement. Another issue was, and still is, the abusive power imbalance. The fact that my father, like many fathers, brothers, uncles, and other authority figures, as head of the family (or whatever power position they hold, such as priests, teachers, coaches, doctors), could violate his duty of moral transmission and get away with it is an attack on a child's soul. This scene, which I had repressed, was not the only blow to my soul. There were others, such as the time my father threw a chair at my mother and it hit me on the head instead, leaving a scar that remains today, and the nights I spent at the top of the stairs, afraid to go to sleep and ready to run out the front door if my father came home drunk. By the time I was ten years old, a strange man exposed himself to my friend and me on a quiet neighborhood street, and I was so confused, I thought it was funny. Recently I read that child-abuse survivors can experience a long list of psychological disorders as adults. One of them jumped off the page—an inability to establish meaningful intimate relationships. That was another reason why I had found it so easy to be a Heaven's Harlot and so hard to be a wife. My psyche had been wounded at a very young age, and no one came to help stop the bleeding. There had never been any healing. Perhaps this was the bloodied little girl who had appeared to me in Italy.

When I eventually discussed this with members of my family, no one but my sister Ruby gave me any emotional support. On the contrary, as is typical when only one child remembers abuse, I was discredited. One of my siblings suggested it could have been the typical Freudian *fantasy* of a female child in the oedipal stage, which is commonly known as "penis envy." My family insinuated that I was imagining the incident, and at the same time they said, "Well, it wasn't that bad! Lots of drunk men expose themselves." They were right—child abuse often involves much "worse" intrusion than mere exposure, and drunk men are notorious for indecent exposure. Some children are more resilient than others. However, the fact that I buried this incident so deeply in my subconscious, and that it returned with such emotional violence in dreams and visions, indicates that I was profoundly affected.

Perhaps I had become a "deep feeler" for the sufferings of the downtrodden masses, but I was also an "unfeeler" of my own pain. Perhaps I had been eager to dissociate from myself so I would not feel the pain. Perhaps in locking up pain, I had also locked up morals and values. Wasn't it the universal moral taboo of incest that had caused my pain to begin with? What better way to rid myself forever of that pain than to discredit the taboo. If I had not been a mother also, I probably would have remained oblivious to morality. Now that I understood my original wound, I questioned God even more earnestly: "What is the meaning of this? Why would you, God, allow this to happen over and over again?"

For some children it is much worse. Some children don't make it through.

To this day, any incident of child abuse that I hear about causes profound feelings of pain to surface, and I often weep to the point of emotional exhaustion. When I read about the two girls who were found dead in a Belgian farmhouse, having been subjected to sexual abuse for months, I almost completely lost faith in any concept of God. The parents and townspeople had prayed for months for the protection of these kidnapped girls. I questioned everyone and did not find a suitable answer as to why any God would let this happen. I don't know how God the Father thinks, but God the Mother would not let this happen. Even after being indoctrinated by Family principles of morality for years, after internalizing the belief that sex is natural and should be shared with all, and after giving my body, in the end I was not willing to give my children. Fortunately, I had enough decision-making power left to decide to take my girls away from eventual abuse. How could an all-powerful, all-knowing God allow continual abuse to happen in His creation? So who or what is God? I want to know!

My mother was living with me at the time I had the dream/ revelation. Although she had played a significant role in that incident of my childhood, by being absent, I knew she was not guilty of neglect. Actually, she was a survivor herself, and I now recognized that my detached attitude in life was modeled after my mother's. I had perfected the coping mechanism by becoming dissociated. I was now able to identify the signs indicating that my mother used whatever she could to survive her pain and abuse.

She had been trained to be a scholar and socialized to live a middle-class lifestyle. Instead, she married an alcoholic who could not keep a job, and being a devout Christian, she allowed him to father her six children. Nothing had prepared her for parenthood by herself, and even more tragic, nothing had prepared her for the abusive relationship inherent in being married to an alcoholic. Her religion told her that she could not divorce, and so she did not. Instead, she bore her burdens by forgetting them. My mother forgot almost all the dramatic incidents that I remember in detail. During her first pregnancy, she developed epilepsy, and she has taken phenobarbital and Dilantin ever since. Perhaps this had something to do with her memory loss, but it also helped her to survive her life in hell. The Christians certainly did not help enough. When her own father suggested she get away from my father, offering to help her start a new life in Germany, she refused. She told me later that she stayed with her husband because of her convictions.

Memories seem to collect cobwebs like an unused attic, but I had to start cleaning out the rooms. I have lived too long with vague memories. I remembered all along that my father had been abusive, only I did not consistently remember. As a child I had recurrent nightmares of a "boogeyman" in my bed, and sometimes I would wake up and see a tall figure leave the room. I asked my mother to sleep with me until I was a teenager, and I even wet the bed once at sixteen years of age while I baby-sat at a neighbor's house. All these are serious disturbances, but I did not look for a cause. When Mo advocated sexual activities with children, I allowed the memory of my father's actions to resurface as something that was *not* morally wrong. However, when I saw the results of abusive sexual relationships, through the drawings of Judah's child, I finally made my own decision that indeed it was terribly wrong. But again I blocked out my own sexual abuse. All power abuse cuts to the heart and soul. And as children, who have nowhere to run and hide, all we can do is let our heart bleed and hide our soul!

I think my mother, who stumbled into this abuse as an adult, hid her emotions. I know she suffered greatly because she stayed with my father. When I was five, right after my second little sister was born, my mother's fourth child in less than eight years, she had a nervous breakdown in front of her children. We were living in a hotel on the highway, and she took the baby and sat in the middle of the street screaming like a lunatic, while the other three children, myself included, stood on the side of the highway waiting for help. The police came and put her back into the hotel room. She doesn't remember the incident. She was one of the silent survivors of a society that allowed patriarchally sanctioned abuse. Abusive husbands in the 1950s were supported by the law, while abused wives were silenced. I was not going to perpetuate this grim silence. I wanted to scream to God—to the world—*"Why do you let this happen?"* But I couldn't scream yet. I couldn't even find my voice.

Through books, I learned much about the correlation among suffering, searching, and knowing oneself. In *Women Who Run with Wolves*, Clarissa Pinkola Estes talks about the women who die a thousand deaths and are constantly reborn:

Having lived through a gross repression causes gifts to arise that compensate and protect. In that respect a woman who has lived a torturous life and delved deeply into it definitely has inestimable depth. Though she came to it through pain, if she has done the hard work of clinging to consciousness, she will have a deep and thriving soul-life and a fierce belief in herself regardless of occasional ego-waverings.

I had lived through an emotionally torturous childhood. As a young adult I joined a repressive authoritarian subculture, and I lived most of my adult life allowing myself to be manipulated by men. Somehow I hung on to consciousness, and I was ready for a thriving soul-life, sensing that there was more to learn. Little did I know that my oldest son, the love of my life who gave me the utmost joy and was the unwitting cause of my most intense pain, was going to be the key to a deeper spirituality.

Thor came to live with me in 1995. With a hard-earned French degree in math, he applied to graduate schools in America. After scoring a perfect 800 on his GRE, he received an assistantship at one of the best schools in the South. The time we spent together was priceless, and I discovered that my twenty-two-year-old son was a spiritual seeker of great depth. His own sufferings, which only he can write about, and his essential search led him to an Eastern form of meditation, a spiritual discipline known as *Sahaj Marg*, or the "natural path." He explained this practice to me patiently for many months, and I started the meditation sporadically at different times, but because there was a "master," which reminded me too much of my cult experience, I was always wary. In fact, during one of my rare conversations with the "master" of this particular discipline, I expressed to him my distrust of any type of leader or guru. He suggested that I "just meditate."

I have not become as involved in the Saharj Marg practice as Thor has, but as a result of the meditation I have done, I began to experience more dreams and visions. First, I rejected these as too "cultish," because the Family had put so much emphasis on dreams and visions, especially those received by Moses David. However, I wrote them down, and they have been a source of inspiration for me, since they were usually messages about myself. It also is a way for me to counterbalance the nonspiritual world of academia. I had become so absorbed in external struggles, such as the economic one, that I found I had little time for self-reflection. Yet self-awareness, like morning dew, is life-sustaining.

When I began to meditate, I was doubtful that it would yield any benefits, but because I wanted to be part of my son's life in whatever way I could, I did it. Sitting still for an hour was very hard, and thinking "no thoughts" was even harder. No one gave me any indication as to what should happen during meditation, or that I would "see" anything. However, as I concentrated on the inner light as a focal point, I began to feel more peaceful. My first visions during meditation were of beautiful colors and designs that I had never seen before and could never reproduce. Another time I saw a multitude of robed people, stretching out across eternity. One day I envisioned an evolution regression, seeing an ape change into a fish and finally into some microscopic organism in which I felt intimate energy. Sometimes I saw things that I recognized as "my story" in symbolic form; other times I received images that gave me inspiration or revelations about something that was bothering me. The meditation practice helped me during a difficult period in my life. I was a single mother, with four school-age kids, and going full-time to college. I felt I was just keeping my head above water. Then one night, while sleeping at Thor's apartment, I had the "dream." I will recount the dream exactly as I wrote it down early in the morning, with tears still streaming down my face.

I was living next to a big old house, almost a mansion in size, and it seemed that I knew this house intimately. Maybe I lived there before. I now live next to the house with my children. I know that the people who were living in the big house had left and the house was now empty. But I heard a baby crying in the house. At first the cry was very faint. Sometimes it would go away. This had been going on for months now [as I knew in my dream]. I thought the child must surely be dead, if there really was a baby in there.

I often asked myself, "Why don't I go in there and look?" But I was afraid. I was afraid of that house. Something had happened to me in there. But tonight, in my dream, I hear the baby distinctly. I hear her crying louder and louder in desperation. I know I will have to go in and look for her or else I will go crazy!

I do not want to go alone, so I wake my oldest daughter, Athena, and tell her about the baby crying next door. She believes me, although she cannot hear the crying, and she says she will come with me to look for the baby.

The old house is connected to our house somehow, and we climb through the attic and into the house next door through an attic trap door, since I do not want to go in the front main entrance. Once in the big house, I feel oppressed with fear, but the sound of the baby crying keeps me going. I must find her.

I start looking everywhere in the attic, and I can't find the baby anywhere. Then I stop hearing the cries. "She must be dead," I think, but just then I hear the crying coming from downstairs. Athena thinks she heard something but isn't sure. I hear it distinctly; however I don't want to go downstairs. Athena thinks we could save the baby. So we go to the next floor and search everywhere, but again the cries stop, and again I hear them coming from down further. Each time I search a level, I can hear the cries on a level below. Finally, Athena, who has never really heard the cries, thinks we should give up.

We are on the floor above ground level now. It is the floor of the master bedroom and the library. The furniture is of an old, massive type and very heavy to move. I pull drawers out frantically to look for the baby behind the big dressers. In the library, I madly rip the books off the shelves, looking inside and behind them. Athena is beginning to think I am losing my mind.

"I am sure the baby is dead by now," she says, almost trying to help me give up my frantic search before I go crazy.

We are in the master bedroom now. I can't even hear the baby cry anymore, and I am about to give up, when I hear the baby breathing. I can hear her better than I hear my own breath; in fact, it feels like it is my breath I hear.

"No, she's in here," I say excitedly. "I hear her breathing. She might be on her last breath and she doesn't have the energy to cry anymore."

Athena cannot hear it, but she believes me. I get down on my hands and knees since I think the sound is coming from below a great old-fashioned wardrobe. I peer underneath it, and there in the back is a tiny fragile baby, covered only with a small blanket and lying on her stomach. I gently pull her out. She is so small she fits in one of my hands. Her skin is translucent and she is glowing like a star or a crystal. She is breathing very faintly, and I am thinking how wonderful it is that I have found her. I will take her home and nurture her back to health. I am filled with an amazing love for this glowing baby.

Just then, a man comes in downstairs. I look over the stairway and he comes up the steps. He is a sophisticated-looking man in a nice gray suit, but his face is without emotion. He is accompanied by a little lady, and he tells her to go up to the attic and shut the trap door. Then he looks at me with an evil smirk, as he takes the baby out of my hands and throws her disinterestedly over his shoulder.

"So you found her," he sneers. "Well, she's mine. And now you are going to suffer for finding her."

I remember thinking that I should not have brought Athena with me. This seemed to be my destiny, and I should not have brought Athena into it. I am overcome with such a fear for Athena that I wake up.

I wrote the dream down right away, but even in my wakeful state, I was strangely afraid, especially for my children. I told Thor the dream, and he thought I should see a Jungian psychologist, trained to interpret dreams.

In wonderful synchronization, my friend Ruth told me about a Jungian psychologist whom she knew in Paris and who now lived in our city. I contacted her and made an appointment.

The psychologist, a woman, forced me to draw the explanation out of myself. The house is myself, my life, and the baby is my soul, who has been abused and neglected for many years. I was forced out of my house by this man, and perhaps kept out of it at different times, in different situations, by different men, but now I was ready to come back in and take possession of my house. My soul had always known its birthing place. Now I had found my soul, and my journey was just beginning! Meaning, purpose, understanding—they were mental processes, paths through the head, and I felt I could now learn the way of the heart. This is my continuing journey!

13

○ ○ ○

The Swan Symbol of Paramatman (Supreme Self)

The Family

The following statistics were taken from a 1987 Children of God publication:

Total membership: 12,162
Number or COG homes worldwide: 1,080
Number of children: 6,470
Number witnessed to: 910,080
Number saved: 92,750
Number loved [through FFing]: 218,722 (to date)

According to a COG publication from April 1990 (Stats Analysis):

Total membership: 18,000
Average number of children per couple: 4.5

In May 1996 the Family distributed a publication in which they claimed that there was nothing wrong with "flirty fishing" since the motivation was not money or power; however, the practice was discontinued in 1987 in order to "emphasize other means of ministering the Word of God to others" ("Women in the Family" :10). Those who left the Family after 1987 claim that although its use was greatly reduced, it was not completely eliminated. The Family does *not* deny that sexual sharing is still allowed among consenting adults. "A married member is free, after receiving the agreement of their spouse, to have sex with another partner" ("Women in the Family" :18). However, certain boundaries have been established:

No sexual contact between adults and minors
No male-with-male sexual activity (female-with-female sexual
   activity is allowed with mutual consent)
No sex with those outside the family
Sexual activity between adults must be done with full consent
   and done in private ("Women in the Family" :19. This information can also be found on the Family's website at
   www.thefamily.org).

Moses David reportedly died in 1994. Maria and a group of elders were given his position of absolute authority. Meanwhile, Maria suffers from an eye illness, which causes her great pain if she opens her eyes in the light. Therefore, she sees only in the dark, but she continues to write letters to the worldwide Family. Due to reorganization of the group, membership rules and regulations were tightened, and in a publication of 1996, the group, now called simply the Family, claimed it had 3,000 full-time *adult* volunteer members, 6,000 children, and 20,000 associates working in over sixty countries. This implies that there were close to 30,000 people associated with the Children of God in some way at that time.

I found an article on the Family's website that stated, "Our present fellowship does not go by the Children of God name because that organization was literally dissolved . . . the Children of God movement represented a substantially different organization with a very different leadership" (1/9/98).

There are various websites that mention the Family. One of them, at www.religioustolerance.org, writes, "In 1987, incest and sexual abuse of children was specifically banned," and "current membership estimates from non-COG sources vary from 9,000 to 12,000" (1/9/98).

This same site also states, "It is our assessment that accusations of criminal activities by the Family are unfounded. . . . No evidence of sexual abuse of children was ever found . . . former members frequently refer to a book, *The Story of Davidito*, which was written by David, son of David Berg's wife, Maria. Although the book does discuss his witnessing of sexual behavior within the group, and their encouragement of him to explore his own sexuality, there is nothing in the book related to adult molestation or abuse of children" (1/9/98).

I have access to the "Davidito" book, and have seen pictures of an adult child-care worker caressing Davidito's private area when he was a child, and of Davidito, as a young boy, sucking on the breast of an adult woman. Perhaps this is not regarded as child molestation by the writers of the above-cited "objective" website on religious cults. As a social science student, I also try to be as objective as possible. The following stories from young people are not an assessment but descriptions.

I cannot vouch for anything that happened in the Family after I left in 1988. Nor can I know what happened in homes other than where I lived. However, I have heard hundreds of stories from adults and children who have left in the past ten years. Many talk of serious physical and sexual abuse. The evolutionary process of perversion in the Family is clearly established as people who won't put up with sexual aberrations leave, and therefore only those who do remain. Many left with the first wave of sharing and "flirty fishing"; others, like myself, finally left when sexual abuse of children became an undeniable reality. I believe these reports are true since it would seem that those who remain have either denied the abuse consciously or unconsciously, or believe it is acceptable. As I hear the stories of children and parents separated indefinitely, corporal punishment in public of teenagers and adults, mind manipulation, sleep and food deprivation, and more, I wonder how a person can ever hope to live a sane life again. Then I remember—this is also my story and my hope!

Here, at the end of my story, I want to tell you what happened to the various players in this story, some who woke up to life and some who didn't.

After the Family

Esther, the unknowingly wicked Queen in this tale, was reportedly excommunicated by Moses David, her father, in the late 1970s. According to her own account, she was ultimately expelled from the Family because she did not want to give in to his incestuous desires toward her. All of her children and the man considered her mate at the time left with her. She wrote a book about her experiences as Mo's daughter, *The Children of God: The Inside Story* (1984), which was published by a Christian publishing house. I read her book and realized that she too had been victimized, but I am disappointed that Esther did not acknowledge the extent of her own role as victimizer and abuser of the immense power entrusted to her as our "Queen." Perhaps she had not yet found answers to her most tormenting questions at the time she wrote the book. Today she is associated with a strict fundamentalist group in California.

Rahab, who had married Esther's brother, the one who "fell" off a mountain in Switzerland, left the Family and became a nurse. However, her oldest daughter, Hannah, who is Mo's granddaughter and Esther's niece, remained in the Family until a few years ago. This young woman, who was left without parents and raised in Mo's house, wrote about her ordeals in an ex-cult newsletter, *No Longer Children* (November 1992). Her sad testimony reveals that she endured dozens of intrusive sexual encounters with her grandfather, the first before she was twelve years old. She wrote that she was beaten with a rod, spanked in public at fourteen years of age, tied to her bed at night, and accused by Mo of being possessed by Satan himself. Hannah eventually wound up in a mental institution in Macao and was sent to California to live with her grandmother (Mother Eve), who no longer lived in the Family. Today she lives with her aunt Esther, for reasons I cannot fully explain, instead of with her birth mother, Rahab, who finally found her lost daughter.

Jacob, Esther's first husband, a top leader of the group, and the one who "helped" me by committing adultery with me, left the group with his second wife, the wealthy former socialite, Pearl. They are now divorced, and Jacob runs a prosperous business in America. Coincidentally, many of his early employees were teenagers who had recently left the Family. When Jacob attended the 1994 reunion for ex-COG members, I heard from others present that he had apologized for his shortcomings as a leader in the Family. I was not in the room when this was said to have happened; however, I talked with him for a short period in private, and he never said he was sorry for what he did to me. I did not mention it to him.

Ruth, the young southern belle whom I first met in Ellenville and who worked with me in Paris, had also been separated by Jacob from her first husband, the father of Thor's childhood friend Chiara. Jacob had attempted to include her in his growing harem in Italy, but instead she was sent to Paris to be part of the Show Group, and was one of our first women given in marriage to a "king," in this case to our music producer. She eventually left the Family due to what she calls a moral decision—the Family no longer needed her husband, but they expected her to leave him and return to become one of the flirty recruiters. She broke contact with the group and stayed with the French producer, who was now the father of two of her children. After what she calls "one of the longest-lasting 'flirty-fishing' experiences in the Family (eighteen years)," she, too, following years of emotional, psychological, and even physical abuse while trying to be a "good Christian wife," decided to leave her husband. With three children she made her way back to her hometown in America, arriving from France about a year after I did.

Ruth has recently returned to college, pursuing degrees in foreign languages and psychology, and she is very interested in trying to understand the disparate reactions of ex-members upon leaving the Family. From her own experience, she has become aware that there are many women like herself who leave the Family and fall into similarly controlling and abusive situations, which tend to perpetuate the experiences that they had while in the cult. Ruth, like myself, is seeking a way to use her own cult experience and subsequent journey to self-awareness as a source of help to the many who leave and who find themselves totally lost in a world they have not been prepared to live in, especially those who were born and raised in the group.

Jon, my former dance partner who traveled with me to Nice and Rome, left the group and started a new life with his family in California. He returned unabashedly to a gay lifestyle, but he kept up a warm and loving relationship with his wife and children. They eventually divorced amicably. When he read an article I wrote for a reunion newsletter, he called me and said he was hurt that I did not say hello to him in my regards to various former members.

James, the most lenient leader I ever met in the Family, and whose home I stayed at while in Paris, left COG and returned to his hometown in Canada. His wife remained in the cult, but he took his two oldest children with him and raised them for many years as a single father. Today he owns his own music video production company, and he sends me original compilations of music tapes for inspiration. James understood that I am soothed and nourished by music, and thanks to his concern, I now listen to more than Bob Dylan.

Abraham, the unfortunate former husband of Breeze (who as far as I know is still in the Family), left with a Frenchwoman he recruited into the group. They had two children and lived in Texas until she divorced him and married a wealthy Texan. Abe became a "Dead Head" and followed the Grateful Dead around America while selling tie-dyed T-shirts. He visited my home when the Dead played where I lived in 1992.

Gabriel, the multitalented musician who was recruited back into the Family in Puerto Rico, stayed with the cult until 1992. His wife was mated to another brother and lived in a separate home so that Gabriel could be free to use his business and technical talents for the group around the world. Living with top leaders, Gabriel became one of the first victims of the "victor camps," which were set up in the early 1990s to break anyone who still had a strong-willed spirit. After what he described as "incredibly harsh methods of mental, psychological, emotional, and even physical abuse," the leaders in Japan finally gave him a ticket to return to his parents, since they suspected he was about to become a serious mental problem. After months of therapy, Gabriel spent a few years attacking the Family publicly in television interviews in the United States and in countries where he had lived, but his emotional state and mental condition by this time were so strained that he gave up his fight. After he admitted on national television to engaging in pedophilia, in the hopes that his confession would convince the authorities that the Family should be investigated, his plan backfired and he was depicted as a pervert by the cool, calm, and well-trained Family public relations men. Gabriel spent the rest of his life on prescription drugs and committed suicide in June of 1996.

Rose and Bishop, the two former members who started the tradition of yearly reunions, left before the height of sexual activity in the Family. Rose, who had joined in 1969, lived in the same commune (or compound) as Mo during her first years in the group, and was married by him to a man she did not want to marry. Eventually, she left with a husband she chose, but she felt a sense of failure, rejection, and isolation upon leaving the group that had defined her identity. "Nine years of an intense lifestyle and indoctrination can be hard to put behind you," she contends. She feels that encouragement and support are important for people when they leave a cult, proposing that "sometimes the best person to talk to is someone who has experienced the same things that you have." She and her husband have now become the connecting source between former members of the Family, borderline members who are contemplating leaving but are not sure what they will do, and those who are still in the Family and whose children are trying to contact them. They would like to see a retreat where families with many children, single parents, and young, inexperienced teens who leave the Family could rest and acquire the resources to tackle the work of living in the real world. The need for such a place became one of their main concerns after hearing the stories of those who left the group in recent years, especially the teens.

Jesse's mother brought him into the group when he was six years old. She quickly rose to leadership position, and Jesse lived ten years with what he claims were experiences of sexual and emotional abuse that taught him little about right and wrong. When he left the Family at the age of sixteen, he found it too hard to adjust to society and ended up spending years in prison. Jesse told me that while he was in jail, he was so lonely he wrote to the Family and asked someone to please write him. He received dozens of letters, and after prison, he began visiting their homes again. His mother and sister are still in the cult.

A Family publication numbered GN 480 DO, from October 1991, published a letter from a teen in their group named Tony, also called Zack Attack. He complained about having a problem with being under constant supervision and restricted from being able to ride "a skateboard or a horse or go ice-skating or roller-skating or even climb a tree." In response, he received "Dad's Blast after hearing about Zack Attack," which stated, "Give him the ultimatum! Tell him, 'Tonight at our next meeting, you're going to get up and weep and pray and cry for mercy and grovel on the floor and confess that you're all wrong in front of all the teenagers and everybody, and beg for mercy." ("Grumblers Get Out!" 2716). This was the type of environment that many members were subjected to at what became known as the victor camps. Adults found it hard to leave because of their connections to their children and spouses in the Family, but teens, who had been raised in the group, had nowhere else to go. Even so, some left and tried to locate distant relatives or to make it on their own.

Teddy, Andrew, and their first sister, Shirley, the three oldest children of Jeremy Spencer, whom I took care of when they were young, left the Family on their own. I read about Andrew, who did not use his father's famous name, in an article from a London paper, and it appeared that he was interested in going to college. However, according to testimony from former COG members, one of Jeremy's daughters who left the Family now works as a stripper. A case in point is that of River Phoenix, the young actor who died of a drug overdose in 1993. His parents joined the Children of God when River was only a young boy—according to some sources, age two—and they became Family missionaries in Venezuela. Like many COG children, River sang on the streets to help support his family until they left the group and returned to America in 1977. His childhood experiences in the Family certainly must have contributed to what became a troubled adulthood (one author described him as a "disillusioned innocent") and ended in a drug-induced death at the age of twenty-three.

Hopie, Mo's second daughter, wrote in a Family-published article on "reaction to childhood sex" (1988) that "daddy made me feel good all over . . . I don't think it perverted me . . . but it sure converted me to *His* call." She came to America for health reasons after her father's death, but it was rumored that she was having conflict with the leadership, especially Maria, who had taken Mo's place. In America, Hopie started living with a former male member of the cult, and they have been together for a while, purportedly out of the Family. I learned through reunion sources that before coming to America, Hopie had been sent to Siberia by the Family, and while there she established a food supply chain across the Russian wilderness to feed the forgotten starving Siberians. This involved negotiations with Russian officials as well as the Russian mafia, according to her own testimony. In 1996 she called me and asked if I would like to help her in Washington, D.C., with her fund-raising effort for the Russians in Siberia. I declined, but I wished her luck, and I heard she is doing well.

Cal/Jerry, Thor's father and my first husband, had three daughters and one more son with his second wife (exactly as I had, and pretty much around the same years). Thor is therefore the older brother to six girls and two boys. Cal eventually divorced his wife, and the children live with him in Colorado. We call each other occasionally and are on good terms. While writing this book, I asked him if he would like to relate some of his own story. The following is what Cal wrote to me from his own memory, but his perceptions of the Family, why he joined and why he stayed, were the same as mine:

For me, the intentions and motives I had weren't wrong, and I believe there were many others who were sincere, who held the beauty and light of their personal vision, and stayed hoping to change what the reality was becoming. Many times I thought, I questioned, and doubted things, but we had been conditioned to resist such thoughts, so our behavior became more radical and consequently more fanatical in some. Maybe we were just plain old afraid to "go back out into the world." Whatever the reason we stayed and obeyed will always be a bit of a mystery. Why people like us join something like this I think is clear—it's the historical climate of the times. We were idealists: "some of them were dreamers/some of them were fools/they were making plans and dreaming of the future/On the brave and crazy wings of youth/we went flying around in the rain/till our feathers once so fine grew torn and tattered" ("Before the Deluge" by Jackson Brown).

When the whole FFing era started I was pretty anxious. We had been prepared for the ultimate sacrificing of our mates to the crucifix of the bed of love. For months the letters just became more and more specific. I didn't really have a say the first time. It hurt bad. I felt we had lost something in our union. Our union wasn't so good at that time because for months the anxiety just built on me seeing clearly where all these new letters were leading. As the months passed I behaved more and more erratic—possessive, fear of losing my most precious loved one. Anyway, I got used to it and persuaded myself that this was the ultimate sacrifice. Then in time we were more manipulative and motives and intentions became less honorable. Within the group the fatherless population grew, bad treatment—bad karma— bad press.

How did I feel about being a pimp for God? At first I had been sincerely persuaded of the power of love—and the attraction of a pretty woman to win souls. There was always a tinge of jealousy and hurt. Always I participated vicariously, imagining I was the stranger experiencing for the first time the fruits of my wife's love. It made her more attractive and desirable and therefore I couldn't wait until she came home to me. My own emotions, however, made me blind and insensitive to her needs and lack of desire toward me—due to fatigue and probably disgust at times because her experience had been distasteful. To my heart and mind at these times, I hurt because I thought it was me. "I let you sleep with strangers and you reject me?" It was a problem and created a communication breakdown dividing us.

I believe we were deceived innocents. I hope you don't carry any guilt feelings from the past. I am sure that all of us who have gone through these things and survived are better people for the experience.

What made me finally leave? It was seeing what happened to poor Sharon. When I heard about her video, something snapped inside me. Of course I had been thinking of leaving for years by then, but knowing what happened to Sharon, I snapped.

While I was writing this book, Mara, the third in our threesome marriage and Cal's second wife, called me. She appears to have gone through her own long journey to self-awareness, and she answered my questions with realistic honesty.

I asked Mara to write me more on why she joined the cult and why she stayed during FFing. The following is taken from a letter she wrote me.

I joined this group while deeply into a spiritual search, and what I now know to have mainly been a search for myself, my true values. In the world I saw corruption, where power and money seemed the name of the game, and where I thought there was no room for me.

Why did I accept FFing, in spite of my original disgust at the practice? Certainly because it was challenging and revolutionary, and that word always struck a chord in me. Going beyond morals, transcending the taboo of sexuality in Christianity seemed very appealing. Now that was the intellectual approach, and I must say that my body could never quite follow. I wasn't free sexually and it made it hard to win people to Jesus that way. Of course, money also being involved made it quite degrading at times.

Looking at it now, I can clearly see my immaturity and lack of confidence, and that I covered up with a display of culture and savoir-vivre. I was very proud, often felt smarter than others, but at the same time very inadequate.

More than the beliefs, it's the human warmth that attracted me in the group, so when I left it wasn't hard for me to cut emotional ties, and go back to my first spiritual interests in Hinduism and Buddhism. Today I feel so different than during that time of my life, that I feel that I am writing about someone else. I can only assume that the serenity and balance I found today are a fruit of all the questions and deep searching that followed that period. It led me to psychotherapy and now meditation.

Mara, now forty years old and divorced from Cal, lives near her children in Colorado.

My Family

My older brother, Steve, has spent most of his life in prison. He currently is finishing a twenty-year sentence for unarmed bank robbery (he reportedly smashed his arm through the teller window and demanded money). No one was hurt but himself, when he cut his arm on the glass; however, since he had already had more than three strikes on his record, he is in the same ward with murderers and rapists. I asked him recently if he ever hurt a person in any of his robberies. After a few minutes of contemplation, he told me that the only person he ever hurt was me.

"I punched you in the stomach once when we were kids. I think we were wrestling and you kicked me, and it hurt so badly that I punched you. You started crying and I have felt sorry about doing that all my life," he explained.

Although all my sisters believe in the Christian perspective of God, none have become very "religious." Perhaps my sister who died in a car accident at the age of twenty would have been. My other sisters all live in Florida, have steady jobs, own their own homes, and seem to be happily married. They are typical Americans and lead typical American lives; however, I will leave it up to the reader to define "typical." They do not talk to me often about my time in the Family, and they encourage me to stop talking about it also, so I hope they don't read this book. Only my sister Ruby, who was in the Family for a short time in Paris and knows how manipulated I had been, understands why I would not want to stay with the father of my children.

Ruby told me years later that when I first joined the Family she was only nine years old, and she had always looked up to me as the big sister. She hated the COG for taking me away and saw that it hurt my mother a lot, so she swore she would get back at the Family for doing this. As she grew up, she watched TV shows about cults and believed that the people in cults were brainwashed; however, when she visited me in Paris, she thought that the Family was just like a group of peace-loving hippies. It was fun in Paris, especially since her sister was in the Show Group and danced onstage. Ruby enjoyed singing on the streets and living with other young people. When she heard about FFing she thought, "I will never do that." She thought the idea of showing one man God's love was nice, but she would never do that with lots of men. "I liked their beliefs in the Bible, and their witnessing methods—distributing literature on the streets and singing at cafés. I felt more like an observer and was just having a good time in Paris. But nobody was going to convince me to FF. I was real careful not to get brainwashed."

My mother continues to live with me as an ever-present grandmother to my children. She visits her other daughters in Florida a few times a year, and talks with her son on the phone every week that he is not in the "hole." She continues to pray every morning, goes to church weekly, and spends many of her waking hours translating German sermons into English. Although she has come to a few ex-COG reunions, and has met many of my friends who were former members, we do not talk much about the time I spent in the cult.

I divorced Paolo after three years of separation. He runs a profitable business and lives close to our home. He has a good relationship with the children and me, thanks in part to counseling he receives from a men's group and from his pastor. Paolo feels comfortable in a church environment, and I am happy for him. I am also delighted that he has done so well in his business, something that never happened while he was with me. I often wonder if it was my fault. Although I have written about my bad experiences with Paolo as my husband, now that I am no longer his wife, we both treat each other better. I don't blame Paolo for anything. In fact, I take the blame for using sex and marriage as a witnessing tool—but in the end, it worked for him. I don't think that Paolo would be capable of living such a rewarding and constructive life as he now leads had he continued his use of tranquilizers, and stopping them was a prerequisite for marrying me. Eventually, I had to deal in my own conscience with the complex issue of annulment, which even the Catholic Church allows in exceptional cases. I believe my marriage was an exception. When I asked Paolo what he thought of our marriage in the Family, he said that he saw it in the context of the "one wife" view that the COG held. For that reason he never gave me a ring, and he called me a "mate" instead of "wife." However, he did not join to share with other women, and he did not particularly like that aspect of our beliefs. He accepted it perhaps because he too was a former hippie who was willing to try out alternative lifestyles.

Once out of the Family's doctrinal hold, we both discovered our true personalities. Paolo is basically a traditional man, with a conservative outlook, and capitalist proclivities, which have helped him to develop a successful business. I am a nontraditional woman, with a radically liberal outlook, nonmaterialistic values, and an eternally questioning mind that attracts me to scholastic pursuits. Even though we are worlds apart philosophically, I do respect his beliefs and his chosen way of life.

My dear children are the only reason I could continue to live during my most despondent times and despairing moments. I hope when they read this book (which they are not to do until they are eighteen years old), they will understand that the woman I am writing about is not the mother they know: the mother who they complain is "too protective," "too old-fashioned," and "doesn't know anything." They don't know me as the Jeshanah in this book, although they are aware that they were born and lived in the Family. They have also gone to the reunions and have met the children of other ex-members. They have heard the stories, and they have probably heard *my* story from other people. I remember Thor's heartbreaking reaction to hearing about me from his father. Since I will probably never be able to sit down with each one and tell them my side of the story (they would never sit still that long), this book will eventually let them know why I was at one time a Heaven's Harlot. But most of all, they should know that it was worth it all in order that I might have had each one of them, and that it has only been through them that I know how to love.

Thor, my firstborn, who explains life to me better than anyone, is now half a foot taller than I but still asks for hugs and kisses. I see him as a performer, scholar, philosopher, and mystic, but he would say that he's only living a life.

Before Thor left to study in Germany for a year on an exchange program, I spent some time alone with him. Both vegetarians, we talk after a leftover meal of broccoli and pasta. The night falls, and we stay there talking about alienation and meaninglessness, about Jesus and other spiritual masters, about Eastern religions of the heart and Western philosophy of the mind. I tell Thor about the little old lady I see when I meditate who informs me that she is wisdom, and I ask him what it means to climb the spiritual Himalayas. As I listen to his answers, I know that he is going farther than I. On the morning of our last day together, I am worried about his future in Germany. Besides the fact that I will miss him again, it seems like an unnecessary difficulty for my son, now twenty-four and working on his doctorate in math, to be an exchange student in Berlin. He doesn't even speak German, and the scholarship he will receive is considerably less than he got in America.

"It's the mountain, Mom," he told me, with a smile that remains in my mind forever. "The mountain was there on my path so I had to climb it."

I knew exactly what he meant. I had been coming to a deep abyss, knowing that I must cross it.

Although I have not been a perfect mother, I have been a flexible one, and I have imparted the concept of an expansive God to my children. This was so wonderfully illustrated to me when we were answering questions one night around the dinner table. Jordan, at twelve years old, wondered why the American Indians were close to nature, living in tents and eating the food from the earth; whereas the Europeans lived in houses and were advanced in technology. The answers offered by her two sisters were that Indians were closer to God, or that God wanted to see how different cultures would be.

The next question came from Michelangelo. "What is the meaning of life?" asked my ten-year-old.

I did not answer him—he was so young—but as I asked him to answer that himself, I remembered when my own search began.

Epilogue

Three of my children were born in Europe, and the first two were raised there since they were one year old. In the summer of 1997, I took my four younger children to Europe to visit their paternal grandmother and to rediscover their roots. Back in Italy, visiting the places where we had lived, my kids had the opportunity to explore and remember who they were as young children, and thankfully, *their* memories were joyful.

Meanwhile, my memories, like cobwebs in a corner of my mind, were glistening in the misty light of the past. While in Italy and France, I recalled the gray ghosts that I had left in those places, and who were waiting there to greet me. Some of them I dismissed, and they vanished. Others clung to me, begging for existence. Sometimes I gave in, such as when I saw Salim walk by while I was sitting on a bench in Monte Carlo, drawing pictures of exotic trees.

I don't think he recognized me, although he looked back my way three times while walking at a quick pace with another well-suited gentleman. He himself had changed considerably, but I knew his eyes.

Salim was not always in Monte Carlo, I don't remember him ever *walking* anywhere, and I was only there for one day, so the fact that he passed by was too fortuitous to be a coincidence. Thinking over the reason for this, I decided I should let him know that I was writing this book. He had been so helpful in finding my son years ago, for which I will be forever grateful. Therefore, I left him a note at the Hôtel de Paris, not even sure that he still had a suite there. The concierge recognized his name immediately and said he would give the note to Salim's secretary. I wrote that I was visiting the area and, if he had time, I would like to talk to him about a book I was writing. I was not sure if he would remember who I was, and all I had for a return address was "in care of" the American Express office in Monte Carlo, since I was traveling. When I checked back the next week, there was a message from him with a phone number to call.

It had been over ten years since I had last seen Salim, and I was a little apprehensive about what he might think of my contacting him again. But I thought he deserved an explanation for my actions in the previous years. I thought he might like to know that I had finally broken free from the cult's clutches—for surely he must have known that I was in a cult. And most of all, I wanted him to know how much I appreciated his help in finding my son and to tell him that Thor and I were together again! Still, I was nervous when he answered the phone.

"Hello, this is Miriam."

"Who?" he asked in a thick Lebanese voice that I recognized immediately.

"Miriam. I left you the note. I used to be called Jeshanah."

"Oh yes, I remember. Yes, I was surprised to get your note. How are you?"

"Fine, thank you. I—"

"Yes, can you come see me?"

"Well, yes, I'd like to talk with you."

"I don't want to talk. I hear you are writing a book, but I don't want you to interview me. You know . . . I want to relax with you . . . like we used to do."

"Oh, Salim," I laughed rather heartily, so thoroughly unexpected had been his comment. "I don't do that anymore. That's what I wanted to talk about. . . ."

"Well, I really don't have time to talk, you see. If you want to relax with me, give me a call. Otherwise, I wish you the best of luck with your book."

"Okay. Well . . . thank you. . . . Good-bye."

I hung up the pay phone in a daze. I was so sure he was a friend that I never thought to question his motives. Why was I so naive? Going back to the hotel room, I was thankful that the children were in Italy with their relatives. It gave me time for contemplation and meditation, and I desperately wanted to explain myself to me.

"I can't explain myself, I'm afraid, sir," said Alice, "because I'm not myself, you see." Alice in Wonderland told this to the Caterpillar, who sat on the mushroom smoking a hookah. She had been through quite a number of changes and found it hard to explain who she was. I also found it difficult to explain myself. I remembered a Zen saying, "There is no better explanation than actual experience." Sitting quietly on my bed with a view of the terra-cotta rooftops of Nice, I relived the experiences of my lifetime in my mind, observing and absorbing each impression. As I contemplated the concept of meaning, I asked the question, "Who defines the meaning of anything?" Continuing along this line of questioning, I arrived where I really wanted to be.

"Who defines me? Who will give meaning to my life?" I should, of course! Perhaps that was one of my first mistakes. I had lost the meaning I gave to myself, the definition of me, and I accepted other people's meaning. No wonder it never fit right. I arose from my bed, and in the light of the midnight moon, I walked down to the beach, searching for a memory of me. Intuitively, I knew that the beach at night had been the scene for many of my turning points. Perhaps the memory of who I was and who I am would come back to me through the timeless rumbling tide of the sea. She once took my thoughts far away, but eventually she would wash them ashore again.

I listened to the waves' steady roar, mentally searching the shore for my memory. An illuminating awareness surrounded my thoughts, and I understood that I had lost not my soul but my self during those years in the cult; yet I have tried to explain myself through the story of my experience. And the story has now come full circle; I was back at the same place where I had stood twenty years ago, when I let my own thoughts drift out to sea and accepted the concept of sacred prostitution.

Whenever I had tried to define myself during those years in the cult, someone always took the self-defined me and threw her over-board. Now I had taken back the captainship of my soul, but it was a long process finding the *self* that had been thrown out to the sea. It required the coordination of time and space and thought and in-tuition. It took crossing the ocean and talking to Salim on the phone before I understood that I still had to reclaim a part of me that had been lost somewhere in Monte Carlo. It meant meditating for hours as I let my thoughts take wing and fly down into the abyss of noth-ingness where meaning can be created. And I had to follow my in-tuition to go back to the sea. That starry summer night, standing alone on the windy pebbled beach the Côte d'Azur, where it all started, I called my self back. Eventually, she came—a cold, shiver-ing, confused young girl, but still alive, just as my soul had still been breathing underneath the wardrobe. I took my trembling self inside the warmth of my heart. I understood her perfectly. Wide-eyed, in-nocent, and silent, she had been waiting to be reunited with my body.

Before calling Salim, I was still a naive, peace-loving woman who craved deep friendships and believed in idealistic love for others. I had been the clueless girl who had idealized the Family and desired a close relationship so much that I allowed them to define who I was. Now I was the captain of my soul—not a captive of some other person's ideology. This time, when Salim made his offer, I answered with my own words, as one who knows who I am. After discovering my childhood secrets and taking control of my "house," I now could affirm who I was.

"No, I am *not* a prostitute!"

Those words were spoken for me and from me—a woman who had found her soul. Those words said that I was now creating my own identity, that I was not an object of sex—not for my father, or hus-band, or a millionaire, or a leader, or even "God."

In the process of defining myself, I have had to establish precise moral imperatives. For instance, never have I condoned any form of abuse of children, especially sexual abuse by adults, or even sexual promiscuity among children. Nor have I ever been anti-Semitic, how-ever my involvement with the Family might seem to negate these positions. As I have tried to explain, and as has been confirmed by many ex-COG members who have written about their experiences, we had willingly given up control of our lives when we joined the cult. The majority of us were still in our teens. All of us were extremely idealistic—and in a practical sense, extremely naive—and I believe that most of us had been sexually, emotionally, or physically abused as children. We were victims as children, and as adults we unconsciously chose to continue to be victimized.

However, I do accept responsibility for having manipulated men, for having allowed the emotional and physical abuse of my son, and for having permitted him to be exposed to sexual issues at too early an age.

I take responsibility for having allowed perversions in the group to continue by not taking a definite stand against what I read in the Mo letters, but when it came to a point where the perversions were in my own home, and I believed they might be perpetrated against my own daughter, I finally realized what responsibility meant. I was not willing to be responsible for child sexual abuse in my own home, so I left it. That was the breaking point for me. Abuse victims, we often read, continue the cycle by becoming abusers themselves. If only they would take responsibility now for their actions, the cycle could be broken. I intend this book to be an act of taking responsibility for my behavior, of setting an example by one person who did break the cycle.

I want to be absolutely sure that the above point is understood, especially by all ex-COG members who now live with the torment of hiding/explaining/forgetting/remembering what they once gave their lives to. Living in a closed society, we unconsciously reinforced each other's sentiments, believing that everything we did was for love, not for lust or vanity, until at last, we were worse than brainwashed— we were self-less, beings totally vulnerable to manipulation. Valuing only some abstract ideal of love, we had little respect for ourselves, and therefore little respect for others. Fortunately, the lives of my children held greater value for me, and thus I was somehow able to snap out of my ideological stupor.

As for the accusations of anti-Semitism in the Family, I really thought it was more a question of strict Christian identity, and since there were so many Jews in the Family, I did not believe it possible that we could be anti-Semitic. I know that I never was, and I often witnessed to Jews. However, in order to confirm my feelings, I called a former member who was Jewish and who had lived with Mo from the very beginning of the group's history. He believes that being

Jewish gave one "extra clout" in the Family, and he remembers sitting around the television watching reruns with Mo and the first disciples and cheering on the Israelis during the Six Day War in 1967. He emphasized that Mo often claimed to be part Jewish and envisioned living in Israel to help establish God's Kingdom on earth. In addition, he contends that Jews in the Family always had a bit higher status, being considered God's original elite. They were sort of the elite of the elite.

There remain many issues for me to resolve, and new issues continue to emerge periodically, and by no means have I reached the end of my journey. I am still dealing with having lived fifteen years of my life in an oppressively fanatical religious environment dictated by a sexually obsessed megalomaniac, followed by four years of floating in a fundamentalist purgatory. However, I don't believe Moses David could have had any power over my actions, my mind, or my body, had I not previously been indoctrinated by the church to believe that the greatest goal in life was to serve God, and had I not been taught by my culture that men have been ordained the figures of authority, epitomized by the fact that "God" is always represented as a man or at least as the male principle. So many of us, especially the self-sacrificial, the idealists, and the altruists, are conditioned to let someone else take control our lives. I am only beginning to establish my boundaries and to sink my roots deep into the ground to take in the nourishment I need.

Some people will protest that because I had Jesus in my heart ever since I was a child, and because my devoutly Christian mother continued to pray for me, it was the Christian faith that protected me and helped me to survive all along. I really cannot deny that; however, the infinite universe I have found inside me is not in the doctrine I was taught by my church. There is Jesus and more, and I think that He would agree with me. Yes, during what I perceived as a demonic attack in Italy, my faith in the name of Jesus helped to keep the demons at bay, but it was the subsequent realization of the strength within myself that caused them forever to vanish. I don't doubt that there are multitudes of Christians who have found truth, meaning, love, God, and whatever answers they need in their religion. What I have discovered is that all dogma is too small to hold even one universal truth that my soul and my self reveal. Since America is basically a "Christian" country, I supplicate all well-meaning re-ligionists to consider Matthew 22:37–39 before judging my life and conclusions: "Love God; love they neighbor; love thyself." I have spent half a lifetime loving God and loving my neighbor—I will now learn to love also myself!

I wish I could provide the answer that all the hurt adults and suffering children who have passed through this and other cults need to hear. But as trite as this might sound, the only truth I have dis-covered that has helped me is that the answers lie within yourself. Peter Townshend wrote, "There is no blood like the blood that flows within one's own body, and no dreams like those that spark from one's own mind." There is also no truth for yourself like the one that dwells within your own heart. Find your soul and love your self.

Glossary

Family Lingo

BABE—a new disciple or new member in the cult

BACKSLIDER—one who has left the cult

BAIT—analogous to the bait used on a fishing hook. In the Family method of "flirty fishing" this was the lure to attract men to the hook or the message. The bait was usually women who would eventually give the men sex.

BATTLE—an internal spiritual struggle, supposedly between good and evil

BROTHER—any male member of the cult

BURDEN—a heavy, usually sorrowful, spiritual load to bear without complaint

BY FAITH—usually meant without visible means of support and used in phrases such as "living by faith," living without a salary; "healed by faith," become better without going to the doctor or using medicine; and so on

FAITH TRIP—an extended excursion made in order to witness or distribute literature and usually undertaken without money, transportation, or room reservations

FAMILY—the Children of God, later called the Family of Love, and finally just the Family

FF—verb signifying the giving of sex in order to tell the person about God's Love

FFING—short for "flirty fishing"

FISH—a person who is being witnessed to through the method of FFing

FLIRTY FISHING—a method of recruiting men or women into the group by attracting them with sexual activity or innuendos of a sexual nature; eventually used as a way to tell the message of salvation by asking Jesus into one's heart

FORSAKE ALL—to give up all worldly possessions for the community of the Family to use as needed

GET THE VICTORY—an expression used to insinuate that the person addressed was not in a good spiritual state and needed to pray or seek the Lord in order to become more spiritual minded; often this expression was directed to members who were not obeying leadership or were having doubts about what the Mo letters were saying.

GOAT—a person who does not want to hear the Word of God

HALLELUJAH—an exclamatory expression used in much the same way as "Praise the Lord" (see below), but employed more often in the sense of glorifying God

INSPIRATION—a time of songs, dancing, and telling stories and motivational speeches

IN THE WORD—reading and studying the Bible and later the Mo letters

KING—a person outside the cult who helped the group in some way, usually through money, housing, or political influence

LEADERS—sometimes called shepherds or servants, the persons with authority and final decision-making power

LITERATURE—Family publications of letters from Moses David, advice from the leaders, and testimonies from the group around the world. This was classified as DO, "for disciples only," and GP, "for the general public." GP literature was distributed on the street while asking for donations.

LITNESSING—a method used by the Family to collect donations. It involved distributing Family literature on the streets and asking for money; LITNESSERS are those who go litnessing.

MO—Moses David

MO LETTERS—the letters written by Moses David to the Children of God, which were distributed around the world and eventually bound into volumes; the sacred text of the group

ONE WIFE—term used to connote the concept of everyone being married to everyone else

PRAISE THE LORD—an exclamatory statement often heard in evangelical church meetings but which became a common expression in the Family: employed to emphasize a statement made by either the speaker or the audience, to contribute to the general inspirational atmosphere, to fill in awkwardness in speech (much as the word "like" or "uh" is used in general conversation), and also in a commandlike interrogatory sense, as when a leader is asking someone to do something that is not being accepted. For example: "This is God's will—Praise the Lord, sister?" The answer in the affirmative was "Praise the Lord" (see "Hallelujah").

PROVISIONING—asking for something for free or at a greatly reduced price; begging

QUEEN—Moses David's daughter, our top leader for a while; later a title given to any woman who was close to Mo

REVOLUTION—a term repeated often at inspirational meetings as a motivational force, which signified that the speakers were in a spiritual revolution against the society. A common expression was "Revolution for Jesus."

SAVED—having gained salvation through asking Jesus into one's heart

SERVANTS—sometimes called shepherds or leaders, the persons with authority and final decision-making power

SHARE—most often used as the verb meaning to have sexual relations

SHEEP—a person who supposedly wants to hear the Word of God

SHEEPY—the adjective describing a person who wants to hear the Word of God

SHEPHERDS—sometimes called leaders or servants, the persons with authority and final decision-making power

SISTER—any female member of the cult

SYSTEM—the world outside the cult environment, especially the capitalistic societies

SYSTEMITE—a person who lived in the system and followed a system way of life, such as having a regular job, marrying one person and raising a family in one's own home, saving money for the future, and consistently putting individual and family needs above the needs of the community; used in a derogatory sense in the COG

TESTIMONY—a personal story, often one's own salvation experience or the story of how one met and joined the group

THREESOME—the term used for relationships involving three adults who live as one marriage unit, either two women and one man or one woman and two men. As in many marriages in the COG, this was not legally binding and was often broken.

TITHE—10 percent of all income, which should be sent to world headquarters

TRIAL—a lighter version of a battle, or an internal spiritual struggle

VICTORY—what one achieves when the good overcomes the evil after an internal spiritual struggle

WITNESSING—a method used to tell people the message of salvation and eventually the Family message of forsaking all and joining the group, usually by going on the streets or to public places and starting up a conversation with strangers; WITNESSERS are those who go witnessing.

WORLD SERVICES—the main organizing center of the group to which reports and tithes were sent and from where each home received the Mo letters, *Family News*, and other cult publications